Worcestershire Under Arms

'March and carye your rest with your Musket'. An early 17th century musketeer by Jacob De Gheyn, 1607. (Brown University Library, USA).

Worcestershire Under Arms

An English County During the Civil Wars

Malcolm Atkin

Pen & Sword
MILITARY

Worcestershire County Council

First Published in Great Britain in 2004 by
Pen & Sword Military
An imprint of
Pen & Sword Books Ltd
47 Church Street
Barnsley
South Yorkshire
S70 2AS

ISBN 1 84415 072 0

A CIP catalogue record for this book is
available from the British Library

Typeset in Ehrhardt 10 on 12 point by
Mac Style Ltd, Scarborough, N. Yorkshire

Printed and bound in England by
CPI UK

For a complete list of Pen & Sword titles, please contact
Pen & Sword Books Limited
47 Church Street, Barnsley, South Yorkshire
S70 2AS, England
Email: enquiries @ pen-and-sword.co.uk
Website: www.pen-and-sword.co.uk

Cover photographs by Susanne Atkin, featuring the 'Fairfax Battalia' and 'The Troop'.

Contents

Preface		6
Chronology		8
Chapter One	The military establishment in Worcestershire before the Civil Wars	11
Chapter Two	Conflicting loyalties 1642	29
Chapter Three	Raising an army 1643–44	60
Chapter Four	Maintaining an army	87
Chapter Five	Losing an army 1645–46	111
Chapter Six	A Parliamentary Militia 1647–60	133
Chapter Seven	The Militia at the Restoration	151
Appendix 1:	Muster Roll for Worcestershire 1641	157
Appendix 2:	Gentry assessed for Horse 1642	174
Appendix 3:	Royalist gentry 1646	177
Appendix 4:	Worcestershire regiments in the Civil Wars	179
Further Reading		189
Abbreviations		190
Acknowledgements		191
Notes		192
Index		203

Preface

From the plundering of soldiers, their Insolency, Cruelty, Atheism, Blasphemy and Rule over us. Libera nos Domine [God Deliver Us]
(Henry Townshend at the siege of Worcester, 1646)

Worcestershire saw the first and last clashes of the English Civil War in 1642 and 1651. The present study is not a narrative history of the course of the Civil War in the county.[1] Instead, it focuses on the origin, development and relationships of the forces that garrisoned the city and county during the conflict. Large numbers of local men were recruited into the Royalist army in the First Civil War, many from the pre-war Trained Bands. Many of the regiments were recruited from the farms and villages scattered throughout the countryside, but Worcester had its own 'Town Regiment' of part-time militia which was a successor to the pre-war county Trained Bands. In maintaining the garrisons, however, there were enormous tensions between the officers, men and the civilian population. The uneasy relationship between the troops and the citizens ranged through indifference to militant neutrality and finally open resistance – as former neighbours increasingly became oppressor and oppressed. This is also a story of the tensions between city and county, burgesses and gentry, between different areas of the county as represented by loyalties to the various gentry leaders and even between sections of the Royalist army. In particular, the study highlights the, at best, ambivalent attitude of the City of Worcester towards the Royalists – in sharp contrast to the image of the 'Faithful City' that was cultivated at the Restoration. The late Philip Styles (whose work on the Royalist administration of Worcester has contributed so much to the period) believed that only a high sense of loyalty could have maintained the citizens during the four years of hardship up to 1646.[2] The present study will conclude that Worcester and the county as a whole was an area under military occupation in which personal loyalties counted for little.

No part of the county was spared the ravages of war. Worcester was the principal Civil War garrison and headquarters of the Royalist war effort in the county. Other important garrisons were at the town of Evesham and the moated manors of Hartlebury, Madresfield and Strensham, with troops also regularly billeted at Bewdley, Pershore and Droitwich, as well as at a small number of country houses. All looked to Worcester as a reservoir of troops and the headquarters of the army command, and the rest of the county became regarded merely as a means to maintain that army. This is made clear in the surviving parish accounts, with their repeated lists of charges for quartering troops and the plundering by the soldiers.[3] The reader might like to consider the present work within the wider study of the Royalist war effort in the region as published by Hutton, and also the comprehensive study by Wroughton of war on the civilian communities in the adjacent counties to the south.[4]

A great deal of the documentation is incomplete and scattered: some of the details conflict. This is especially true of the period immediately before and during the First Civil War and reflects the fact that the county was then on the losing, Royalist, side. The history of Worcestershire in this period is, however, fortunate in the survival of the diary written by Henry Townshend, a justice of the peace for Elmley Lovett and a Royalist Commissioner.[5] This records the administration of the war effort in great detail but in his personal comments he also conveys the grinding effect of the war and the huge expense of maintaining the garrisons. By the end of the war his exasperation with the military is all too clear. There was more to be gained from making claims against Parliament during the Interregnum, and a good series of claims for losses survive in the Commonwealth Exchequer Papers from Worcestershire parishes against the costs of monthly contributions, free quarter and plundering.[6] Although directed against one side alone, they may also be taken as representing the types of suffering caused equally by the Royalist and Parliamentary forces.

Chronology of the English Civil Wars

1642

9 January	King Charles I leaves London
5 March	Parliament issues the Militia Ordinance to claim control of the army
22 August	King Charles raises his Royal Standard at Nottingham to start the war
16 September	Byron occupies Worcester for the King
23 September	Skirmish at Powick: Royalist victory
24 September	Earl of Essex occupies Worcester for Parliament
20 October	Earl of Essex withdraws all but a small garrison
23 October	Battle of Edgehill: inconclusive outcome
15 November	Parliamentary troops evacuate Worcestershire
	Sir William Russell garrisons Worcester for the King

1643

3 April	Prince Rupert wins Battle of Camp Hill and slaughters inhabitants of Birmingham
13 April	Battle at Ripple: Prince Maurice defeats Waller
29 May	Siege of Worcester: William Waller unsuccessful and forced to withdraw
5 July	Battle of Lansdowne: Royalist victory
13 July	Battle of Roundway Down: Royalist victory
27 July	Fall of Bristol to Royalists
10 August– 5 September	Siege of Gloucester: held by Parliament
20 September	Battle of Newbury: Parliamentary victory

1644

Early April	'Tinker' Fox raids Bewdley and captures Sir Thomas Lyttleton
4 June	Massey takes Tewkesbury on Worcestershire border
	King's army enters Worcestershire, pursued by advance guard of Waller
5 June	Pershore and Evesham Bridges demolished by Royalists: area occupied by Waller's army
	King's army camps at Worcester
10 June	Sudeley Castle surrenders to Waller
11 June	Evesham bridge repaired by citizens to assist Waller
12 June	Waller at Abbots Morton
13–14 June	King at Bewdley: bridge is demolished
	Waller's Foot at Bromsgrove and the Horse at Stourbridge

15 June	Skirmish at Kidderminster
	Waller faces Bewdley, where the Royalists attempt to demolish the bridge
16 June	Royalists return to Evesham and try again to demolish the bridge
17 June	Waller's army at Droitwich
18 June	Waller at Worcester and then marches to Evesham
	Pershore Bridge demolished by Parliament
	Evesham defences and bridge demolished by Parliament
	King retreats to Oxford
20 June	Waller at Gloucester
29 June	Battle of Cropredy Bridge, Oxfordshire: Royalist victory
2 July	Battle of Marston Moor: Parliamentary victory
13 July	Battle of Corse Lawn, Eldersfield: Parliamentary victory
23 September	Parliamentary Militia Committee for Worcestershire authorised to raise new army from the county
11 November	Skirmish at Pinvin, Worcestershire: Royalist victory
December	Royalist Association formed to raise local troops from Worcestershire and surrounding counties

1645

20 January	Samuel Sandys becomes Governor of Worcester
5 March	Meeting of Woodbury Clubmen in north Worcestershire
March	Clubmen rising in Herefordshire
22 April	Battle of Ledbury: Royalist victory
May	Charles marches through Inkberrow, Droitwich, Bromsgrove
26 May	Battle of Evesham: seized by Parliament
31 May	Royalists take Leicester
14 June	Battle of Naseby: Parliamentary victory
24 September	Battle of Rowton Heath: Parliamentary victory
8 November	Skirmish at Trimpley, Kidderminster: Parliamentary victory
31 October	Battle of Denbigh: Parliamentary victory
11 November	Clubmen meet on Bredon Hill, East Worcestershire
December	Clubmen of Worcestershire unsuccessfully attack Prince Rupert and Prince Maurice

1646

5 February	Chester falls to Parliament
February	Samuel Sandys resigns as Governor of Worcester
21 March	Battle of Stow on the Wold: the last Royalist field army is defeated
26 March	Parliamentary army arrives before Worcester but depart for Droitwich
30 March	Garrison at Worcester clear the suburbs in preparation for siege
19 April	Skirmish at Worcester
5 May	King Charles surrenders to Scots
6 May	Banbury surrenders to Parliament
8 May	Newark surrenders to Parliament
10 May	Dudley surrenders to Parliament
16 May	Hartlebury surrenders to Parliament
20 May	Siege of Worcester begins
27 May	Ludlow surrenders to Parliament

21 June	Madresfield surrenders to Parliament
24 June	Oxford surrenders to Parliament
23 July	Worcester surrenders to Parliament

1647

3 February	King Charles handed over to English Parliament by the Scots
	Broadway Plot by disgruntled parliamentary officers
11 November	King Charles escapes to the Isle of Wight but is captured and imprisoned

Second Civil War

1648

23 March	Revolt in Wales
26 May	Kentish revolt fails
8 June	Revolt in Essex
July	Colonel Dudley's rising in Shropshire
5 July	Battle of Willoughby, Nottinghamshire: Parliamentary victory
17 August	Battle of Preston: Parliamentary victory
26 August	Rising at Colchester is defeated
	Rising in Herefordshire
6 December	Pride's Purge of the House of Commons

1649

January	Riot in Worcester against the Excise Tax
20 January	Trial of King Charles begins
30 January	King Charles executed
	Further plotting in Worcestershire
22 March	Surrender of Pontefract Castle to Parliament
17 March	Monarchy abolished by Act of Parliament
19 March	House of Lords abolished
1 May	Army mutinies
19 May	England proclaimed a Commonwealth
15 August	Cromwell begins campaign in Ireland

Third Civil War

1650

| 26 June | Cromwell replaces Fairfax as Lord-General of the Parliamentary Army |
| 3 September | Battle of Dunbar: Scottish Army defeated by Cromwell |

1651

1 January	Charles II crowned at Scone
1 August	Charles II marches on England with Scottish army
21 August	Scottish army enters Worcestershire
22 August	Skirmish at Ombersley, Worcestershire
23 August	Scottish army occupies Worcester
27 August	Parliamentary army rendezvouses at Evesham, Worcestershire
3 September	Battle of Worcester: Scottish army defeated
16 October	Charles flees England

Charles II was finally restored to the throne in May 1660.

Chapter One
The military establishment in Worcestershire before the Civil Wars

The English Civil Wars mobilised thousands of men across England, Wales, Scotland and Ireland, yet before the outbreak of war there was no standing army. This chapter will therefore consider the type of force that was available to the warring factions in England, using Worcestershire as a case study. By the early 17th century, all counties had a part-time militia under the command of the Lord Lieutenant, and it was composed of two forces – the Trained Bands and the general levy of the *Posse Comitatus*. In addition, there were periodic levies of men to form troops for foreign service. Whilst in theory the men of the Trained Bands were supposed to be excused from impressment for such active duty, they were increasingly chosen in preference to untrained men. The disputed control of the Trained Bands was a significant national and local factor in leading to the outbreak of war and they continued to play a role in the war as well as shaping the nature of the forces that engaged in the fighting.

The Trained Bands of the Tudor and Stuart periods were intended to be a middle-class force, comprising yeoman farmers and urban artisans and were funded by a local tax. Their gentry officers were under the command of the Lord Lieutenant and his deputies. The officers were expected to be 'men of honourable worthy and virtuous disposition', chosen on the basis of social rank rather than any military experience.[1] They were to organise their men 'sorted in bands, and to be trained and exercised in such sort as may reasonably be borne by a common charge of the whole county'.[2] The Trained Bands were principally designed to deal with any potential internal disorder and riot but also formed a nucleus of trained soldiers who could be drawn together into ad hoc regiments during a national emergency (as with the Armada crisis of 1588). They were largely composed of Foot, but also included troops of Horse provided by the gentry and wealthy freeholders. The Foot were normally organised geographically by hundreds and parishes into companies, nominally of *c*.100 men. Each parish in Worcestershire supplied from 2–12 soldiers. The surviving Worcestershire muster rolls for 1641 do suggest, however, that there was not a strict division into hundreds but rather as was necessary to apportion sufficient men and resources to the companies (see below, p. 25). One of the most unpopular responsibilities of the Petty Constable of the parish was to produce the quota of men, arms and armour for the periodic musters from their neighbours, as demanded by the Lord Lieutenant. Apart from providing the men, each town or village on a shared collective basis, and individuals with property over £5 (together with certain of the clergy), were required to supply a specified amount of weapons and equipment. These were stored under the control of the Constable and were typically kept in the parish church or in a town magazine. The details of men and their equipment were then recorded on muster rolls which were checked by the muster master at the beginning of each muster (see Appendix 1). The parishes were also expected to contribute to a rate to fund the costs of musters and other expenses.

With the principal role being that of local riot control, the gentry commanding the Trained Bands were reluctant to allow them to serve outside their own county. Indeed, in 1590 the Privy Council had reminded the Earl of Pembroke that men of Worcester were not to be forced to muster outside the City. The Trained Bands from neighbouring Warwickshire even refused to leave the county in 1588 and join the national defence against the attempted Spanish invasion. Such parochial concerns

Map of Worcestershire in the early 17th century by J. Speed. The inset of Worcester shows the line of the medieval defences that were to be restored during the Civil Wars, and also the already extensive suburbs that were to be destroyed by the Royalist garrison.

(Worcester City Museum)

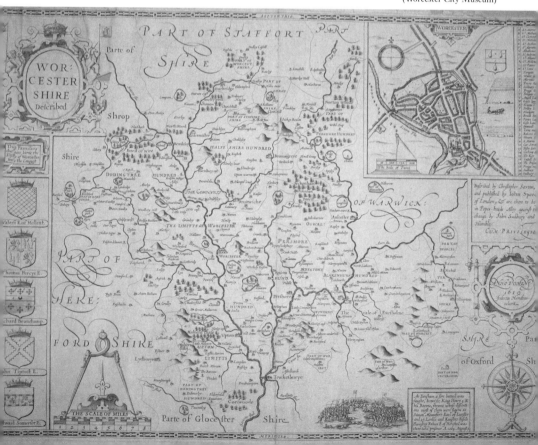

were to become a major issue in the years leading up to, and during, the Civil War (see below, p. 44).

Nonetheless, there was also a regular need to provide troops for periodic foreign service during the late 16th / early 17th centuries. Around 100,000 men were drafted for foreign service from 1585–1603 alone, including 1,151 men raised from Worcestershire.[3] The order to raise the required number of men would be passed from the Privy Council down through the Lords Lieutenant and the chain of local administration to the Petty Constable of the parish. The middle-class Trained Bands were supposed to be exempt from service and the parish constables tended to use such occasions as an opportunity to round up local vagabonds and vagrants. Thus the active service contingents were likely to be less well trained or motivated than the body supposed to be the 'bulwark' of the defences of the kingdom. Where the scouring of the countryside for 'undesirables' did not suffice and men of more substance were chosen, it was possible to pay for a substitute. Not surprisingly, there were frequent attempts to desert en route or at the embarkation ports. The county was responsible for the costs of feeding and billeting the levy until the men reached the port through a 'Coat and Conduct' tax. The Crown paid the men thereafter. In 1601 Wichbold, Dodderhill, Elmbridge, Upton Warren and Cookesley parishes were rated at £3 for sending 50 soldiers on the seven-day march to Chester for service in Ireland. The majority of the troops were musketeers armed with the earlier, lighter, form of the musket called the caliver. The rest were divided equally between pikemen armed with a 16–18 foot-long pike and those armed with the cheaper, if less effective, 6–8 foot long bills.[4] The threat was a regular one. In 1625 it cost the county £17 16s 8d to muster the 166 soldiers (one or two per parish) who had been sent for service alongside the other impressed men who formed the core of the *c*.9,000 – strong English army under Count Mansfeldt – the general of the English and French forces attempting to recapture the Palatinate.[5] Just two years later, in August 1627, a further tax had to be levied in Worcester for the costs of pressing into service twelve soldiers who were sent to Hull for shipping abroad for the Rhe expedition.[6]

Despite tradition, the forcible impressment of members of the Trained Bands into the foreign levies became increasingly common in order to supply the foreign expeditions of Charles I. In 1631, 150 men of the Worcestershire Trained Bands formed part of a contingent of 6,000 men who were raised for service in Sweden under Lord Hamilton. Their officers were Captain Fielding, Sergeant Major Fowler and Captain Talbott.[7] A Captain Fielding was later to serve with Lord Sandys' regiment in the Civil War, although there is no evidence to suggest that they were one and the same. Other individuals from the county also volunteered for service. John Lyttleton, the younger brother of Sir Thomas Lyttleton of Frankley, served as a captain of horse in the Netherlands and was killed there in 1629. Army service might provide a useful occupation for the younger sons of gentry who might lack an inheritance, but not all volunteers were gentlemen adventurers. In the early years of the century, Richard Higgins, a labourer from Worcester, served two years in the Low Countries in the English Brigade under Sir John Vere and then volunteered for a further two years as a mercenary in the service of Venice.[8] One might wonder about

a)

b)

c)

Early 17th century pikeman (a), shot (b), and musketeer (c) as illustrated by Jacob De Gheyn (1607). His illustrations represent the ideal of the middle class and well-equipped troops of the Trained Bands. By the outbreak of the Civil War the reality was very different. The Shot is armed with the light caliver and the musketeer with the heavier musket which was used with a rest at this time (although dispensed with during the Civil War).

(Brown University Library, USA)

the personal history of Henry Chamberlain of St Michael Bedwardine in Worcester who volunteered as a substitute for service in 1628 despite being married. His deserted wife was refused maintenance by the parish on the grounds that her husband had volunteered for service rather than be impressed![9]

Although most arrived as unwilling conscripts, the English soldiers won a good reputation on the continent during the Thirty Years War. Their practical experience was later to prove very important to both sides in the Civil War. But many of those who were forced to serve abroad never returned: they died of disease or from the fighting. Any wounded man that survived to return was liable to become a burden on the local parish. By an Act of 1592/3 each parish had to collect an assessment to pay a weekly pension to a maimed soldier, as determined by the Quarter Sessions. This was the basis of a principle followed by both sides during the Civil Wars. The records of the Worcestershire Quarter Sessions suggest that the casualties suffered in Ireland had been considerable. In 1607 William Holland of Castlemorton petitioned on the basis that he had received 'many incurable distempers' following his service there.[10] James Browne, a linen weaver of Arley Kings, claimed in 1617 that he had been pressed into service as a sergeant in the Bands of Sir Thomas Williams and Sir Henry Folliott and served in Ireland for eleven years. He had been wounded and eventually the parish provided a cottage for him.[11] Another Worcestershire man, Richard Coitte, also served as a soldier and in 1621 tried to claim a pass from the Worcestershire Quarter Sessions to go to the King's Hospital in London because whilst on service in Ireland he had been made 'lame and impotent' from 'lying on the ground'.[12] The parish of Blockley tried to avoid paying the 9d per week pension of wounded William Gough because they were already paying the costs of other maimed soldiers and because Gough had been jointly provided as a hired soldier by Prior's Cleeve, Wickhamford, Harvington, Cutsdon and Scomle (*sic*).[13] Only limited funds were available for payments to maimed soldiers. John Sampson had served eight years in the army under Elizabeth I and had been 'divers times wounded' but had to wait until the death of the next pensioned soldier before receiving a full payment.[14] With such a history, it is perhaps no wonder that troops of the later 17th century were reluctant to serve in Ireland!

The 17th century saw dramatic changes in the equipment of the Trained Bands from a force initially equipped with pike, bills and bows. From the early 17th century, musketeers (initially armed with the caliver) formed around two thirds of the Worcestershire foot when levied for active service. The rest were divided evenly between pikemen and billmen but by 1640 the short bill had been completely replaced by the 16 foot-long pike as far as the formal muster requirements were concerned. Nonetheless, the pike was still considered to be the most gentlemanly division of the Foot. The distinction was present even within the privileged ranks of the Worcester City Council. In 1638, the twenty-four members of the Grand Council were instructed to equip themselves as armoured pikemen whilst the forty-eight strong Common Council had to provide themselves with muskets.[15] It was the desire to preserve the social stratification that meant that the early peacetime Trained Bands still retained a ratio of 1:1 musketeers to pikemen.[16] But by 1641, in the climate of the Bishops' Wars and a move to more of a war footing in the Trained Bands, the power of musketry meant that the muster list for two companies in Worcestershire had a musket: pike ratio of 1.5:1 and 1.8:1. During the Civil War, the fighting regiments had a musket: pike ratio of at least 2:1. The musketeers were to become the real killing machines of the Civil War armies. With a rate of fire of two rounds per minute and firing in successive ranks, a well-disciplined regiment could maintain an almost continuous rate of fire with shot that could pierce a pikeman's armour at 100 yards (although in practice a 17th century battle proceeded at a more stately pace). When they were close enough to fight hand-to-hand they would swing their muskets around to make vicious clubs. In action, the main purpose of the pikemen was essentially to protect the musketeers from cavalry and also to be used as a terror weapon in a measured advance, with the hedge of deadly points aiming at the eyes of the enemy. The musket (either a full 12 bore or a lighter 'bastard' musket of 17 bore) was supposed to replace the lighter, 20–30 bore, caliver for general service from 1618. To save costs, the intention was to introduce the new guns as the old ones wore out. Some calivers were, however, still in service at Worcester in 1642. Swords are not mentioned in the local accounts, although these were regarded as the badge of a soldier (otherwise only allowed to be carried by the gentry) and are invariably shown in contemporary woodcuts of pikemen and musketeers prior to the war. But they were very much a secondary weapon in the hands of the common soldier and may not have been a priority for purchase. They are not mentioned in the lists of arms to be provided by the Worcestershire Trained Bands or in purchases made by Sir William Russell for his regiment in 1643 although he did obtain a number of wooden clubs as a cheap weapon for his men.

The musket was a noisy and dirty weapon, used by 'rude mechanicals', and there was still a widespread nostalgic reluctance in the country to finally give up the skills of archery: archers comprised 17 percent of the late 16th century Trained Bands. In East Anglia in the 1620s it was even suggested that a return to longbows might so shock invaders from a larger and better-equipped foreign enemy that it would give the smaller English Trained Bands an edge of surprise![17] Locally, in 1627 there were complaints that troops in St John's, Worcester, were not bringing longbows and arrows to musters or training with them regularly: there were warnings from the Constable that the butts at Holt and Cotheridge were ruinous. Better prepared, the parishioners of Northfield (now outer Birmingham, then in North Worcestershire) paid 4d in 1620 to repair their butts and built new ones in 1623 at a cost of 1s.[18] In 1628–9 the Statute of Henry VIII requiring archery practice was restored and as late as 1633 Charles I issued a new order for the use of bows in the Trained Bands, with training to be provided by a master bowman.[19] Indeed, a company of pikemen also armed with bows (the 'double-armed man') was formed in Herefordshire in 1642. But despite such efforts, the age of the longbow had passed into that of gunpowder and longbows saw little service during the Civil Wars.

The social elite of the Trained Bands were the Horse (cavalry). Horse at the beginning of the 17th century comprised heavy cavalry equipped as Lancers, and Light Horse armed with wheellock pistols. By the time of the Civil War they mainly

Extract from the Droitwich Borough Accounts for 1642 showing payment for 16 yards of 'broad ribbon' at a cost of 8s, with which to make colours for the Trained Bands.

(Worcestershire Record Office)

consisted of Light Horse armed with pistol or carbine and a sword, and wearing armour of back and breast plate over a heavy buff coat. In Worcestershire a small troop was provided by the gentry of the shire but they were expensive to maintain and it was difficult to recruit the required numbers. This was partly because the deputy lord lieutenants were reluctant to press any financial charges against men of their own social class and acquaintance – especially as the basis for doing so was based on an imprecise royal prerogative rather than having the force of law. As well as front-line troops, support services were also catered for within the Trained Band system. For every 1,000 men, there was also to be provided a company of 100 pioneers equipped with spades, pickaxes, shovels, hatchets, bills etc for building camps and fortifications. Such duty was unpopular with the soldiers and might also be used as a field punishment. In practice, local men and women would also be conscripted in the field to carry out any hard labour that was required (as they were in Worcestershire throughout the Civil War).

There was a strong tradition in the 16th and early 17th centuries that Trained Bands should be issued with uniform coats, partly paid for out of the local 'Coat and Conduct' tax and then topped up by the Crown.[20] In neighbouring Gloucestershire, the Trained Bands were smartly turned out in blue suits with yellow trim. Blue and red were favoured colours – not least because they were cheap colours to dye. A special effort was made to clothe the levies that were sent on active service. In 1616 the 25 pressed soldiers from Worcestershire were issued with jerkins. Clothing, probably a uniform coat, was also provided for the Worcestershire Trained Bands sent on service to Scotland in 1639 and 1640. From 1626, the levies were also supposed to be issued with 'snapsacks' in which to hold their rations and personal possessions.[21] The manual *Directions for Musters* (1638) simply stated, however, that troops should muster in their best clothes and there is no surviving evidence of any general issue of uniforms in Worcestershire. In the summer of 1642, the Droitwich soldiers of the Trained Bands were provided with 16 yards of broad ribbon, at a cost of 8s with which to make 'colours' – probably to decorate the company flag but possibly to decorate hatbands or armbands as a field sign. In 1638 the parish of Northfield paid 3s-1d 'for ribbininge, the souldiers'.[22] There is no evidence during the Civil War itself for any clothing issue at all to the militia of the Worcester Town Regiment, the successors to the Trained Bands. The City Council was stretched even to provide arms and pay for the officers. Indeed, most soldiers of the Civil Wars would have envied the uniforms provided for Elizabeth I's army in the Netherlands where the winter issue consisted of cassack (overcoat), doublet, breeches, hat, two shirts, three pairs of hose and three pairs of shoes.[23]

The scale of the Trained Bands in the county declined dramatically in the first half of the 17th century. In the early years of James I, the Worcestershire Trained Bands amounted to 2,500 Foot (caliver, pike and bill), 230 Pioneers, 20 Lancers and 85 Light Horse, all expected to provide their own arms and armour. In addition there were another 5,600 'able' men to act as a reserve.[24] However, from 1624 until the Civil War the Trained Bands numbered only 800–900 men, possibly indicating the overwhelming need to provide active service levies. In 1621 Worcester was allowed a limited autonomy in organising its contribution to the Trained Bands, although still part of the county structure. In that year, the Lord President of the Marches and Lord Lieutenant, William, Earl of Northampton, conceded the responsibility for mustering the Trained Bands of the city to the mayor and two other aldermen in return for a fee of £21 5s.[25] This seems, however, to have been limited to the funding of the musters and organising the delivery of men and equipment, ward by ward, to the county officers. The Council did not exercise any distinct military role. Worcester's desire for autonomy was not unique and reflects a general unwillingness of towns to muster with their counties, and re-kindle their privileges of the late 16th century (see above, p. 12). Neighbouring Gloucester succeeded in winning full autonomy to arm, drill and appoint officers to their own Trained Bands in 1627, but the failure of Worcester to win similar rights proved to be of great significance in the stance that the city took against the county gentry in the months leading up to the Civil War.[26]

The origin of the 800 men included in the 1621 muster suggests that the Worcestershire Trained Bands were organised in nine companies of 60 men and above, with one or two companies per Hundred.[27] The Worcester return of over 161 men was included within Oswaldslow Hundred although no details were provided. The company was the principal unit of organisation, under a captain. Ideally, each company would then have been divided into five squadrons, each under the command of a corporal and further divided into files of six men grouped from neighbouring parishes under an experienced 'file leader'. This therefore allowed (in theory at least) for a progression of training from a local to a Hundred and then county level.

Generally, service in the Trained Bands was not popular amongst its intended members, although poorly paid substitute labourers probably found it

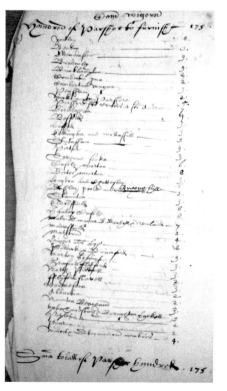

Extract from 1621 Muster Roll for Worcestershire showing the 175 soldiers raised from Pershore Hundred.

(Worcestershire Record Office)

The muster of the Worcestershire Trained Bands in 1621

Oswaldstow Hundred	267 men
Pershore Hundred	175 men
Blakenhurst Hundred	60 men
Halfshire Hundred	178 men
Doddingtree Hundred	120 men
TOTAL	800 men

more attractive. It might provide an occasional holiday for the training musters and a reasonable rate of pay for those days, but otherwise it interrupted a normal livelihood and, despite assurances to the contrary, carried the risk of impressment into any army gathering for foreign expedition. John Genifer, a saltpetre maker of St John's in Worcester drew a knife and threatened the constable when he was summoned to a muster in 1601. A similar charge was made against Thomas Clarson of Alvechurch, as a man of 'badde behaviour and ill disposition' in 1604.[28] There were continual problems in maintaining any form of military standard in terms of training or adequate equipment. When Charles I acceded to the throne in March 1625 he wanted to reform the system and create a 'perfect militia' and in 1626 the Trained Bands were optimistically called 'the sure and constant bulwark and defence of the Kingdom'.[29] There was indeed a brief interest during this period in organising musters and in London, and elsewhere, watching the Trained Bands being drilled remained a popular social activity. Military Yards were established in a number of towns including Colchester (1621), Norwich and Bristol (1625) and Gloucester (1626). But in many shires, including Worcestershire, where the total cost of the muster in 1614 was £108 18s 4d and where in 1624 it cost £17 16s 8d to muster the Worcester men of the Trained Bands, the cumulative costs could be off-putting, with persistent grumbles about the legality of such demands.[30] In 1628, the miller John Hide from Acton Beauchamp, refused to pay his share of the 60s 4d demanded for the musketeer's match, the Muster Master's pension and other expenses of training.[31]

New initiatives around this time included establishing permanent magazines for ammunition and weapons storage, encouragement of the use of artillery grounds for training and an attempt to raise the standards of the Horse (always expensive to maintain). This was on top of an earlier plan to progressively upgrade arms – discarding the old fashioned caliver in favour of the more modern musket as the former became unserviceable. A comprehensive system of drill was approved by the Privy Council to maintain and train the Trained Bands. Drill was to be carefully structured with training progressing through files, squadrons, companies, county regiments and then ideally regional musters. The traditional site of the county muster was at Pitchcroft on the north outskirts of Worcester where the men were supposed to be ready to muster at one hour's notice. The state of the roads and the fact that the common soldiers were expected to make their way to the musters on foot does, however, make this an optimistic assumption.[32] The gentry officers were also, in the main, not skilled enough to instruct their men. Recognising the problems of relying totally on an amateur force, the counties employed a professional soldier as a part-time Muster Master to supervise training. The one-time soldier, Gervase Markham described a muster-master as 'a man of faire vertue, good birthe, temperate and myld nature; of great skill and good judgement'. He was to set a good example and to 'expound the mysteries of warre' by 'encouragement, gotten by exercise, that must make men and commandment, mixt with severitie, that must force arms'.[33] From 1621–1640 the Muster Master for Worcestershire was Edmond Woodward of Sambourn, just across the county border in Warwickshire, who owned a mill in Worcestershire.[34] He was given a substantial annual salary of £50 per annum. This was an unpopular post, widely regarded as being an informant for the Lord Lieutenant and also expensive to maintain. In 1626 Charles I also ordered that the muster masters should be assisted by experienced sergeants who had seen service in the Thirty Years War. They were originally intended to undertake an intensive training programme of just three months, paid a minimum of 6s per week and maintained at the hospitality of the local gentry. During this time, there was to be daily training of officers, instruction of three corporals from each company and drilling groups of men twice a week.[35] It was an unenviable and impossible task. Weather-beaten NCOs, used to the privations of campaign, had to teach both their social superiors and the ambivalent common soldiers. The training schedule could not be maintained and in Worcestershire, as in many counties, sergeants Peter Wetherall, James Guyatt and Fitzwalter Hungerford remained until 1630.[36]

One spur to the interest in training during the late 1620s was an invasion scare in 1626 which lead to widespread mobilisation of the Trained Bands. In that year, the Lord Lieutenant established a new magazine at Worcester (at the Tolsey from 1629) and stocked it with 2½ lasts of powder (1 last = 24 small barrels: in total equivalent to 2.6 tons), 2½ ton of match (the fuse for firing muskets) and 2½ ton of lead (for the manufacture of musket balls).[37] The powder cost 10d per lb.[38] This was a larger stockpile than was present even in the run up to the Civil War. As a consequence, Worcester City Council spent many hours during the year deliberating on the costs of the training of the Trained Bands and their inspection. In March, a tax of a double fifteenth had to be levied towards the cost of the soldiers, their powder and wages for the forthcoming muster (as well as the repairing of the town wall). At the same time, a survey was made of all the arms held within the city. It was agreed that the mayor 'shall assigne everie man to finde armour accord[ing] to his abilitie and power'.[39] By April the muster had taken place and they were confidently described as 'nowe trained' but on 16 May there was a further inspection of the troops and their armour, suggesting that some deficiencies had been noticed in the March/April muster. But the demands of maintaining the Trained Bands continued to mount and in August the Chamber agreed a new double fifteenth to supply powder, lead and match 'for the defence of the relme'.[40] Roger Goughe, John Tillam and Edward Waring supplied this material. The Council was still worried over the cost and therefore suggested that instead of paying the troops their allowance for the training day, they should be excused the payment of the fifteenth.[41] The soldiers were evidently still not happy about not receiving money in hand and in September the Chamber had to reverse their previous decision not to pay the troops at their musters and agreed to pay them 12d per training day. In return, however, the soldiers were expected to also pay the assessment.[42]

The King repeatedly tried to raise uniform standards of drill and equipment and build up stocks of powder, match and bullets.[43] But the cost of maintaining such a system with any regularity quickly became a source of resentment for the local community. They could see little direct benefit in a time of peace for maintaining the Trained Bands beyond subsidising a periodic social outing for some of the men of the parish. For most people, interest in the Trained Bands – either in terms of making a commitment for training or equipment (or indeed the maintenance of town defences) – could only be justified at a time of immediate crisis.

Until the outbreak of the Civil War, any system of structured training then appears to have collapsed completely in the county. Local

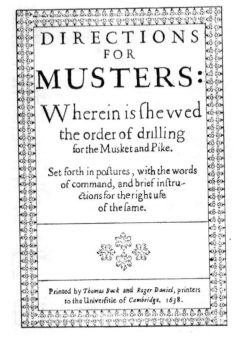

Cover of *Directions For Musters*, 1638. One of a series of drill books capitalising on a gentry interest in military drill and tactics.

(Partizan Press)

references in the Chamber Book of Worcester City Council to the training of the Trained Bands disappear from 1627 to 1639, with only occasional inspections of arms. The personal interest of Charles I in improving the Trained Bands also appears to have waned. This is despite a rash of training manuals that were produced to feed the new interest of some of the gentry in the theory of combat and public shows of drills in the capital and elsewhere. In 1638, 80 gentlemen of the Artillery Gardens in London 'where the choice and best-affected citizens (and gentry) are practiced and taught the Rudiments of our Militia' performed an elaborate three-hour long drill display entitled 'Mars: his triumph', but this formalised display bore little relationship to the desperate efforts of the muster-masters and their sergeants on muddy fields across England.[44] *Directions for Musters* (1638) summarises the various instructions of the King and Lords Lieutenant and represents an idealistic vision just before the Civil War. It details how the companies were to be divided into files of near neighbours, under the best men as file leaders. This was supposed to make it easier for the separate files to drill weekly regularly on 'holy-dayes or other convenient dayes'. This must have been difficult, with only 42 percent of the parishes listed in the 1641 Worcestersire muster providing a full file of six men or more (see below, Appendix 1). Each musketeer was supposed to be supplied at the rate of 2lb of powder, 6 yards

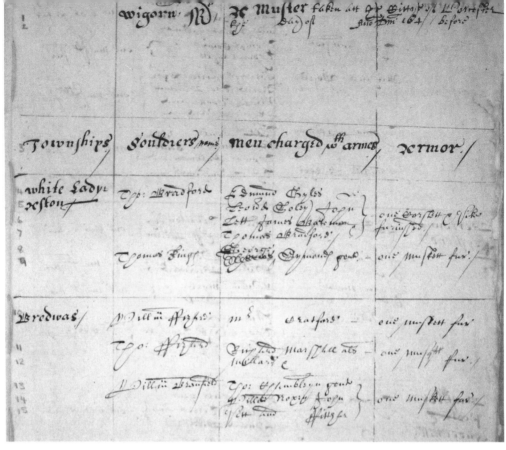

Extract from the 1641 Muster Roll showing the allocation from White Ladies Aston and part of Broadwas. The names of the soldiers are given together with those responsible for providing their arms and the nature of the arms themselves – either the 'corslett' (armour) and pike or a musket. See also Appendix 1.

of match and 24 musket balls per year.[45] For the weekly drills, however, the musketeers were only to be issued with enough powder to flash their pans as part of the process of learning to fire their weapons safely. For the monthly company drills there was live firing at targets. There was then supposed to be an annual regimental muster, although this tended to clash with harvest-time. Such an ideal was rarely met, at least outside London, and according to contemporaries the troops at musters were prone to sneaking off into the local inns or simply absenting themselves during the harvest-time! This was despite the threat of 10 days imprisonment or a 40s fine for absence from a muster.[46] Only rarely did the musketeers actually fire their muskets and in some counties the officers were reluctant to issue any amount of black powder as being too dangerous! This was not surprising as the tactician William Barriffe complained that, despite the careful theory of the training structure, few musketeers knew the correct amount of powder with which to charge their muskets.[47] Such a lack of training could easily have led to a major disaster in the ranks and manuals of the day focused heavily on learning postures by rote in order to minimise risks. The musketeers had to be trained to be able to progress from learning the over thirty-five separate movements to load a musket safely, to the three battlefield commands of 'Make Ready – Present – Give Fire!' The high cost of powder also meant that the local gentry were unwilling to purchase adequate stocks, and in Worcestershire, the Lord Lieutenant complained that the costs of its transport from London was as much as the cost of the powder itself.

Robert Ward, in his *Animadversions of Warre* (1639), thought that the monthly training sessions were a waste of time as 'matters of disport and things of no moment' without the ability 'to make one good soldier'. The troops drifted in slowly from the villages so 'by the time the arms be all viewed … it draws towards dinner time'. This was certainly a complaint of the Worcestershire muster in 1640 (see below, p. 27). Ward blamed the officers who 'love their bellies so well as they are loath to take much pains about disciplining of their soldiers'. But such men were soon to become the officers of the early Civil War armies. Ward advocated meeting just twice a year for three or four days; similarly, Barriffe, in his manual 'for the bettering of the souldier's knowledge of the trained bands' recommended a six-day programme of structured training at Company level and above. Whether this was ever taken up is doubtful.

As well as training musters, there were also supposed to be regular inspections of the arms and armour; but after another inspection of armour in the city at the Guildhall in 1628, any interest by Worcester City Council in the Trained Bands seems to have been completely lost until 1635 when it was agreed that each of the twenty four aldermen should provide armour, and each of the 48 Common Councillors a musket by 24 August.[48] Some evidently did not comply and the order was repeated in September 1638 when the arms were ordered to be inspected again on 1 November. Defaulters risked a fine of 20s (for the 24 members of the Grand Council), or 10s (for the 48 members of the Common Council). Other commoners were expected to provide arms as appointed by the mayor and aldermen with a fine of 6s 8d if they did not comply. But no mention is made of actual training until May 1639 and the start of the Bishop's War. By then the costs of training the soldiers in the city and contributing to sending 14 men to the campaign in Scotland soared to £71 3s 4d.

The surviving partial muster roll for Worcestershire in 1641 (Appendix 1) gives details of how the troops immediately before the Civil War were supposed to be equipped. Most of the arms and armour was provided for the named soldiers by groups of 2–4 individuals, combining the value of their assessments. For those too poor, an assessment might be levied on the township as a whole to provide extra arms (typically a single musket). Only in a minority of cases (6 percent) did a soldier provide his own equipment, but frequently helped pay for someone else's weapons instead. It may be that this encouraged the arms to be viewed as communal rather than personal property. In Tibberton, the son of Thomas Hooper provided a musket for his father. The social status of the soldiers is not given in the document, although providers included a number of local gentry and also a considerable number of widows. Only a minority of the soldiers can be identified from the records of the Quarter Sessions or from wills, where they are typically described as yeomen or

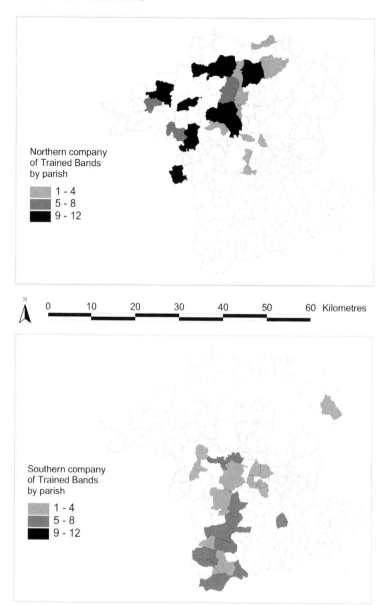

Map showing the origin, by parish, of two companies of troops listed in the partial 1641 Muster Roll. These represent the company of Captain Clent in the north of the county and that of an un-named officer in the south. Men were, in the main, drawn from adjacent parishes, whatever Hundred they were in. There are, however, some inconsistencies, with some troops in the south company taken from a detached part of Pershore Hundred lying in the northeast of the county.

(Worcestershire Historic Environment and Archaeology Service)

husbandmen, with the occasional craftsman such as a glover and dyer and including the Sheriff's bailiff of Belbroughton, Thomas Goffe. This would tend to support the complaints made by the army that by now the Trained Bands were composed mainly of property-less labourers rather than the yeoman ideal. Parishes might provide up to twelve soldiers for the Trained Bands, although it was more commonly between one and six. By this stage, it is clear that the companies were not organised on a strict Hundred basis, hindered by the fact that in Worcestershire the Hundreds were not divided in coherent blocks. Thus, Captain Clent's company of 177 men (114 musketeers and 63 pikemen) was drawn from over 30 parishes scattered from the adjacent parts of Halfshire, Doddingtree, Oswaldstow and part of Pershore Hundreds.

It had proved continually difficult across the nation to recruit men of the expected calibre. There were particular problems in recruiting the Horse because of the additional expenses of maintaining the mounts, and it proved difficult to recruit the Council of State's ideal of younger sons and brothers of gentlemen or the sons of farmers.[49] Frequently the selected Trained Band members paid for substitutes of poorer status to attend and the arms provided were of similar low quality. The reports of the conditions of weapons of the Worcestershire Trained Bands in August 1642 makes it clear that the instructions for the troops to arm themselves with 'compleat' arms of the 'best modern fashion' (*Directions for Musters*) had been ignored on a wide scale. There was no mention of the pikes and armour meant to have been provided by the parishes in 1641 and the appearance of hedgebills and sheep pikes are suggestions more of a force of farm labourers than the middle-class ideal.

The substitutes may have lacked the sense of 'stake-holders' in the country's defence, as intended in the original conception of the middle-class Trained Bands. Service also increasingly carried the real risk of being forcibly impressed into temporary foreign service.[50] It is, therefore, hardly surprising that discipline became a problem during the musters. In 1640, prior to being sent off to the Bishop's War in Scotland, men of the Worcestershire Trained Bands destroyed the Worcester gallows – possibly erected as a warning to them to behave during their muster on Pitchcroft![51] John Corbet, in neighbouring Gloucestershire, expressed a commonly held view when he described the Trained Bands as 'effeminate in courage and incapable of discipline, because their whole course of life was alienated from warlike employment'.[52]

The Trained Bands were therefore in a sorry state in the years leading up to the Civil Wars. Although William Barriffe described the Trained Bands in 1635 in traditional language as the 'last refuge' and 'chiefe Bulwark' of the country, he also bemoaned their lack of training that left the country 'dull and snoring' in the face of danger, and an object of ridicule in the eyes of Europe.[53] Charles I's initiative in trying to improve their training had failed. Barriffe complained that 'our souldiers are scarce called forth to exercise either Posture or Motion once in four or five yeares'.[54] The 17th century poet, John Dryden, in cynical mood later described the Trained Bands more poetically thus:

> The country rings around with loud alarms,
> And raw in fields the rude militia swarms;
> Mouths without hands; maintain'd at vast expense,
> In peace a charge, in war a weak defence;
> Stout once a month they march, a blustering band,
> And ever, but in times of need, at hand.[55]

In 1639 and 1640, with the onset of the Bishop's War in Scotland, the threat of having to mobilise and undertake active service on a much wider scale than seen before became very real. Those who had been attracted to warfare as mercenaries on the continent were very much in the minority. The rest had been unwilling conscripts who had come to fear the widespread disease that followed the army as much as the bullet or sword. In early 1638 the number of Trained Bands in the country amounted in total to 93,718 Foot and 5,239 Horse.[56] Around 30,000 of these men were mobilised for service in 1640.[57] For many in the country, the forcible pressing of the Trained Bands, to serve not just outside their county but even in a foreign country, without any clear statutory basis (as opposed to Royal prerogative) to do so, became one of the principal grievances against the King.

There was also an economic cost to consider. In the face of war, the costs of maintaining the Trained Bands in Worcestershire rocketed from £11 17s 7d in 1638 to £48 17s 7d in 1639, together with an additional charge of £40 19s 7d for sending fourteen soldiers on active service to Scotland and providing their 'apparull' (clothing).[58] Much worse was to come. In 1640 the constables were instructed to select the fittest 600 men from the Trained Bands for impressment into new army regiments raised for the campaign in Scotland. This amounted to *c*.75 percent of the total trained military strength of Worcestershire. To ensure maximum choice and to make up the resultant deficiency in the regular military strength of the county, each man was expected to bring two more for new training (which carried on throughout the year). The selected soldiers came from over 50 parishes, mainly from the South Worcestershire Trained Bands but also included Captain Boys' company from north Worcestershire and 36 men from Worcester City.[59] Elmley Lovett was instructed to provide four soldiers but eventually only supplied three, at a cost of £7 10s. Two were Henry Powell and Rowland Edwards, a tailor, but for some reason a replacement had to be found for Christopher Stutty, and Richard Crow, a mason, was eventually not sent.[60] After mustering at Worcester at 9am on 25 April, the chosen men were divided into five companies of 100 men or more and billeted for two months in Droitwich, Evesham, Pershore, Bewdley and Worcester until early July. The men were given training on one day a week, for which they were paid 8d but were expected to find work to support themselves for the rest of the week. Not surprisingly, there were huge problems in keeping such a large number of idle men together without a regular income for such a period. With over 150 men billeted in the city, Worcester appears to have escaped lightly in the arson attack on its gallows! It was probably with considerable relief that the officials of the county, in early July, finally saw the men start their march northwards, guided by the beat of their drummer, John

Massey. Other counties were not so lucky. There were mutinies in neighbouring Warwickshire and Herefordshire. The Trained Bands from the latter were described as 'for the most part a naked, poor-conditioned people, and of the meanest sort'.[61] This was a long way from the ideal of the middle-class and respectable force, with many men evidently sending substitutes in their stead. The King had to deal with even more serious problems in the Dorset Trained Bands. They hanged one of their officers after a dispute at Faringdon in Berkshire whilst on the march and then a number deserted.[62] Sir Jacob Astley, who commanded the contingent that the Worcestershire Trained Bands joined at Selby, described his army in despair as the 'arch-knaves of the country'.[63] Some went to extraordinary lengths of self-mutilation to avoid active service. In 1639 the commander of the Lincolnshire Trained Bands was accosted by the wife of one of his men who presented him with the big toe of her husband, wrapped in a handkerchief.[64]

Loath to report until the last possible minute, the unwilling Worcestershire recruits drifted in to their training sessions throughout the day, consequently exasperating the officers by interrupting their training schedules. Some men were then declared unfit and it might take three or four attempts to find suitable replacements. Some, like Henry Sherrard of Belbroughton in north Worcestershire, only waited to be issued with their 20s worth of new clothing before deserting. Eventually their exasperated officers had to put the men under guard to prevent them absconding.[65] Although details do not survive, the costs suggest that a cheap set of coat and breeches was being provided. Coventry provided 33 blue coats at 15s each and 24 blue breeches at 8s each.[66] This was, however, not necessarily so, and it was likely to have been a motley army that marched northwards. Apart from the soldiers, the county also had to supply 17 carters and their carts, and 50 horses to the train of artillery.[67] In all, it cost the county £1,200 (including £200 from Worcester city) to equip and send these soldiers and support to Newcastle. The imposition on the counties of the costs of maintaining the army during this war and then the cost of disbanding it was one of the charges that John Pym laid against the King.

The soldiers returned home from the war at the end of 1640 and with much relief the cost of maintaining the Trained Bands in Worcester fell to the sum of only £7 6s 6d in 1641. The surviving muster roll for 1641 may be incomplete but still over 300 men were mustered in that year (Appendix 1).[68] This recent experience of war (both human and financial) may well have coloured the unenthusiastic response of many men in the county to the rising danger of war on a much larger scale.

The other pre-Civil War force in existence, but only as a last resort of defence, was the *Posse Comitatus*. This was a levy of all able-bodied men between the ages of 16 and 60 that were supposed to be called out in an emergency and to act as an untrained reserve (especially if the Trained Bands were mobilised for service elsewhere). Unlike the Trained Bands, they were supplied with weapons rather than being expected to provide them themselves. In view of the difficulties in equipping the Trained Bands these are likely to have been primitive, such as bills and clubs rather than any more up-to-date equipment. Nonetheless, there were regular, if desperate, attempts in times of emergency throughout the Civil War to continue the

---

Order to mobilise the *Posse Comitatus* 1643

To all Constables, Petty Constables and all other his Majesty's loving subjects within the County of Worcester.

Forasmuch as there are a multitude of armed men come within this County of Worcester and against the City of Worcester this 29th day to the great disturbance of this County and the hazard of the loss of the said City from their loyalty and obedience, these are to command you suddenly upon receipt hereof and with all haste to summon all persons within 16 and 60 years of age to repair with all such arms and weapons as they have to the City of Worcester to help, assist and defend the said City and County from all opposition whatsoever. And that every person bring with him three days' provision at the least. And hereof fail not at your perils. Dated this 28th day of May 1643.

Sam Sandys

---

mobilisation of the *Posse Comitatus*. In Worcestershire they were summoned in 1643, 1645 and 1651 but to little effect. In May 1643, the governor of Worcester, Samuel Sandys, faced with the threat of a siege by Sir William Waller, optimistically commanded the men of the county to appear with their arms and also three days rations (the standard expected to be carried in a soldier's snapsack), and the similar call made by Charles II in August 1651 was almost universally ignored.[69] By then, as an untrained, poorly equipped levy, the prospect of facing up to the professional and battle-hardened New Model Army must have been a totally unappealing fate!

Chapter Two
Conflicting Loyalties – 1642

There had been a background of widespread complaints regarding the King's government for much of his reign. In trying to rule without Parliament from 1629–40, Charles I had been driven to rely on a number of extraordinary forced loans and taxes that were imposed without parliamentary consent. The levy of 'tonnage and poundage' (duties on imports and exports) reduced profits for merchants and not surprisingly, therefore, the trading classes, centred on towns such as Worcester, were amongst the fiercest opponents of the Crown. This opposition also created a suspicion amongst some sections of the gentry that the merchants were trying to usurp their traditional position in society and so helped further polarise opinion between town and county. Objections to the Ship Money tax eventually affected a

very broad section of the community as the tax to refurbish the fleet was extended from coastal ports to the whole country. Worcestershire ranked sixteenth in the Ship Money tax of 1636. The Kidderminster preacher, Richard Baxter, described how this had caused 'a wonderful murmuring all over the land, especially among the county nobility and gentry'. The Ship Money tax was extended by 'Coat and Conduct' money in 1639 to pay for the army's campaign in Scotland but it seems to have been the Ship Money that remained the focus of agitation. Baxter, with a characteristic disdain for the lower classes, explained how 'The poor ploughmen understood

Engraving of Charles 1 (1600–49), after Van Dyck.

but little of these matters, but a little would stir up their discontents when money was demanded'.

Complaint was more than simply against what was considered unfair and excessive taxation during a time of economic uncertainty. The imposition of taxes without the consent of Parliament was also feared as a signal of the absolutist ambitions of Charles I in wanting to rule completely without Parliament. Even so, there were many who still believed that the King's majesty was sacrosanct and it was the duty of Parliament simply to serve rather than pursue its own ambition. Political loyalties polarised with the King's attempt to remove five of his worst critics from the Houses of Parliament forcibly in January 1642.

There were similar divisions regarding changes in the direction of the established Church. On the one hand the greater ritual in the Laudian reforms seemed to be heading towards Roman Catholicism, but on the other hand there was fear of the intentions of those promoters of radical puritan reform. Religion played a central, passionate, part in the life of the country, whipped up by the partisan sermons of the clergy. There were some pockets of Catholicism in the county, associated with key families such as the Sheldons of Beoley, the Lyttletons of Frankley and the Russells of Little Malvern and Strensham, but the numbers were not great and few others would have supported outright Catholicism. However, fear of 'papists' led to a rash of rumours about plots in the county and at Bewdley in November 1641 rumours 'caused them all in the town to be up in arms, with watch all night in very great fear'. In December 1641 an order was sent to the Constable of Mamble ordering a watch to be kept at the crossroads for 'wandering soldiers' possibly carrying letters between conspirators and in February 1642 the Trained Bands of Doddingtree Hundred were ordered to be ready to muster at one hour's notice.[1] The stories of massacres of Protestants in Ireland had heightened the fear of Catholic plots against a reformed Church of England. As King Charles, with his own personal sympathies and a Catholic wife, tried to raise an army to quell the Irish rebellion, the fears intensified as to whether he could be trusted with an army which might ultimately be used against the English Parliament and Anglican Church.

If so obliged, the choices that people were to make in supporting one side or another in the developing crisis were a complex mixture of general economics, religious belief and mistrust, but they were also driven by more local grievances and loyalties. In Worcestershire, issues of city versus county and clothier versus employee could be just as important, allying with whichever side seemed most likely to support their cause. Many of the inhabitants of the Vale of Evesham had a particular complaint in that the government from the 1620s repeatedly tried to suppress the local, but extensive, tobacco-growing industry in order to protect the interests of the new colony in Virginia. In Malvern Chase and Feckenham Forest, the deforestation, division, and sale of the royal forest to raise money for Charles I in the later 1620s and early 1630s upset the poor cottagers who feared the loss of their common pasture rights, right to timber from the waste, and the blocking of routeways. The Royal Commissioners faced armed riot![2] All combined to produce a suspicious and quarrelsome atmosphere of rising rancour. It was a difficult time for many as they wrestled with their

Timetable to War in Worcestershire

1642

5 March	Militia Ordinance to raise the Trained Bands for Parliament
27 May	Commission of Array to raise the Trained Bands for the King
mid-July	Quarter Sessions refuse to support the Commission of Array
21 July	Commission of Array appointed for Worcestershire
2 August	Worcester buys arms
3 August	Quarter Sessions now agree to support the Commission of Array
5 August	Sir William Russell makes an inventory of arms in the county
11 August	Warwickshire Commission of Array requests support from Worcestershire
12 August	Worcestershire Trained Bands and volunteers muster at Pitchcroft but will not serve out of county
14 August	County gentry agree to raise a troop of 89 Horse for the King for three months
17 August	Volunteers sought for service out of county
20 August	Charles I orders a further search for arms in the hands of suspected Parliamentarians in Worcester
21 August	Charles I unsuccessfully requests the Worcestershire Trained Bands to march to support Warwickshire
22 August	**Charles I raises his standard at Nottingham – the Civil War begins**
	Muster of the Worcestershire Trained Bands and volunteers in five companies
23 August	The Worcestershire Commission of Array again declines to support Warwickshire
25 August	Inspection of arms at Worcester
28 August	Charles I am worried that the Parliamentary faction in Worcester is receiving arms from London, orders a new search for arms and gives free reign to mobilise Royalist volunteers.
29 August	Worcester buys cannon
2 September	Worcestershire Commission of Array declines to Associate with Shropshire, Denbigh, Flint and Chester because of the dubious loyalty of Worcester
3 September	Worcester City is asked to define what it intends to do in support of the Commission of Array
4 September	Worcester Trained Bands and the Mayor refuse to allow the Commission of Array to recruit in the City
5 September	Commission of Array is formally given new powers to raise volunteers. Sir Thomas Lyttleton appointed commander of the County Horse and Foot

13 September	Worcester raises its own militia for Parliament
16 September	The Royalist, Sir John Byron occupies Worcester with a small force and camps at Powick
23 September	**Skirmish at Powick**
24 September	Worcester occupied by the Parliamentary army of the Earl of Essex
19 October	Earl of Essex's army leaves the city
23 October	**Battle of Edgehill**
15 November	Royalists occupy Worcester

consciences, splitting class and family, and in some eyes threatening an imbalance in society itself. But above all, the majority of people in the country tried to steer a peaceful path between the strident calls of the small cliques of activists.

Despite its serious faults, as the only organised military force in the country, control of the county Trained Bands and their stocks of arms was vital as the activists of both sides jockeyed for power in the months leading to the outbreak of Civil War in 1642. Neither side could count on the automatic support of the Trained Bands whose allegiances depended heavily on that of their local gentry officers and their polarisation through any local issues. On 28 January 1642 Parliament petitioned the King for him to hand over control of the Trained Bands. In Worcestershire, they proposed that command be given to Edward, Lord Howard rather than the existing Lord Lieutenant, Thomas, Lord Windsor. Not surprisingly, the King refused to accept this attack on his personal authority, with the whole legal basis of the maintenance of the Trained Bands resting largely on the royal prerogative rather than by statute. Nonetheless, on 5 March Parliament issued the Militia Ordinance to order counties to muster, arm and train troops to its command. They appointed new Lords Lieutenant, with the power 'to make colonels, captains and other officers to lead, conduct and employ the persons aforesaid arrayed and weaponed, for the suppression of all rebellions, insurrections and invasions' under the direction of the Lords and Commons assembled in Parliament.[3] Sympathetic MPs then tried to ensure that the counties actually implemented the instructions.

Such an attack on the authority of the monarch could not be tolerated and the King replied on 27 May by ordering his subjects not to co-operate with this presumptuous order of Parliament. Frustrated by his lack of control of the mechanism of government that was available to Parliament, he was, however, obliged to retaliate via a revival of the old medieval device of the Commission of Array to muster troops under, hopefully, sympathetic peers and gentry to whom he gave new commissions. In Worcestershire, the Prince of Wales (later King Charles II) was the nominal head of the Commission, led in practice by Edward, Lord Dudley and Thomas, Lord Coventry (of Croome D'Abitot) and other prominent local gentry. The 27-year-old Samuel Sandys of Ombersley (1615–1685) countersigned the summons of the militia, suggesting that he may have been with the King in Doncaster – an early indicator of his importance in

17th century altar rails in St Eadburga's Church, Broadway. The presence of altar rails became a focal point of religious disagreements – symbolising the separation of high-church clergy from their congregation. In many churches they were removed. INSET: contemporary illustration of removal of altar rails.

(Author Collection)

Worcestershire Commission of Array[5].
▲ = known Royalist Army officer during Civil Wars

Charles, Prince of Wales	John Littleton
Edward, Earl of Dudley	William Child
Thomas, Lord Coventry	Edward Pitts
Sir T.C.	John Nanfan
Sir John Packington ▲	Henry Townshend
Sir Edward Sebright	Samuel Sandys ▲
Sir William Russell ▲	Joseph Walsh ▲
Sir Edward Littleton	Edward Vernon
Sir Ralph Clare	Sherrington Talbot
Sir Henry Herbert ▲	Francis Finch
Sir John Rous	Henry Ingram ▲
Sir Rowland Berkeley ▲	Thomas Savage ▲
Sir Henry Spiller	

Tomb of Thomas, 2nd Lord Coventry (d.1661) at Croome Church. He was one of the heads of the Royalist Commission of Array in Worcestershire during 1642. He did, however, anger Charles 11 by excusing himself from joining the King at Worcester in 1651.

(Susanne Atkin)

the Royalist establishment within the county. No member of Worcester City Council was included in the Commission and we must be careful in reading too much into the affiliations of who were named. Inclusion was in part intended to encourage waverers, rather than being in itself a measure of loyalty or commitment. Only a small number of activists within the Worcestershire Commission eventually took up arms for the Royalists. Similarly, it has been calculated that over 40 percent of the Commissioners in the north Midlands remained neutral during the war.[4]

Their purpose was to secure the county by raising the Trained Bands, to arrest Parliamentary activists and to raise a new national army for the King. For its part, Parliament saw the Commission of Array as a virtual declaration of war and retaliated immediately by issuing an Order declaring:

Whereas it appears that the King, seduced by wicked counsel, intends to make war against the Parliament ... It is therefore ordered by the Lords and Commons in Parliament that the Sheriffs shall suppress the raising, and coming together of any souldiers, Horse or Foot, by any warrant, commission, or order from his Majesty without the advice and consent of the Lords and Commons.

In an attempt to avoid the charge of treason, the blame for the crisis was therefore put on the 'wicked counsel' but anyone who tried to execute the King's Commission of Array was still declared to be 'disturbers of the peace of the kingdom'.[6] War was clearly in the offing.

As the local authorities scratched their heads and tried to decide what to do in the face of such conflicting instructions from King and Parliament – each declared to be treasonable by the other – in Worcestershire, as elsewhere, the small number of partisans of both sides tried to win over the uncommitted majority. This was a confusing time and by August events were moving at a rapid pace, fuelling drunken rioting on the streets of Kidderminster and Worcester and raising fears of a general breakdown of law and order. The Royalist faction in the county was led by a small number of influential county gentry, led by Sir Thomas Lyttleton of Frankley (1593–1650), Sir William Russell of Strensham (1602–1669) and Samuel Sandys of Ombersley (1615–1685). These activists were the traditional leaders of their communities but they met apathy from many of their fellow gentry and more overt resistance from at least the well-to-do citizens of Worcester whose Council had, as we have seen, its long-running intention of winning greater independence from such traditional leaders of county society.

Control of the Trained Bands became an important symbol of this struggle. In 1641 Worcester had tried again, unsuccessfully, to get full independent control of its Trained Bands.[7] Although this move failed and in 1642 it was given no role in the command of the county muster, the development shows the city already pointedly looking for a lead towards Parliament rather than the King and the local Royalist establishment. In December, the City Chamber decided not to pay their £3 share of the annual salary of the muster-master — unless ordered by *Parliament* to continue

The Commandery, Worcester. This was the home of the Wylde family, bitterly divided by the Civil Wars. It served as the headquarters of the Duke of Hamilton during the Battle of Worcester in 1651.

(Author collection)

it.[8] The role of the muster-master had become a constitutional issue as much as a simple resentment against its costs. The posts were seen as part of the patronage of the Lords Lieutenant and with no legal standing for their enforced funding. The long-standing desire for independence remained fundamental to Worcester's resistance to the county-dominated Commission of Array in 1642 and its uneasy participation in the Royalist muster of the Trained Bands.

In June 1642, preparing for the worst, Worcester decided to buy new arms although claiming in a spirit of militant neutrality that these were only for the defence of the city and were to be held under the control of the city council.[9] Such a statement also announced that the city was ready to negotiate with either party! The city did finally purchase the private stock of weapons belonging to Lord Windsor, the late Lord Lieutenant of the county, on 2 August 'for the generall use and defence of the cittie'. Their parochial stance was reinforced further as the arms were not to be used except 'by consent of the Chamber'. The national crisis deepened further from 12 July when Parliament resolved to raise its own national army under the Earl of Essex 'for the safety of the King's person, defence of both Houses of Parliament, and those who have obeyed their orders and commands'.[10] This formal profession of loyalty to the King whilst actively opposing him remained a feature of Parliamentary language throughout the course of the war but this could not conceal the enormity of such a rebellious action. In mid-July 1642, an unusually crowded Midsummer Quarter Sessions seemed to throw the lot of Worcestershire in with Parliament and they refused to support the execution of the orders of the Commission of Array. The latter had commanded the mustering of the Trained Bands and other volunteers at Worcester Town Hall on 13 July, with Samuel Sandys to be appointed as commander of the Horse. Existing officers who had supported the earlier Ordinance of Parliament were to be removed and other Parliamentary activists to be arrested by JPs within the Commission.[11]

The refusal to support the Commission had been engineered by the two Worcestershire MPs, Humphrey Salway (of Stanford-on-Teme) and Sergeant-at-Law John Wylde who had rushed back at the last minute from London to pack the Grand Jury with their supporters. Thus it was that the Grand Jury declared the Commission of Array illegal 'with a great acclamation of the company then present' and raised a petition to support the Parliamentary Militia Ordinance – boasting that another ten thousand people would have signed if time had permitted.[13] Little can be said about the men who signed the petition, although Townshend dismisses them as not being of the gentry. There may, therefore, be signs here of a popular resistance to the Royalists. Playing on the fears of impending war, Wylde and Salway accused the Royalists of having 'a designe, hope and probability ... to have made the countie a place of war'.[14] In a panic on seeing the strength of feeling, one of the leading Commissioners, Sherington Talbot of Salwarpe (near Droitwich), fled the county to avoid possible arrest. The planned muster had to be cancelled and it appeared that Worcester, that 'faithful' city of later legend, was ready to side with Parliament.

But this was merely the first stage in a campaign marked by wavering from one side to another. None of the local gentry had signed the anti-Royalist petition and

The King's instructions for the Commission of Array in Worcestershire (23 July 1642)

Charles R.

Right trusty and right well beloved, and trusty and well beloved, we greet you well. Whereas we have lately by our Commission of Array trusted you with your service for our County of Worcester and are informed that some persons have presumed in contempt of us and our authority to despise and vilify our said Commission and to menace and threaten our Commissioners, We do hereby require you according to your duties speedily to publish our said Commissions so necessary at this time for the peace and safety of our good subjects, and to proceed in the full execution thereof with all possible industry and alacrity. And if the High Sheriff shall be absent, or neglect to perform his duty being present, that you proceed in the service, and if you find any persons so malicious as not to yield obedience to our said authority, that you proceed against them by imprisonment or otherwise according to the direction and power of the said Commission, of the legality whereof we being so well assured notwithstanding any abets to the contrary, we think that rule the best for you to proceed by and shall protect you therein, and all such who shall dutifully submit to our authority with our through power, and with the hazard of our life. And that you remove all such persons from any command over any part of the militia whom you find unfit for the service, especially those who have executed the pretended ordinance *[of the militia – deleted]* so expressly against our consent, and the known law of the land. Against whom we shall shortly proceed in an exemplary way for such their transcendent presumption. Except you find them sensible of their former error and desirous to obey our commands. And our pleasure is that our trusty and well beloved Samuel Sandys, Esqre, of whose affection to our service and to the public peace of the kingdom we are well assured, shall command the Horse of this our county. And because notwithstanding the large power in our commission to array such of our good subjects as shall be fit for the service, we well know you will out of due regard to our people only summon such, except extraordinary occasion happen, who have been usually or are of our trained bands, yet we think fit in this time of so public distraction that you receive without summons all such who shall voluntarily offer themselves to train and muster. And that you in our name signify our very good acceptance of that expression of their affections, and use them with that regard as such forwardness and zeal to ours and the publick service deserves. And we do further require you our said Commissioners, or so many of you as are Justices of the Peace within that our said County that you make inquiry after such seditious preachers, and other persons of what degree soever, who endeavour by their sermons, counsels, and discourses to lessen and deprave our just legal authority, and to incense our good subjects against us, and that you proceed against them as stirrers of sedition and promoters of rebellion against us, especially against those who shall presume to execute that pretended ordinance, which at this time we interpret to be no other than levying war against us. And that you give all encouragement and assistance to those whose zeal and affection is eminent to our service, and we do hereby authorize you and every of you our said commissioners to receive such subscriptions as any of our loving subjects of the county shall be willing to make for the assistance of us by men, horses, or otherwise, in this great distraction of the commonwealth, and to receive such money as any of our good subjects of the said county shall be willing to lend us upon these our urgent occasions for the defence of our person and for the religion and laws of the kingdom, and any acknowledgment given under any two of your hands of the receipt of such monies shall be an engagement upon us to repay the same with interest after the rate of.~'8 per cent., which we shall punctually perform, and shall moreover acknowledge it as a most seasonable testimony of their affection and loyalty unto us, which we shall never forget. Lastly our will and pleasure is that you take into your custody the arms of all recusants within your county, and so the same safely keep. Given at our Court at Doncaster the 21st of June 1642 in the 18th yeare of our reign.

To our right trusty and right well beloved and to our trusty and well beloved our Commissioners of Array for our County of Worcester.

the remaining members of the Commission of Array, undismayed by Talbot's action, continued their work in sending out instructions to parishes to raise the Trained Bands for the King. The early success for the Parliamentary faction turned out to be short-lived. In a roller coaster of manoeuvring, the activists within the local Royalist gentry organised themselves and applied their own pressure in turn; a new, more sympathetic, Grand Jury was empanelled on 3 August at the Assizes which issued warrants to search suspected Parliamentarians for arms and to again summon a muster of the 'trained, freehold and clergy bands' and the horses and arms of the gentry. This muster was to take place on 12 August on the meadow at Pitchcroft, on the outskirts of Worcester. The Sheriff of Worcestershire, members of the City Council, justices and leading gentry, now all subscribed to a loyal Declaration for 'putting the County in a posture of Arms' and denounced the former opposition to the Commission of Array of just a few weeks ago.[15] But this was still a declaration of moderation in favour of constitutional monarchy, calling on the king to 'preserve the freedom and just priviledge of parliament' and 'attend His Majesty in all lawfull ways'. The Declaration therefore fell short of outright support for the Commission of Array. This change of stance was not unanimous and a counter-petition in favour of Parliament 'by the best Freeholders of the county' according to their supporters in London, was also collected at the Assizes. This was, however, rejected by the judge as being 'contrived and prepared for them by some few persons, not well affected to the peace and quiet of the country'. The reaction of Parliament to this snub was to

The Commissioners of Array warrant to the High Constables for forwarding to the petty constables of the parishes (1 August 1642)[12]

We his Majesty's Commissioners of Array for the County of Worcester whose names are subscribed send greeting.

Whereas the King's Majesty by his Commission under the great seal of England bearing date at Beverley the 23rd day of July last past in the eighteenth year of his Majesty's reign have authorised us amongst others in the said commission named to array, train and muster the inhabitants of this county in these times of distraction according to the tenor of the said commission and instructions sent to us from his Majesty under his hand. These are therefore to will and require you forthwith upon receipt hereof you issue forth your warrant to all the petty constables within your limits and division thereby requiring them to give warning to all the trained and freehold and clergy bands within their constablewick both horse and foot that are charged with armes to come and appear before us or any three or more of us upon the twelfth day of August next being Friday in the morning by nine of the clock, at and in the great meadow called Pitchcroft near the City of Worcester completely armed and arrayed, And you are to take notice yourself and give warning to the petty Constables that neither you nor they nor any of the said trained band horse or foot fail of their appearance upon pain of such penalties as shall fall thereon.

And further we do require you and every of you to signify unto all such as are well affected to this service that so many as will voluntarily come in at the day and place appointed with their armes or otherwise shall be well received and perform an acceptable service to their king and country. Dated at Talbot in Sidbury, the first day of August in the 18th yeare of the reign of our Sovereign Lord Charles by the grace of God King of England Scotland France and Ireland Defender of the Faith etc.

13 signatures are obliterated

order Wylde and Salway to seize the 'Coat and Conduct' money in the county so as to hinder any mobilisation of the Trained Bands against them.[16] The overwhelming impression throughout this manoeuvring is of small groups of activists on both sides vying for position whilst the majority of people in the county bent with the prevailing wind of power and tried to keep the war away from their homes for as long as possible.

Nonetheless, outside the heady confines of the Quarter Sessions and Assises, there is evidence of wider divisions in the community for whom the developing national crisis provided a focus for local grievances. At Kidderminster, the leading burgesses of the newly incorporated town of 3,500 inhabitants were strongly puritan. Byelaws of 1640 forbad 'tippling' and the playing of unlawful games on Sunday; constables were sent out to search alehouses for those trying to escape Sunday services. The

Petition of the Grand Jury 13 July 1642 in support of Parliament

That with all thankfulness and from the bottom of our hearts we acknowledge that exceeding great favour the Parliament hath been pleased to shew unto us in declaring the illegality of the Commission of Array intended at this present to be executed amongst us, and we do most humbly beseech these to whom the ordinance of the Militia of this country is intrusted that they would be pleased speedily to put the same in execution, That so his Majesty's royal person, the Parliament and kingdom may be secured which as we are now fully persuaded are in great danger, by reason of the plots of the malignant party, and persons ill affected to the King and state ...

Signatories:

Paul Rumney	Richard Cosonett	John Poolehouse
Thomas Turbeville	Richard Saunders	John Spooner
Thomas Moore	John George	Christopher Gillam
Richard Yarnold	John Palmer	Simon Cowley
John Best	Thomas Taylor	Richard Cotterell
John Marshall	William Styles	

views of this influential, but small, alliance of clothiers and minor gentry was not welcomed by all and the lower classes saw political and religious opposition as a means of venting their economic and social grievances against their masters. As a reactionary gesture, they therefore allied themselves with the Royalist gentry. When an attempt was made to remove the crucifix from the churchyard cross Baxter claimed 'a crew of the drunken riotous party of the town (poor journeymen and servants) took the alarm and run altogether with weapons to defend the crucifix'.[17] This 'rabble' also supported the reading of the King's Declaration of 27 May 1642 against the Militia Ordinance. Similarly in Worcester during the summer of 1642, Baxter dismissed the rowdy group of Royalists near the Cathedral who shouted 'Down with the Roundheads' as a drunken rabble.[18] It was a common accusation by supporters of Parliament that the Royalists consisted principally of the gentry with the support of servile classes.

As the county and nation drifted into outright war and with signs of social order breaking down in drunken riots, on 5 August Sir William Russell compiled an inventory of the ammunition stocks held in the county for the use of the Trained Bands. This amounted to 44 barrels of gunpowder, 1½ tons of lead (for casting musket balls) and 2,276lb of match (lengths of cord soaked in saltpetre used to ignite the charges of muskets) held in the magazines of Bromsgrove, Droitwich, Bewdley and Kidderminster, the largest store being at Evesham. In addition there were 5 barrels of gunpowder, 500lb of lead to make musket balls and 112lb of match in Worcester. The total in Worcester would have been greater had not John Wylde already removed some of the stocks to Droitwich, fearing that under the influence of the local gentry the city's loyalties might turn towards the King. A small number of individuals also had significant private stocks including the prominent Parliamentarian Walter Devereux of Leigh Sinton. But at this stage in the conflict there is no evidence for any mass movement of support on either side. Even the fervent puritan, Richard Baxter, explained his flight to Coventry as a desire to avoid the conflict 'with a purpose to stay there till one side or other had got the victory and the war was ended, and then to return home'.[19]

Time was running out for peace. By 15 August 4,800 Foot and 11 troops of Horse were on the march from London to Warwick and Coventry to secure the Midlands

Sir Ralph Clare (1587–1670), one of the leading Worcester Royalists but an opponent of Sir William Russell during the bitter Royalist infighting of 1643.

(Worcester City Library)

Sir William Russell's inventory of ammunition in Worcestershire (5 August 1642)[20]

A note of the Magazine powder, match and lead heretofore provided for this County, and how it is now placed. The gross sums. 44 Barrells of powder, 1 tun and a half of lead and 2276 lbs. of match, beside the magazine of the city of Worcester.

At Evesham	powder	12 barrels, match 600 weight.
At Droitwich	powder	6 barrels, match 300 weight.
At Bewdley	powder	6 barrels, match 300 weight.
At Kidderminster	powder	6 barrels, match 300 weight.
At Bromsgrove	powder	10 barrels, match 776 weight.

Of lead remaining in the places aforesaid 1 ton and a half.

Sir Walter Devereux	powder	1 barrel and 50 lbs. of match.
Sir Tho. Russell	powder	1 barrel and 50 lbs. of match.
Sir John Rouse	powder	1 barrel and 50 lbs. of match.
Giles Savage, Esq[re]	powder	1 barrel and 50 lbs. of match.
The City of Worcester	powder	5 barrels and 112 lbs. of match and 500 of lead.

for Parliament.[21] Panic ensued amongst the local Royalists. On 11 August (the day before the planned Worcestershire muster), the desperate Warwickshire Commission of Array, with 3,350 of their own county Trained Bands and volunteers now mobilised for Parliament, and with Warwick Castle in the hands of a Parliamentary garrison under Lord Brooke, sent an urgent message for the Worcestershire Trained Bands to march to Warwick and reinforce them.[22] They were to be disappointed. The turnout of the muster at Pitchcroft on 12 August aroused mixed reactions. For the members of the Commission of Array there was relief simply in being able to attract numbers that 'the appearance of the gentry and commons was very great and the acclamation very high for his Majesty's service, not a dissenting voice, but one and all like good subjects for the King's safety and honour.'[23] But a former mercenary from the Thirty Years War, William King, viewed the quality of the turnout with more of a jaundiced, and perhaps honest, military eye. He also described it as being attended by 'a great number of men' but dismissed them as 'of mean and base quality as they seemed to me – and having hedgebills, old calivers [the antiquated type of musket], sheep pikes and clubs'.[24] From the weapons, these were clearly Foot, probably comprising farm labourers and far from the original idea of the respectable middle class and well-armed Trained Bands. King's description provides little sign of the pikes and armour meant to have been provided by the parishes (see

Richard Baxter (1615–91). Vicar of Kidderminster before the Civil War and a leading puritan. He served as an army chaplain in the Parliamentary Army but later opposed Oliver Cromwell.

(Almonry Museum, Evesham)

Appendix 1). It seems likely that, if they ever existed, Parliamentary supporters had indeed hidden arms from the Commission of Array. With war in the offing, we can perhaps imagine the mixed emotions running through the minds of the Trained Bands – high excitement at a possible adventure to relieve the tedium of farming life and work for the clothiers, confusion over the issues that were drawing them towards war, and dread of possible death or injury. Inevitably, it seems at such times few would have imagined that the war was going to last any length of time. The phrase 'over by Christmas' echoes through the ages!

The public confidence of the Commission of Array in the muster was clearly based on numbers rather than quality. Concerned about the standard of training and equipment of their men, and also still reflecting the parochial attitude to the Trained Bands, the Commission was unwilling to break tradition and order the Trained Bands as a body to serve out of the county as their beleaguered colleagues in Warwickshire had requested. A second request for support was presented – and again refused. A serious problem in trying to mobilise forces for war on a national scale was already beginning to materialise for the Royalists. In an effort to overcome this problem, on 17 August it was proposed that each soldier in the Trained Bands should bring in a fresh recruit to serve as a volunteer in the new Royalist Army and specifically for 'neighbouring service' to allow them to serve out of county as part of a more mobile army, whilst retaining the existing strength of the Trained Bands for local defence.[25]

In the meantime, on 14 August, the Horse of the Trained Bands were also mobilised. Forty gentry (including seventeen members of the Commission of Array) agreed to provide a troop of 89 Horse, initially for only three months, but this is only equivalent to the number normally expected to be provided by the peacetime Trained Bands in the county.[26] Interestingly, one of the gentry, Edward Rous of Rous Lench became a prominent parliamentarian during the war and so it may be doubted how far this was a serious offer by all of those listed. A revised Assessment was produced later in August to summon another *c*.70 horse. This again included the noted parliamentarians Humphrey Salway, Daniel Dobbyns and Sergeant Wylde; it is unlikely that the numbers were actually realised and such documents cannot, therefore, be automatically taken as measures of loyalty to the Royalist cause. But with no reference to anyone from Worcester City Council it is clear that this was a county and gentry force. Ultimately, it appears that few of the county gentry took an active part in the war, leaving the effort to a small hard-core of Royalist families. Of the local men in the Commission of Array, only eight are later listed as officers in local regiments: Sir Rowland Berkeley and Thomas Savage served in Samuel Sandys' Horse, together with Henry Ingram at the siege of Worcester in 1646 and Joseph Walsh served in William Russell's Horse. Sir John Packington served at Edgehill but was captured. Thomas, Lord Coventry, appears to have become disillusioned during the First Civil War and avoided providing support to Charles II at Worcester in 1651. Of those ninety seven men assessed to provide Horse in 1642, only ten (10 percent) are included in the surviving lists of officers of local regiments, although others may have served elsewhere (see Appendices 3 and 4) and from the surnames it is clear that other members of their families did serve (i.e. the Savage and Blunt families). Indeed, of the 44 Royalist gentry seized at the end of the war in 1646, only 15 (34 percent) can be positively identified as having served as officers in the army. Others, like Henry Townshend, had remained civilians throughout the conflict, although he served the cause as a civilian Commissioner of Array. In all, there are just *c*.25 names of local gentry that

A representation of a soldier of the Trained Bands c.1640. He wears civilian clothes and is armed with the primitive form of musket called the caliver. These should have been replaced in the 1620s but many of the Worcestershire soldiers were armed with these at the muster of August 1642.

(Author Collection, with thanks to the Fairfax Battalia of the English Civil War Society)

re-occur during the Civil War which might be taken as representing the hard core of Royalist activists in the county.

1642 Worcestershire Trained Bands

Companies of	Training at
Captain John Clent	Bewdley
Captain Philip Brace	Worcester
Captain John Speite	Pershore
Captain Scudamore Pitt	Droitwich
Captain Richard Pitt	Worcester

Popular support for the mobilisation was no more forthcoming than that from the gentry. On 22 August, the day that war was formally declared at Nottingham, there was a second muster on Pitchcroft. This gives the clearest indication of the structure of the pre-War Trained Bands before their re-organisation. They were divided into five companies of Foot, totalling *c.*500 men to train in Worcester, Bewdley, Pershore and Droitwich under local captains.[27] This was considerably less than the establishment of just two years before, marking a growing reluctance to become involved in the impending conflict. Two companies, comprising *c.*200 men, were to muster in Worcester but neither of the captains were members of the City Council. The company of Richard Pitt was funded to the sum of £270 by the High Church clergy of the diocese, continuing the tradition of clerical funding of the Trained Bands.[28] (The clergy went on to also fund a troop of Horse in James Hamilton's regiment.)[29] Pitt later served as Quartermaster in Lord Goring's Horse and eventually became Provost Marshall in the city at the time of the Restoration. It is perhaps significant that, despite the presence of the magazine, the east Worcestershire Company trained at Pershore rather than at Evesham. There may already have been a suspicion of the Parliamentary tendencies of the town and its puritan mayor, Samuel Gardiner, which were to emerge later in the war.

Despite such efforts, and even with a third plea from Charles I on 21 August to send troops to support an ever more desperate Warwickshire, on 23 August the Commission were obliged to write to the Secretary of State to apologise for their 'weak and imperfect endeavours'. They said that they were more fervent in their affection than having any real power, thwarted by lack of arms and ammunition.[30] Their repeated inability to support the Warwickshire Royalists, with a Parliamentary army now indeed on its way from London, may therefore have been a contributory factor in Charles I having retreated to Nottingham, where he raised his standard on 22 August to begin the Civil War formally. The troops at the Worcester muster on 22 August were no better armed than when they had mustered two weeks earlier. An exasperated Commission therefore wanted to know where the arms that they were supposed to carry (as listed in the Muster Roll of 1641) had disappeared to. Consequently, all men in Worcester that were liable for service were ordered to bring their weapons for inspection to the Tolsey in Worcester on 25 August or face a fine.

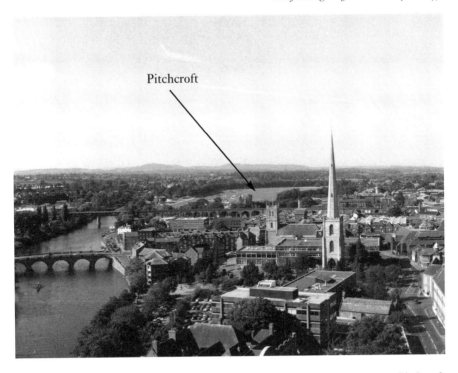

Pitchcroft

The traditional location of the Worcestershire musters of the Trained Bands was at Pitchcroft outside the city to the north. The Scottish cavalry also camped here in 1651. The photo is taken from the top of the Cathedral tower, giving some sense of what Charles 11 would have seen as he surveyed the opening scenes of the battle of Worcester in 1651.

(Author Collection)

There must have been substantial numbers of defaulters for on 29 August the City was able to buy new cannon, using the money collected from the fines.[31] The magazine was also to be restocked with six barrels of gunpowder and a suitable quantity of shot and match. But it was again stressed that this was 'for the defence of the cittie' rather than as part of an allegiance to one side or another and the purchase of cannon was no substitute for the missing armour and muskets for the Foot.

The difficulty in raising sufficient numbers of men and the repeated failure of the efforts to mobilise the Worcestershire Trained Bands outside of their county, together with similar experiences elsewhere, meant that the King quickly realised that the men of the existing Trained Bands were not likely to be of great use in the war. On 28 August Charles wrote to the Commission of Array urging them to mobilise whatever forces they thought necessary, beyond the confines of the traditional organisation of the Trained Bands.[32] In many counties the King simply disarmed the Trained Bands in order to equip new regiments that would form the basis of a new, more mobile, field army. In Worcestershire, Trained Bands and volunteers were combined to form the core of a new system of regiments of Foot,

Horse and Dragoons (mounted infantry). Offers were enthusiastically made by the local Royalist gentry to raise this new army for the king. The 49-year-old Catholic, and current High Sheriff, Sir Thomas Lyttleton of Frankley, offered (in principle at least) to raise a regiment of Foot and a troop of 89 Horse.[33] On the basis of this offer, he was rewarded on 3 September by being appointed colonel of all the Trained Bands and volunteers, with the intention of combining the Foot so raised into a new single regiment.[34] Despite the earlier commission to Sandys, the more senior Lyttleton was also put in command of the Horse, so becoming the commander of all Royalist troops in the county. He was then summoned to Shrewsbury to advise the King.[35] But Lyttleton may have been over-optimistic in his ability to raise and fund such a commitment and there is no evidence that any regiment was ever raised in his name. Despite this position of early power, and possibly because of the inflated claims that he had made and his age, Lyttleton became quickly overshadowed by other, younger, local gentry and drifted into a more minor role. He also suffered the distress of having his home at Frankley burnt down by his own side (Prince Rupert) simply to avoid it being garrisoned by Parliament, causing the move of the family seat to Hagley. He was made governor of Bewdley but was not mentioned in the Council of War held there in February 1644. He was captured there during a daring raid by 'Tinker' Fox in April 1644 and spent the rest of the war in the Tower of London. (He died in 1650 and is buried in Worcester Cathedral.) Lesser gentry also provided support according to their means such as Edward Broad of Dunclent, near Kidderminster, who obligingly raised a new troop of Horse for his son Edmund to command. The enthusiasm of at least a number of the gentry to create this new army, as a means of signalling and increasing their status in the community, masked a problem that was to dog the King throughout the war – how to pay for such forces in the long term. In the lead-up to war, and even in the early stages of the war itself (expecting that it could only last a single campaign season), it was hoped that funding could be achieved simply by requesting voluntary contributions from such supporters but as the war dragged on it became clear that a more organised system based on local taxation would be required (see below, chapter 4).

Based on a core of former members of the Trained Bands, along with labourers, servants and the unemployed, the men of the new regiments were certainly no better trained at the start of the war than their predecessors in the Trained Bands. John Corbet described the equivalent (Parliamentary) Gloucestershire volunteers as 'a cake not turned, a kinde of souldiers not wholly drawn off from the plow or domesticke imployments, having neither resolution nor support suitable to the service; but the greatest defect was the want of able and experienced officers'.[36] The dangers of what this might lead to are well illustrated by an incident at the siege of Basing House, Hampshire, in 1643. Here, the unfortunate front rank of the Westminster Trained Bands were shot in their backs by the second rank who had panicked and fired before their comrades had been given a chance to clear the firing line! Another Royalist officer bemoaned the fact that because of accidents 'we bury more toes and fingers than we do men'.[37] The Worcestershire gentry may well have been avid readers of *Directions for Musters* or the other theoretical military manuals, but had shown little actual interest in the training of the Trained Bands. This was, in any case, no substitute for actual service and there is no record of the local officers having served an apprenticeship on the continent in the Thirty Years War.

The creation of the county volunteer regiment lead to a further deterioration in relations between city and county. Neither of the two commanders of the Worcester companies of the Trained Bands mustered in August 1642 had been members of the city council. Philip Brace came from Doverdale and was a Justice of the Peace and a Tax Commissioner. The amalgamation of the Trained Bands and volunteers under Lyttleton could therefore only serve to increase county control at the expense of the city. The known strong Roman Catholic influence amongst the leading Royalist gentry – the Lyttletons and Russells – in the county would also have fuelled the rumours amongst the puritan city council that the King was planning to re-establish his power with the aid of an Irish Catholic army.

Thus it was that Worcester was even less forthcoming than the rest of a largely apathetic county in providing support for the King in this opening stage of the Civil War. There were some undoubted pockets of strong Royalist feeling in the city, especially it seems amongst some of the lower classes whose loyalty could be bought for the price of a drink and a chance to vent their feelings against their puritan employers, but this was not a sign of a popular groundswell in favour of the King and few citizens were prepared to go further than shouting slogans. As a consequence of a continuing lack of co-operation from the city, King Charles was repeatedly forced to order those 'factious and disorderly persons' that supported Parliament in Worcester to be disarmed.[38] Resentment against the Commission of Array and its efforts to recruit new troops under a Catholic leadership had bred an atmosphere of non-cooperation. The City Council ignored the Commission's enquiry of 30 August as to what total number of volunteers the city might raise, how many troops could be billeted, or what number of armourers could be supplied. Their eventual reply was not what the King was hoping for. On 4 September, the citizens and Trained Band members in Worcester delivered a petition to the mayor, Edward Solley. Fuelled by rumour of events elsewhere, they complained that:

> Cavaliers and soldiers in divers parts of the kingdom (where they come) have plundered the towns, bloodily killing the king's peaceable subjects, rifling their houses, and violently taking away of their goods and in some places deflowered women.[39]

Once again declaring the Commission of Array 'unlawful', the petitioners wanted the 'strangers, gentlemen, delinquents and papists' who had arrived in the city, presumably ready to mobilise in the new regiments of volunteers, to be expelled. On top of the traditional antipathy to the county gentry there was now a pragmatic fear that the presence of 'cavaliers' would bring disorder and simply attract the attention of the new Parliamentary army, hastening the arrival of war to their county. Regarding them as being divisive, the petitioners demanded that the King's Commission of Array should be barred from the city, as well as an end to recruiting and billeting of troops there. They wanted 'those troopers and all Adherents to the unlawful Commission of Array, which daily appear here to the terror of the citizens, the hindrance of our trade and market, and tend to be dividing of the King and Parliament' to be thrown out of the city.[40] Having received their petition, the response of the mayor, Edward Solley, to the Commissioners, although he had signed the Royalist Declaration of August, was only marginally more diplomatic. He asked the Commission to 'forbear' to meet in the City and took the opportunity to again make the political point (no doubt as a bargaining counter for the future) that the City should have control of its own Trained Bands.[41] Unable to rely on Worcester for support, the Royalist Commission of Array was therefore forced to meet just outside the city boundary, at the Talbot Inn in Sidbury (part of the county parish of St Michael Bedwardine).[42] This was not an auspicious start for the Royalist efforts to recruit in the city and bears more resemblance to Hutton's 'determined neutrality' than to the mythology of the Civil War 'faithful' city.[43]

Less than two weeks later, opposition to the Commission of Array in Worcester took an even more serious turn. Not having received an answer to the Mayor's suggestion that the City should control its Trained Bands, the City Council now decided to raise its own militia in opposition to the county volunteer regiment. At a cost of £5, the Town Clerk was dispatched to London in order to discuss the raising of a militia with Parliament. On 13 September, the House of Commons approved a declaration of loyalty from the 'Commons' of Worcester and agreed to its request to raise a new militia 'for the defence of the King and Parliament', commanded by one of their aldermen, Captain Thomas Rea (another waverer who had also signed the August Declaration). The city magazine was to be seized along with any weapons and ammunition in the hands of the Commission of Array. Already, there was a suspicion that the Cathedral was being used to store arms.[44] But this was an age of irony and despite its origin in strengthening anti-Royalist feeling, it was to be this militia that formed the nucleus of the town regiment which in turn was part of the Royalist garrison of the city throughout the war.

This drama in the first weeks of the war suggests that Worcester, at least, was more ready to support Parliament than the King. But Worcestershire was simply swept along by events as the country drifted into war. The worst fears of the citizens of Worcester as expressed in their condemnation of the Commission of Array were quickly realised. On 13 September Royalist troopers on the boundary of the county plundered the house of William Stephens of Broadway. The troops took money and two silver bowls, and set fire to his hayricks. Worcester could not keep the army out of its gates forever and on 16 September Sir John Byron entered the city with 200 troops guarding a treasure convoy bound for Shrewsbury. Worcester was now occupied by the Royalist troops and was to remain under military control for the rest of the Civil War. Its fate was to be in the hands of others. Byron was reinforced on 22 September with Prince Rupert's cavalry and Sir William Russell also joined the escort. The City spent £1 15s on providing bread and beer for the saddle-weary troopers of Prince Rupert. The Royalists won the sharp skirmish at Powick on 23 September but immediately continued their journey to Shrewsbury, throwing the

Powick Bridge, Worcester. This was the scene of the first skirmish of the Civil War, on 23 September 1642 and also played a key role in the final battle of the wars on 3 September 1651.
(Author Collection)

city open to the fast approaching army of the Earl of Essex. Ironically in view of the recent antagonism of the city to the King's officials and fears of marauding 'cavaliers', it was to be the arrival of the Parliamentary Army on 24 September 1642, overwhelming the city by sheer numbers, and its subsequent behaviour that brought home the reality of war to the citizens of Worcester and the surrounding district. This would have been quickly reinforced with tales from the battlefield at Edgehill and the trail of casualties leading back to Evesham and east Worcestershire.

Many in the Parliamentary army that entered the city thought that Worcester citizens had aided Lord Byron. Fearing retaliation for what may simply have been an innocent misunderstanding at Powick, the citizens had sent a petition to the Earl of Essex via Captain Rea, begging 'that the Earle would not be offended with the Towne, for what they did was merely through compulsion, and feare of the Cavaleers, who had done the Towne great injuries, as likewise most places wheresoever they came'.[45] This declaration of loyalty to Parliament and plea for

Key Events: 1642 – the Skirmish at Powick on 23 September

On 16 September, Sir John Byron and a 150–200-strong detachment of dragoons arrived at Worcester from Oxford, with a convoy of treasure destined for the king at Shrewsbury. He was received with scant sympathy from the city who knew that the 20,000 strong army of the Earl of Essex was only 25 miles away. The men camped beside the Teme at Powick Bridge, guarding the approach from the south.

Meanwhile, the advance guard of Essex's army, under Colonel John Brown, dashed ahead of the main column with around 500–1,000 horse and dragoons in an attempt to cut off Byron. After a bungled attempt to enter the city, they crossed the river and camped on the ridge of high ground at Powick, keeping the treasure convoy under surveillance whilst awaiting the arrival of the main Parliamentary Army.

Brown's men remained in the saddle all through the night of 22/23 September, fearing a Royalist breakout. Then the following afternoon they saw signals from some of the citizens that they interpreted as indicating that the Royalists were decamping. Brown drew down his dragoons who had been keeping watch on the ridge at Powick to form up on Powick Ham whilst an advance party charged across the narrow Powick Bridge. There they unexpectedly came face to face in the next field with part of a force of cavalry under Prince Rupert, sent by Charles I from Stafford to assist Byron. This may be what the citizens had been trying to warn the Parliamentarians about. The *c.*700 Royalists included a number of French mercenaries as well as Sir William Russell from Strensham. Both sides seem to have been equally surprised but the Royalists recovered first and, not waiting to put on their armour, charged. Both sides fired their carbines at point blank range before taking to the sword.

The Parliamentarians broke in a panic. Some men were trampled to death in the lane and others were pushed into the swollen River Teme and drowned. The official Parliamentary figure for their casualties was given as thirty-six dead and twenty-one wounded. The Royalists claimed to have killed eighty. Prince Rupert then gathered up his men and they successfully escorted Byron's convoy back to Shrewsbury via Tenbury and Ludlow. The next day the Earl of Essex occupied Worcester.

The skirmish was quite a minor engagement, but it had a great psychological effect and was considered by contemporaries to mark the first real engagement of the two field armies.

mercy was to no avail. Neither was their provision of a hogshead of Gascony wine and six sugar loaves to the Earl of Essex 'to save the city' (at a cost of £8-13s-2½d). Taking a jaundiced view of Worcester's actions, rankled by their first experience of defeat and no doubt irritated further by the pouring rain and the after-effects of the local perry (so particularly praised by the soldier Nehemiah Wharton), it was decided to make an example of the city that Wharton described as 'so vile, and the country so base, papisticall, and atheisticall and abominable, that it resembles Sodom ... a very den of thieves, and a receptacle and refuge for all the hell hounds of the County'. The city was obliged to pay for the carrying of the soldiers wounded in the skirmish to the Guildhall and for burying the dead (£12 6s 2d) but this was not to save them from further retaliation.[46] The army of the Earl of Essex did considerable damage to the city during their brief occupation until 19 October, including ransacking the Cathedral, which had been used by the Royalists as an arms store. They broke up the organ and smashed stained glass windows, defaced monuments and tore up books in the Cathedral library. Despite all the arguments surrounding their formation, no reference was made to any active participation of the city or county Trained Bands for either side during the first uncertain weeks of the war, only that Essex was reported as 'settling' the militia in the district.[47] Presumably this simply meant an instruction not to get involved!

Sir William Russell was made to suffer for his efforts on behalf of his King. His moated manor house at Strensham was 'pillaged unto the bare walls' by Essex's troops. The Parliamentary army made the most of its time in the city, with Essex commanding his officers to concentrate only on basic training of the men, rather than any ceremonial. No doubt the Royalists had come to the same conclusion with their hurriedly raised army. The necessity was clearly demonstrated on 2 October when one of Essex's musketeers panicked during training; double loaded his musket, and then accidentally shot one of his comrades! The following years saw a new flurry of pamphlets offering advice on training and tactics both from the new generation of field officers and also armchair tacticians.

The army of the Earl of Essex marched out of the city on 19 October to try to intercept the Royal army which was by then en route from Shrewsbury for London. They took with them horses, carts and the carters requisitioned from farms and villages. The armies of both sides became desperate for horses during the war. Thomas Morris at Pershore lost a bay mare, worth £1 11s, to Essex's troops.[48] In Flyford

Robert Devereux, Earl of Essex (1591–1646). Commander of the first Parliamentary army to enter Worcestershire.

(Worcester City Library)

> Our food was fruit, for those that could get it; our drink, water; our beds, the earth; our canopy, the clouds, but we pulled up the hedges, pales, and gates, and made good fires; his Excellency promising us that, if the country relieved us not the day following, he would fire their towns. Thus we continued singing of psalms until the morning. Saturday morning we marched into Worcester ... (Nehemiah Wharton of the Earl of Essex's army, 26 September 1642)

Flavell, William Kaye and Simon Bradley each claimed for the cost of 'two horses that were lost at Edgehill fight and the hiring of the man that went with them' at a cost of 6s 8d, whilst Thomas Maystaffe put the loss of two horses at 15s. But these were evidently poor quality animals as Maystaffe also claimed £5 6s 8d for a third horse taken to draw ammunition to Edgehill.[49] Sometimes there is evidence of clear collusion on the part of those making the post-war claims to parliament. There is a suspicious conformity in the claims for £4 for horses taken for the Edgehill campaign from the inhabitants of Bricklehampton![50]

A small garrison drawn from Merrick's and Lord St John's regiments, under Sir Thomas Essex, were left in the city for a few weeks but was obliged to withdraw on the approach of the Royalist Army following the battle of Edgehill in neighbouring Warwickshire on 23 October. With relief, the city paid £40 to Thomas Essex 'to free the city from plunderings' by the retreating soldiers. The noise of the furious, but inconclusive, battle was heard by Richard Baxter at Alcester. This would in itself have been shocking to 17th century ears, unused as they were to the background noise of motor cars, radios and aeroplanes that we now find commonplace. Against the hopes of the King, the battle was not to provide the single decisive action that would have ended the Civil War almost as it had began. Casualties were heavy on both sides although the Royalists claimed victory by virtue of retaining possession of the field. The Worcestershire Royalists Samuel Sandys and

Worcester Cathedral. Used as an arms store by the Royalists and ransacked by the Earl of Essex's troops in 1642. It was used as a temporary prison after the Battle of Worcester in 1651.

(Susanne Atkin)

payd for two horses that more lost at Edge hill fyght
and the buyrng of a man that went mile from }——0— 6—

Extract from the Commonwealth Exchequer Papers for Flyford Flavell, detailing the loss of horses and cost of a carter (£2 o 6d) by William Kaye at the Battle of Edgehill.

(The National Archives)

John Packington were amongst those who had joined the King's Army and Richard Sandys, younger brother of Samuel, was one of the casualties. The parish register of Warmington, Warwickshire, records one of the casualties as a Captain Richard Sannes, a captain of Foot and 'gentleman of Worcestershire'.[51] In the aftermath of the battle, the Mayor of Evesham, Samuel Gardiner, was paid £160 for the relief of maimed soldiers that had been brought into the town from the battle.

From November 1642 the city and county came back under Royalist occupation and remained so for most of the rest of the war. The first governor of Worcester was Sir William Russell of the now wrecked Strensham Manor. He was presented with two sugar loaves and a hogshead of claret to celebrate his appointment but immediately had to look for funds to support the new garrison. Initially, much of the funding came from his own estate; it included, by the end of December, a sum of £100 to pay men of John Burn's regiment, £75 to Francis Blount's men and £237 18s for 150 dragoons. Enterprisingly, he also collected the arrears of tax originally demanded by the Earl of

Finds of musket balls and cannon balls indicate the site of a possible skirmish documented on 17 October 1642 as being between Stourbridge and King's Norton at Ludeley.

(Author Collection)

Commission granted to Samuel Sandys to raise and maintain a Regiment of Foot (20 November 1642)

Charles R.

Charles by the Grace of God of Great Britain, France and Ireland, Defender of the Fayth etc. To our Trusty and welbeloved Captain Samual Sandys Greeting. Whereas there are now att and near London great forces in levying and monoys raysing towards the charge of raysing and mayntayning an Army or forces by Order of our two Houses of Parliament, not only without Our consent, but contrary to Our several express Commands, published by several Proclamations, Letters and otherwise, Such army or forces what Effects and Consequences they may produce if Tymly Care be not had, we know not, and therefore for the defense of Our royal Person, the two Houses of Parliament, the Protestant Religion, the Laws of the land, the Liberty and Property of the Subject, and the Priviledge of Parliament, Wee do hereby authorize and appoynt you to rayse and retayne one regiment of one Thousand foot Voluntiers, (Officers therein comprised) within our Kingdom of England and Dominion of Wales, and doe give unto you full power and Authority to command, arm, discipline, traine and order in warlyke manner, and with all possible speed to conduct them to such places as you shall be directed either by Us, or by Our Lieutenant General of Our Army for the tyme being; Willing and Commanding all Officers and Souldiers which by virtue hereof you shall retayne, you to obey and readily to recieve and accomplish your Directions Commandments and Summons in all things hereto apportayning and necessary to bee done. As also all Mayors; Sherrifs, Justices of the Law, Commissioners of Array, and all others our Officers and Loving Subjects to bee ayding and assisting herein both unto you, and to all such Officers and Persons whom you shall appoynt under you Hand and Soale for the furthering and Advancement of this Our most special Service. For such this shall bee to you and to those every of them a sufficient Warrant and Discharge. Given under Our signed manuall att Our Court att Reading this 20th of November in the Eighteenth year of Our Raigne.

Essex to pay the expenses of the soldiers. Samuel Sandys was also granted a commission in November to raise a new 1,000-strong regiment of Foot, ready to march to wherever the King commanded, in sharp contrast to the parochialism of the old Trained Bands. It is likely that many of the new recruits would have been drawn from the Sandys estate, drawn by a mixture of personal loyalty, conviction and impressment. With the main garrison for the county established at Worcester, Evesham was also occupied from early December by Sir John Beaumont's regiment of Foot (taken from the field army) to protect the main east to west river crossing.

Once the county was occupied by the Royalist Army, the Parliamentary activists were forced to either keep their opinions to themselves or to flee and join the Parliamentary army. Captain Rea probably left at this time and had certainly lost his place in the City Council by 1643. The strongest local pockets of Parliamentary supporters were mainly in what might now be termed the middle classes of yeomen, craftsmen, clothiers and traders. Supporters of Parliament in Worcester were therefore dismissed, unfairly, by Royalists as 'but of the middle rank of people, and none of any great power or eminence there to take their parts'.[52] The city had a strong trading class based in the textile industry which was under less domination by Royalist gentry and whose clothiers typically tended to support Parliament. Despite the dismissive attitude of the Royalists it was the clothing industry that was most strongly represented in the City Council.[53] In Kidderminster, a number of the clothiers joined the Parliamentary army. Abraham Plimley became a quartermaster in Colonel Purefoy's train of artillery in Warwickshire and later served as a sergeant in Richard Turton's Horse, alongside other Kidderminster men. Baxter reports how 30–40 Kidderminster men joined a troop of Horse at Wem, Shropshire. At Evesham the mayor, Samuel Gardiner, was a puritan who joined the Parliamentary Army under Lord Brooke in December and also provided £1,000 to raise new soldiers.

The majority of the established clergy in the Worcestershire towns also joined the Parliamentary cause, despite the influence of the High Church Bishop, Dean and Chapter. The parsons of St Helen's and St Nicholas's in Worcester (Henry Hackett and John Halater) were described in 1642 as seditious and 'actually joined to the rebels'. Elsewhere in the county, Humphrey Hardwicke, the rector of St Mary Witton, Droitwich, was another local clergyman who joined the army of the Earl of Essex.[54] Mr Burroughs, rector of Oldberrow, was described as a 'great promoter and stirrer up of this horrid and unnatural rebellion'.[55] In Bromsgrove, Charles I went as far as ordering the parish to turn out the vicar, John Hall, as a rebel. In Bewdley, the curate fled to the garrison at Coventry, as did the Kidderminster lecturer, Richard Baxter.

Parliamentary Propaganda Leaflet circulated in Worcester, May 1643

To all gentlemen, and other inhabitants of the City of Worcester
As many of you as are sensible of the danger of your religion, your persons and goods, and the privileges of your Corporation, are desired to declare yourselves sensible of them at this opportunity. It being my errand. (by the help of God) to rescue them from the oppression of your present governors. And I promise that all such as shall appear willing to welcome my endeavour shall not only be releived of free quarter, but protected to the utmost of my power.
May 29th, 1643.

William Waller

True and happy Newes

From *WORCESTER.*

Read in the *Honourable* Houfe of Commons,
Septem. 24. 1642.

Sent in a Letter from His Excellencie
the Earle of *Effex* upon Saturday the 24 of
September, 1642. to the Houfe of
Commons.

Wherein is declared a Famous Victory by Mafter
Fines a Member of the Houfe of Commons over
Prince *Robert*, who came to the faid City with 500.
Horfe, upon Thurfday laft.

Relating alfo the fame Defcription of the Battell
and the number that was flaine on both fides,

Likewife the proceedings of His Maje-
ftie fince his comming to the faid City
expreffed in the faid Letters.

Together with His Refolution concerning the
City of *London*, being happy tydings for all thofe
that wifh well to this happy Refolution.

London, printed for *Tho. White. Septem.* 26.

The Civil War saw the first use of printed propaganda on a large scale. This Parliamentary
pamphlet falsely claimed the skirmish at Powick as a victory for their side.

A small, but significant, faction amongst the gentry also supported Parliament. They included Sir Walter Devereux from Leigh Sinton who fled to Bristol, the former High Sheriff, Daniel Dobbyns, who became a captain in the Parliamentary army, the Presbyterian Rous family of Rous Lench near Inkberrow, the Lygon family of Madresfield, the Lechmeres of Hanley Castle and part of the Wylde family. Despite his earlier support for the Royalist militia, Edward Rous, together with his brother Thomas and Nicholas Lechmere later formed the core of the Parliamentary Committee for Worcestershire (which also included William Lygon and a number of other minor families, some newly-moved into the county). Edward Rous and William Lygon became colonels in the Parliamentary army and in 1644 were given a licence by the 'Committee of Both Kingdoms' to 'beat up their drums in Warwickshire for volunteers for the service of Worcestershire'.[56]

But not all of the Parliamentary sympathisers were in a position to leave Worcestershire and they continued to give only grudging assistance to the Royalist cause. An attempt by Worcester in January 1643 to petition Parliament for peace – whilst declaring the latter to be the 'Malignant party' – met local opposition and was abandoned.[57] In June, there were men ready to distribute propaganda leaflets in Worcester on behalf of Waller in advance of his march from Gloucester. After the siege, Waller was informed that there were 'many citizens of Worcester and likewise county men in the Royal Army who did assist the Parliamentarians.' Some of those sympathisers were identified, arrested and tried by the governor, Sir William Russell.[58] Later events, however, make it clear that there were still a considerable number who were concealing their allegiances and who came to the fore only once it became clear that the Royalist occupation was near to an end. In September 1643, King Charles issued a bitter commission to Sir William Russell, Sir John Packington, Martin Sandys and others complaining that 'many of our subjects traiterously raised armes and levyed against us, and are now in actual rebellion, and divers others have been traiterously aiding and assisting with men, horses, plate, money, ammunition and other things.' He therefore granted Russell and the others authority to investigate whom from the county had joined the Parliamentary army or might otherwise have been assisting their cause and 'seize their land, tenement, or other hereditament, ready money, plate, cattle or chattels real or personal, or debt owing to them'.[59]

Chapter Three
Raising an army 1643–1644

Occupied Worcestershire was valuable to the Royalist cause as a source of manpower, supplies and armaments. Its bridging points over the rivers Severn and Avon also made it a key routeway from other supply bases in Wales, the Forest of Dean and Shropshire to the Royalist capital at Oxford. The county and its route system had to be protected and it therefore became heavily militarised during the war. In doing so,

Map showing the main Royalist garrisons in Worcestershire during the Civil Wars.

(Worcestershire Historic Environment and Archaeology Service)

it relied heavily on locally-raised regiments and in contrast to the situation in neighbouring Shropshire, the forces were centralised in a small number of large garrisons rather than being scattered in small outposts. The main permanent garrisons were within fortified sites at Worcester and Evesham defending the main river crossings across the Severn and Avon; the moated manor sites to the north at Hartlebury and to the south at Strensham acted as bases for mounted patrols. More temporary bases were later established at Madresfield and Leigh Court manor houses. There was also a permanent garrison on the Severn river crossing at Bewdley, and troops were also regularly stationed at Droitwich and at Pershore. Surprisingly, there appears to have been no permanent force at the river crossing of Upton on Severn, and this passed through different hands repeatedly as the armies of both sides marched through.

The main magazine in the country, at the Tower of London, was in Parliamentary hands, so the ill-equipped Royalists were desperate to exploit the iron-working industry of north Worcestershire and the West Midlands as quickly as possible. During the 17th century, around 4 percent of the population of the county were engaged in metal-working, and 18 percent in manufacturing.[1] There were both craft workshops attached to cottages, supplying parts for assembly elsewhere (such as the musket stocks made by John Brancill of Kidderminster), and larger manufactures and foundries organised on an industrial scale. Production was quickly converted to war work; Richard Foley's ironworks at Stourbridge began producing cannon balls as early as August 1642. New industries also developed; Worcester became one of the main centres of Royalist gunpowder production, with the construction of powder mills in spring 1643 financed out of a special levy. The gunpowder was made from saltpetre, charcoal and sulphur, ground together in a mill (water or horse-powered) and 'corned' through a sieve. It was a dangerous and noxious process. The saltpetre was produced from decaying, nitrogen-rich deposits dug from privies, stables etc. and required large amounts of fuel to process it. The government-appointed 'saltpetre men' had the right to enter any premises to dig it out.[2] The gunpowder was then kept in a storehouse in one of the churchyards – to minimise damage in case of an accident!

Large amounts of clothing were also required to equip the troops. It was a Worcestershire man, Thomas Bushell, who organised the new red and blue uniforms for the Oxford army in 1643 and it may be expected that he used his local contacts to arrange the supply of cloth. Worcester was certainly supplying cloth for Prince Rupert's regiment in 1645. The regular passage of the field army through the county would also have brought additional demands to make running repairs on equipment and arms. Horses would need regular shoeing and the matchlock musket was of a basic construction that could be repaired by any country blacksmith. Although simple and with a minimum of moving parts, the English tactic of swinging the musket as a club in hand to hand combat must have meant that damaged locks were a common occurrence.

Shipments of arms to the Royalist capital at Oxford via Worcester began in December 1642. At the end of that month, William Russell paid £5 to William 'Dud' Dudley for the casting of cannon shot from his Stour ironworks. The transport of

The defences of Worcester at the end of the Civil Wars, in 1651, as depicted in a plan of 1660.

1	The Cathedral or Colledge Church	15	Castle Gate
2	St Peters Church	16	Colledge Gate
3	St Andrews Church	17	Sudbury Gate
4	St Martins Church	18	St Martins Gate
5	St Nicholas Church	19	Fory Gate
6	St Clements Church	20	Friers Gate
7	St Albans Church	21	Frog Gate
8	St Helens Church	22	High Street
9	Swithins Church	23	Friers Street
10	St Johns	24	Pitch cross
11	All St Church	25	Bridge over Severn
12	The Fort Royal	26	The Waterhouse
13	Castle hill	27	The Key
14	Bishops Palace		

The Way to London

The medieval city wall of Worcester was refurbished during the Civil War, with a 2–3m bank of earth constructed behind it in order to deaden the impact of cannon shot.

(Worcestershire Historic Environment and Archaeology Service)

armaments from north Worcestershire and the Midlands became regular traffic down the River Severn to Worcester and on the county's roads until 1645. A consignment of pikeheads was supplied in February 1643; in March iron shot, strakes for cannon wheels, mortar shells and hand grenades were taken from Worcester to Oxford. In April there was another major shipment of 95 cartloads of arms, including shot for cannon ranging in size from demi-cannon to robinets, mortar shells, hand grenades and 1,046 pikeheads.[3] In June 1643, 10 iron cannon were delivered. In January 1645 Worcester was expected to provide 8,000 pikeheads at a cost of £150; most of the pikeheads were produced at Foley's ironworks at Stourbridge.[4] In return, supplies of black powder, musket balls and match were regularly sent from Oxford to the garrisons at Worcester and Evesham. A major task of the garrison troops was to protect such convoys whilst in the county and local carters were impressed to carry the goods to the county boundary. One of the first convoys through the county was to transport the mint to Oxford safely: Doddingtree Hundred was ordered to provide it with 20 carts and teams, to be sent to the Talbot Inn, Sidbury in Worcester. There was clearly a shortfall and the irritated Governor, Sir William Russell, ordered them to pay a fine of £3 per cart for those not supplied.[5]

With such activity, the east and south parts of the country also needed protection from what became the increasing threat of Parliamentary raiding parties from Warwickshire and Gloucestershire and from Colonel Fox's base at Edgbaston. Personal loyalties were of little account: property was likely to be seized by 'friend' or 'foe' alike to supply the troops and any man faced the threat of being impressed into whichever army found him first, or depending on the whim of any local constable that he had antagonised. The pattern of the war in Worcestershire also saw the field armies of both sides moving back and forth through the county, funnelling over the bridging points on the River Severn at Upton and the River Avon at Evesham as they manoeuvred for position and also tried to raise new supplies and men from the farms, villages and towns through which they passed. The local garrisons were intended to hinder such activities of the Parliamentary field army and also to act as staging posts and, if necessary, reservoirs of troops for their own field army. At the end of December 1642 Beaumont's regiment from Evesham served as escort through the county for the Welsh regiments of the Marquis of Hertford and were quartered with them for a few days in early January at Stow on the Wold. The overall task of the garrisons was, therefore, to protect a corridor of movement for both arms convoys and field army, to serve as bases from which to clear the region of pockets of Parliamentary resistance and create local centres of administration from which the collection of taxes could be enforced.

Parliament did its best to interfere with the Royalist plan for the county and until 1645, when their efforts became more serious, mounted more or less desultory attacks on the garrisons as well as more wide-ranging raids through the countryside. Only the key garrisons were provided with defences. Nonetheless, despite its defence of an earthen bank and a 5.5m wide v-shaped ditch on the north side and the strong natural protection of the River Avon on the other three sides, the tactic at Evesham seems simply to have been withdrawal on the approach of a serious Parliamentary threat.[6] The garrison may have counted on the likelihood that Parliament would not feel confident enough to occupy the town for any length of time.[7] Parliamentary forces similarly occupied Droitwich temporarily from time to time. By contrast, Worcester was designed to be held: strongly defended by the restored medieval walls backed by 2m–3m wide earthen banks to deaden the cannon shot, re-dug defence ditches up to 16 metres wide and 3.5m deep, and some new earthworks.[8] The form of the circuit of defences by 1651 is shown in a plan drawn up in 1660 but what is not apparent from this is the fact that the garrison created an additional defence from June 1643 by clearing the ground outside the defences to provide a clear field of fire from the city walls. Worcester was besieged for two days by Sir William Waller from 29 May 1643 before being obliged to withdraw on the approach of a relief army. Waller's men managed to reach the very base of the city walls and the decision was therefore taken to burn down the suburbs in order to provide a clear field of fire for the future (see below, p. 107).

The smaller permanent garrisons of Hartlebury and Strensham were based within medieval moated manor houses, their main purposes being to partol the surrounding countryside. At Strensham, gutted as a private residence by Parliamentary troops in 1642, the existing ditch was reinforced by triangular artillery platforms built on the corners to carry light cannon. The garrison seems to have surrendered without a fight in 1645 and was replaced by a small Parliamentary garrison under Captain Dormer. At Hartlebury, the moat may have been widened but it too surrendered after

The ditches in front of Worcester city wall were cleaned out and widened. This excavated section from The Butts was 16 metres wide and over 3.5 metres deep.

(Worcestershire Historic Environment and Archaeology Service)

A small fort was built outside the line of the medieval defences on the east side of Worcester to protect the city from the surrounding high ground. This was rebuilt on a larger scale as Fort Royal in 1651.

(Author Collection)

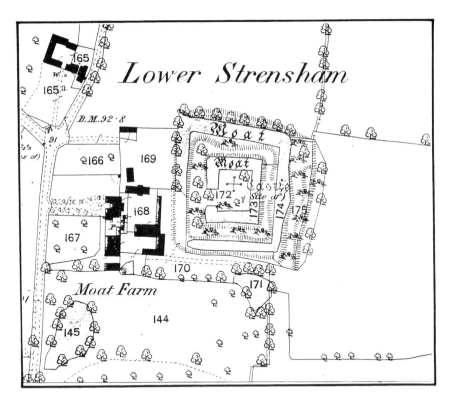

(Top) Plan of the site of medieval moated manor house at Strensham. This was the home of Sir William Russell, re-fortified as a small Royalist garrison 1643–45 and then occupied by Parliamentary troops. Note the triangular extensions to the corner of the banks, built to carry artillery.

(1st edition Ordnance Survey Map, 1885. Crown copyright)

(Bottom) Aerial photograph of Strensham moat, looking north.

(Mike Glyde, Worcestershire Historic Environment and Archaeology Service) a brief siege in 1646. There were other, more temporary, defended garrisons. In November 1645 a small fort was constructed on the high ground at Trimpley, near Kidderminster, and in 1646 the moated site at Madresfield was also briefly occupied before an ignominious surrender. Bewdley appears not to have been provided with defences, relying on defending the bridge over the River Severn and possibly temporary barricades across the main approaches. Although defended by soldiers, much of the work in creating the defended garrisons would have been undertaken by the local civilian population, including the women and children.

Some contemporaries also recommended building camps for armies on the march, clearly based on the model of ancient Rome, but there is no evidence that any were actually constructed and armies probably preferred to use the natural protection of hedged fields or temporary barricades around villages.[9]

The number of troops in the county rapidly increased in the first flush of excitement of the first year of war. In a significant move, on 12 April 1643 all the Trained Bands were ordered to report, at just one day's notice, at Worcester Town Hall in front of the Commissioners.[10] The Committee for Worcestershire had been instructed to ensure that all the weapons of the Trained Bands 'who have voluntarily carried their arms to Gloucester, Warwick or Tewkesbury whilst these held out against us' should be returned to the magazine in Worcester and thereafter not re-issued 'but upon warre and by indenture'.[11] In effect the Trained Bands were being disbanded and their men summoned to join the new regular Royalist regiments.

Local Royalists led by Samuel Sandys and Sir William Russell may have raised up to 7,000 men from the county for the field army and local garrison regiments down to October 1643, including a garrison of around 1,500–2,000 men in Worcester. Together, this amounted to *c.*12 percent of the total population of *c.*57,000. Recruiting would have depended heavily on the influence and pressure of the local gentry. Richard Baxter dismissed the Royalist recruits as 'gentlemen and beggars and servile tenants'.[12] William Russell's troop of Horse included twelve of his servants, dressed in scarlet cloaks 'well-horsed and armed'.[13] Some were volunteers, no doubt urging on their neighbours and promising a short, exciting, campaign after which they could return to their normal livelihoods with tales of daring-do to regale friends in the local inns. They probably included some of the servants and journeymen of Kidderminster whom Baxter despised so much and triumphantly claimed 'when the wars began almost all these drunkards went into the King's army and were quickly killed'.

Other men had simply been conscripted and their recruitment cannot, therefore, be taken in itself as evidence of Royalist support in the county. In November 1643, the King established a formal national system of conscription, threatening severe punishments for any who refused or later deserted.[14] A parish might also be held responsible to provide replacements for any who did desert. Edward Broade tried to raise local reinforcements for Sir Gilbert Gerrard's attack on Stourton Castle in 1644 'telling and threatening divers of the country people that they should be hanged at their own doors if they would not go with him against the said castle'.[15] Most people tried to keep out of the fighting for as long as possible and the situation in

Worcestershire was probably no different to that in the West Country where General Poyntz wrote 'my countrymen love their pudding at home better than musket and pike abroad, and if they could have peace, care not what side had the better'.[16] From the very start of the war, Sir William Russell, as High Sheriff of Worcestershire, had gained a reputation for conscripting men and then imprisoning them in local churches so that they could not escape. He was described as being 'very active for pressing men for the late King, and haven got together a great many psons and pent them in churches for that purpose'.[17] Churches were typically the most substantial buildings in a town or village and so made natural prisons. This practice continued throughout the war and in 1645, the Constable of Droitwich had to spend 15s for guarding men who had been conscripted. There was a financial imperative in this as the county was responsible for paying the 'press money' and costs of clothing and transport until the men could be delivered to the army. The conscripted men were of dubious worth. In theory, the more prosperous were excluded from conscription and, as before the Civil War, local constables saw the practice as a means of removing vagrants, criminals and other undesirables from the locality. Often, if captured, such men would readily agree to fight for the opposite side rather than risk being sent to prison, especially the notorious prison hulks on the River Thames. Baxter gave his verdict on the large number of Royalists who later changed sides and joined the New Model Army

'for the greatest part of the common soldiers, especially of the Foot, were ignorant men, of little religion, the abundance of them such as had been prisoners turned out of Garrisons, under the King, and had been soldiers in his army. And these would do anything to please their officers'.[18]

The new troops were raised as three types of regiment. The Horse were still considered the social elite; theoretically organised in regiments of *c*.400, divided into troops of *c*.70 men. Worcestershire troops could, however, vary in strength from as low as 50 up to 100 men. The Parliamentary Horse operated as independent troops in the early months of the war, although the Royalists developed the regimental structure from the start of the conflict. They were equipped with sword and carbine or pistol, and both sides wore a thick buff leather coat and lobster-pot helmet. Back- and breast-plates were provided if available, although these may have been dispensed with by the end of the war. Dressing identically, the opposing troopers were differentiated by coloured 'scarves' (sashes) tied around the waist. The Royalists tended to wear red and the Parliamentarians 'tawny' orange or blue (the colours of the Earl of Essex and Sir Thomas Fairfax respectively).

The regiments of Foot consisted of *c*.1000 men, divided into companies of *c*.100 men. Royalist regiments were frequently much smaller, particularly towards the end of the war. One of William Russell's companies was reduced to just 43 men in 1643 and a mere 24 men in 1646 (with 4 officers). In the Civil War, two-thirds of the infantry would be musketeers, generally armed with the matchlock musket although some flintlocks (English Lock or Dog Lock muskets) were used for guard duties and by the end of the wars some flintlock companies had been created. The pikemen were used to protect the musketeers from cavalry attack and were also employed as a terror weapon – faced with a hedge of 16ft pikes levelled towards one's eyes it would be a brave man who did not try to break and run. There is, however, some evidence to suggest that bodies of pike were not always provided, especially in the regional armies.[19]

The scale to which the Foot were uniformed on a regular basis during the Civil Wars is debatable. Some Trained Band units continued to operate throughout the War but, apart from the buff-coated Parliamentary regiments from London and the Gloucester 'blue' regiment, there is little evidence that these were generally uniformed.[20] There is no surviving documentary evidence from the Worcester city accounts to support the idea of any regular uniform issue for their Town Regiment. The city was more concerned to fund works on the defences and to meet the expenses of the officers in the garrison, and the militia is therefore likely to have fought in its civilian clothes. At its formation in 1645 the Parliamentary New Model Army was issued with red coats (as being a cheap and easily available colour to dye); earlier some regiments of both sides might be variously issued with red, blue, grey, white or green coats. These were effectively overcoats worn over civilian doublets. Others, particularly the Royalist regiments raised for regional service, may never have been issued with uniforms, fighting instead in their ordinary civilian clothes or

A representation of a fully equipped pikeman of the First Civil War. He is wearing back and breastplate and tassets to protect his thighs and a helmet. The soldiers dispensed with such armour during the course of the Civil Wars at it was heavy and gave little protection against musket fire. Few of the local Royalists troops could probably aspire to this degree of equipment.

(Author Collection, with thanks to the Fairfax Battalia of the English Civil War Society)

those looted from local farms and villages. The armies would therefore have been motley assemblages. To avoid potential confusion, soldiers would follow their company flag (the origin of the present-day 'trooping of the colour' ceremony), and wear field signs of sprigs of greenery, paper or ribbons in their hats to tell friend from foe. In 1651 the Worcestershire Militia was simply distinguished by the use of coloured ribbons in their hats. Ironically, the most detailed description of the dress of men in such units is probably afforded by Charles II's ragged disguise after the battle of Worcester in 1651:

a very greasy old gray steeple-crowned hat, with the brims turned up, without lining or hatband, the sweat appearing two inches deep through it, round the band place; a green cloth jump coat, threadbare, even to the threads being worn white, and breeches of the same, with long knees down to the garter; with an old sweaty leathern doublet, a pair of white flannel stockings next to his legs, which the King said were his boot stockings, their tops being cut off to prevent their being discovered, and upon them a pair of old green yarn stockings, all worn and darned at the knees, with their feet cut off … his shoes were old, all slashed for the ease of his feet, and full of gravel, with little rolls of paper between his toes … he had an old coarse shirt, patched both at the neck and the hands, of that very coarse sort which, in that country, go by the name of hogging shirts …[21]

The shoes were elsewhere described as 'countryman's shoes', probably being calf-length boots . Although comfortable, they were looked down upon as being the dress of country bumpkins and were not officially issued to the army.

The third type of soldiers were the Dragoons: a versatile force equipped as infantry (see above) but mounted on horses (albeit poorer quality 'nags' than those of the Horse) to ride into battle and then dismount to fight on foot. They were especially useful for patrolling and skirmishing. Royalist regiments of Horse tended to include a troop of Dragoons within their structure.

In the early months of the Royalist occupation, Worcester finally achieved its ambition of an

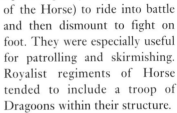

A representation of a Civil War musketeer wearing a Monmouth cap, as made at Bewdley. Note that the soldier's coat is designed as an overcoat, to be worn over a civilian doublet. INSET Some of the powder bottles for the bandoliers had lead tops. These are frequent finds on Civil War sites and a key piece of diagnostic evidence for the period. Upper illustration is of the top to a priming bottle and the lower illustration is the top to a powder bottle.

(Author Collection, with thanks to the Fairfax Battalia of the English Civil War Society).

independent Trained Band or Militia. Whilst the county volunteer regiment was absorbed into new regiments raised by Sandys, Russell and the outsider, Sir James Hamilton, a town regiment was created as the Royalist successor to Rea's militia. Its purpose was 'for the guard and securing of the city'.[22] Martin Sandys, just 18 years old, younger brother of Samuel Sandys and a resident of the Cathedral Close, was appointed as Colonel (see Appendix 4). Now at last fulfilling their pre-war ambitions, the City Council were strongly represented in the command of the Town Regiment. The Lieutenant Colonel was the Mayor, Edward Solley; Lieutenant Sharman and Ensign Hughes were members of the City Chamber and city constables. The city also controlled the administration of the regiment which was paid 'as the said captain [Martin Sandys], Mr Mayor and Mr Aldermen shall thinke fitt'.[23] Organised by wards into four companies, the regiment numbered 300 in March 1643 but enthusiasm waned and numbers had fallen by desertion to only 200 in February 1644. In an apparently dramatic turnaround, the regiment was reputed (by the diarist Richard Symonds) to have comprised 800 men in June 1644 and a massive 1,800 in March 1645.[24] The latter figure would have included most of the adult males in the city. This increase does not betoken a sudden upsurge in enthusiasm for the Royalist cause; it may simply be a confused reference to the traditional summons of the *Posse Comitatus* in the city. As, however, registration in the regiment qualified for tax reductions and avoided conscription elsewhere, the high numbers may also reflect a 'tax fiddle' and a concern to avoid more dangerous activity at a time when service in the Royalist army was becoming increasingly unhealthy! Martin Sandys was also a captain in Samuel Sandys' Horse (it was not unusual for officers to hold multiple commands) and tried to raise a regiment of Horse from the city – the Royalists went to desperate lengths to try to raise men for it. In June 1644 the King and Council of War instructed Martin Sandys to muster all able-bodied men in the city and inform them that it was the King's 'express pleasure and command' that they should enlist in the regiment of Horse or risk being expelled from the city. This threat may also explain the rise in number listed for the Town Regiment in that month but there is no further reference to militia Horse during the First Civil War and it appears that the regiment was never actually mobilised. It is difficult to imagine, given the state of the county and the difficulties in supplying the existing regiments of Horse and Dragoons, where the Royalists expected to find the mounts for the regiment.

The men of the Town Regiment only served part-time. The officers were paid but the common soldiers only received the incentive that they were excused at least part of their tax assessment. Initially, they were excused the whole amount but by necessity this concession was quickly reduced.[25] There were other incentives: they were initially also excused service on maintaining the defences. Thus, on 11 March 1643 they were excused their share of the contributions to pay 60 men who were to work on the city defences (costing 40s per day).[26] The cost of maintaining the regiment continued to rise throughout the war. In April 1644 an additional levy of £5 per week had to be collected to pay the wages of the militia officers. By now, even the soldiers had to contribute to this tax – which cannot have improved their morale! It was agreed that 'the rate of five pouindes by the weeke shall be assessed and collected upon the inhabitantes of the cittie as well souldiers as others towards the payment of Collonell Martin Sandys officers as he shall dispose thereof.[27] By October 1645 this levy had risen to £20 per month. There was considerable opposition to these payments and Sandys was euphemistically obliged to 'assist' in collecting the money, no doubt with armed soldiers behind the tax collectors. Even so, many of the officers were never paid. The drummer, Edward Addams, agreed in November 1645 to waive his arrears of pay in return for being admitted as a freeman of the city.[28] (The drummer was not a boy but a senior soldier, responsible for sounding the various calls of war, passing messages during a truce and also carrying out field punishments.) The means by which the regiments were funded will be considered in more depth in Chapter 4.

The role of the Town Regiment was largely confined to local garrison duties but they did serve in the early campaigns around Tewkesbury, Gloucester and at Warwick. Continued problems with desertion and their half-hearted role during the siege of Worcester in 1646 suggests that this was at best a reluctant force for the Royalists, severely hampered by their part-time service. This must have been a source of great frustration for their commander and his family. The Sandys family was staunchly Royalist throughout the Civil Wars. Martin's brother, Samuel, was governor of Hartlebury, Evesham and then Worcester. Another brother, Richard, had been killed at Edgehill. Their kinsman William, from Fladbury, also served temporarily as governor of Worcester and was then the last Royalist commander of the garrison at Hartlebury; an uncle, John, also served as Captain-Lieutenant in Sandys' regiment of Horse.[29] Such problems were not unique to Worcestershire. Waller described the Parliamentary Trained Bands of Essex and Hertfordshire after the battle of Cropredy in 1644 as 'mutinous and incommandable' and for him, such men were 'only fit for the gallows here and hell hereafter'.[30] By contrast, however, the Gloucester Town Regiment provided sterling service during the siege of the city in 1643 and took a major part in Massey's campaigns in Worcestershire as raiding parties and in the battle of Evesham in 1645.

Control of the Town Regiment was an isolated success for the City Council in its battle with the county gentry. Although the military government of the county was based at Worcester, war-time administration was in the hands of the garrison commanders and those of the county gentry who from March 1643 formed the 'Commission for the guarding of the county' (Committee of Safety), meeting twice weekly at the Town Hall and Cardinal's Hat Inn on Friar Street. The existing local government in the county took a more subservient role to the military. With a similar composition to the former Commission of Array, the principal role of the largely civilian Commissioners was as tax collectors – raising the monthly assessment, encouraging voluntary contributions and listing parliamentary estates for future sequestration (a separate Sequestration Committee was created in March 1644). Although the Commission had a nominal strength of twenty four plus the garrison commanders, real power was in the hands of an inner core of nine, one of whom had to be within a quorum of four needed to make decisions.[31] Almost 50 percent of this inner group had, in any case, taken commissions as army officers.

Commission for the guarding of the county ('Committee of Safety') appointed 16 March 1643

■ = known Royalist army officer
Core Members
Sir William Russell ■
Sir John Packington ■
Sir Edward Sebright
Sir Ralph Clare
Sir Rowland Berkeley ■
Sir Henry Spiller
Samuel Sandys ■
Edward Pitt
Francis Smith
Henry Townshend

Others
Sir John Rouse
Sir John Winford
Thomas Savage ■
Sherrington Talbot
John Keite
Edward Dingley
Francis Finch
Edward Vernon
Thomas Childe
Joseph Walsh ■
William Jeffreys
James Littleton
Henry Ingram ■
Martin Sandys ■

There was also a smaller Council of War of governors and senior officers to deal with military matters in the county, and from February 1644 it met weekly to deal with courts martial. In May, Prince Rupert agreed that members of the Committee of Safety were also entitled to sit on the Council of War, although they could not vote on matters of discipline or punishment of soldiers.[32] King Charles was evidently aware of potential problems of creating a military government alongside the existing civilian structures. His commission to Samuel Sandys as Governor of Evesham included a command 'not to meddle with the civil government of the said town of Evesham, but leave the same in the Mayor or chief Magistrate to whom it properly belongs'.[33]

The scale of the regular garrison in the county in March 1643 is shown by a letter from King Charles: a £3,000 monthly assessment for the county, together with 'such other sums as from time to time shall be agreed upon', was to be divided equally between Sir James Hamilton's combined Horse and Dragoons (then comprising in all nine troops amounting to 620 men), and Samuel Sandys' regiment of Foot of up to 1,000 men.[34] Richard Symonds also believed that Hamilton's regiments were raised 'at the charge of the county' although one troop of Horse was actually funded by the clergy. These were therefore considered to be the core regiments in the county at the time and depended on local recruitment. Hamilton was an experienced Scottish soldier, possibly brought into the county by the King to provide much needed military experience to the leadership. It did, however, prove impossible to limit the county's responsibility simply to those regiments. In any case, the organisation of regiments at this stage of the war was very fluid such as officers holding multiple commissions, particularly in the Horse (where the Troops tended to operate within a very loose regimental structure).

Cardinal's Hat Inn, Friar Street, Worcester. Now substantially rebuilt, this was the site of the weekly meetings of the Royalist Committee of Safety from 1643–46.

(Susanne Atkin)

Samuel Sandys also raised his own 600–700-strong regiment of Horse in 1643, but it was originally excluded from payments out of the monthly Assessment. However, by order of the King in March 1643 quarters were to be provided and their support was made subject to an additional charge at the discretion of the Worcestershire Committee.[35] As the county found continuous difficulty in meeting even the basic Assessment it is unlikely that this proved successful. Symonds went further and claimed that all of Sandys regiments were 'all at his owne charge'. The allocation of the monthly Assessment was the cause of a rift between Sandys and the Governor of Worcester, Sir William Russell (who was also resented for combining the power of High Sheriff and Governor), and encouraged disorder amongst Sandys' men who were left to supply themselves from the people of the county as best they could, taking food, clothing and even bedding. What this meant is illustrated by the case of James Hill of Doddingtree who, on 28 August 1643, was plundered by men under Captain Thomas Simonds of Colonel Sandys' regiment of Dragoons who stole 'certain clothes, woollen and linen to the value of £5'.[36] In December 1643 Prince Rupert again authorised Sandys to levy an additional weekly Assessment to support his men from any of the hundreds between his quarters at Hartlebury and Warwick, as long as they were not already contributing to a garrison. As the Warwickshire parishes were under the control of Parliament this was effectively a licence to plunder the adjoining county (and so reduce the financial pressure on Worcestershire). The Royalists continued to try to levy contributions from the Stratford area as late as December 1645.[37]

There was no further mention of county Trained Bands or the early volunteer regiment from April 1643 and their members were presumably absorbed into this new establishment. Most of the troops were based in Worcester, and there were smaller garrisons at Evesham, Bewdley, Strensham, Madresfield and Hartlebury, and other troops were billeted periodically at Droitwich and elsewhere.

Other regiments were soon created. By May 1643, Hamilton had raised three regiments in the county. As well as the regiments of Horse (400 men) and Dragoons that were included on the county establishment, he also raised a 1,000-strong regiment of Foot.[38] His regiments of Horse and Dragoons had begun mobilisation in December 1642, although there were continual problems in finding mounts, particularly for the Dragoons. However, part of Hamilton's regiments joined the field army in the spring of 1643 and were decimated at the siege of Bristol in July. The regiment of Foot and that of Dragoons were later captured near Devizes. To replace them, Sir William Russell was authorised to raise his own regiment of Horse (*c*.300 men) and a regiment of Foot (originally *c*.700 men although *c*.400 deserted through lack of pay) between May and August 1643. They appear to have been based on some of the local officers of Hamilton's regiments and there was a considerable overlap in their composition. In May 1643 part of Russell's regiment of Horse was quartered at Abberley at a cost of £14 10s 9d to the township. [39] It was impossible even for contemporaries

Sir William Russell (1602–69). He spent a considerable personal fortune on raising troops for the Royalist cause.

(Private possession)

to determine exactly how many men Russell had raised or funded (and from what sources), but he certainly devoted a considerable personal fortune to the Royalist cause as well as distributing the proceeds of the monthly Assessments. Although the enthusiasm to raise troops was welcome and essential to the Royalist cause, it did exacerbate the problem of how to pay and maintain them.

There is no mention of Sir Thomas Lyttleton in this Royalist mobilisation, despite his command of the initial Royalist volunteer regiment. Sandys and Russell proved to be the main powerhouses of local recruitment in the county, but remained bitter rivals and both eventually came into conflict with the Royalist High Command who tried to reduce their influence by importing professional officers from outside the county (see below, p. 83). In December 1643, Russell's regiments marched out of Worcester to temporarily join the field army. This was at the end of a long-running dispute with fellow Commissioners, led by Sir Ralph Clare, over their pay (see below, p. 92), although the Foot were back in the city in August 1644 and were present during the siege in 1646. [41]

The early garrison of Worcester consisted of a nucleus of the Town Regiment with a strong mobile detachment of Hamilton's Horse and Dragoons, and a complement of artillery under the cannoneer, Edward Scarlett. As the principal garrison during the war, Worcester contained the main ammunition magazine for units based within the county. The powder makers, William and Jane Baber (whose family also controlled powder making at Oxford, Bristol, Taunton and Exeter) and

Commission granted to Colonel Samuel Sandys to levy money for the maintenance of his regiment of Horse from Worcestershire and Warwickshire (17 December 1643)

Whereas the Contributions of the Countie of Worcester are for the most part already assigned to his Majesty's Garrisons in the said Countie, insomuch that although your Regiment doe Quarter in the same, you cannot possibly receive or with reason desire anne contributions from them for the mainteynance thereof. Which and therfore by vertue of My power we do authorize and require you and such Officers as you shall therein employ immediately after right and by vertue hereof to assess Levie and raise and receive your weekly contributions for the mainteynance of your Regiment from anne of those hundreds lying between your Quarter and Warwick which are not already assigned to anne other of his Majesty's Regiments of Troopes – And that you maie the better effect this his Majesties Service I doe hereby strictly charge and Command all and everie the High Constables Pettie Constables and other his Majesty's Officers and Ministers of all such hundreds in the Countie of Warwick as are not alreadie assigned by his Majesty Myself or his Majesty's Commissioners for contributior from time to time readilie duelie & punctually to assess levie raise and paie unto you or your Assignees such weekly contributions as you shall in reason impose upon them for the mainteynance of your said Regiment according to the effective number of your Men. Whereof they and everie of them whom it may concern maie in noe way faile as they will answer the Contrarie at their utmost perrills. And for yours and theirs soe doing this shall be to you and them and everie of them sufficient Warrant. Given at Oxford under My Hand and Seale Armes this 17th day of December 1643.

RUPERT
To Colonell Samuell Sandys
Colonell of One Regiment of
Horse, and to the chief
Officer of his Regiment.

James Powell, and the saltpetre maker, William Richardson, were based here as the King ordered new powder mills to be constructed.

Apart from Worcester, the other main garrison in the county was at Evesham to guard the strategic crossing over the River Avon.[41] The first governor was Samuel Sandys, but its garrison troops seem largely to have been brought into the county from elsewhere. A former field army regiment from the Edgehill campaign, that of Sir John Beaumont from Leicestershire (1607–1643), came into the county in December 1642 and then served as garrison regiment for Evesham (under Lieutenant Colonel Godfrey

Key Events: 1643 – Battle of Ripple

In March 1643 the Parliamentarian general William Waller occupied Tewkesbury, forcing Russell's garrison to retreat to Worcester. But Waller was also being pursued by the army of Prince Maurice from the west and so to hinder their advance across the Severn, Waller sent troops to break down the bridge at Upton on Severn. But his demolition team was forestalled by the arrival of the Royalist army. The Parliamentary troops were forced back across the bridge on to the east bank of the Severn and were then pursued by Prince Maurice's army towards Ripple (three and a half miles north of Tewkesbury). There they rendezvoused with a relief column of *c*.1,500 troops under Waller himself). It was here, on 13 April, that Waller decided to make a stand against the young prince.

The two sides met at Ripple Field, on the north side of the village (see plan on p. 79). Waller had advanced through the village on to a ridge known as 'The Bank' or 'Old Nan's Hill' (Ordnance Hill) which runs east to west between Uckinghall village and Ripple Brook. Prince Maurice's army of *c*.2,000 men formed up in front of him on the large flat plain of Ripple Field. Although Waller had the advantage of the higher ground, he soon realised that his flanks were vulnerable. So he decided to beat a retreat back to the village. The plan was to encourage the Royalists to follow his rearguard into the long narrow sunken lane leading back to Ripple where he could harry them from the hedgerows until they tumbled out of the lane into a large open field beside the village. Here they would be confronted by the main body of Waller's troops, lying in wait. The Royalists would then be expected to try to retreat in confusion back up the lane, and be cut to pieces in the process.

As Waller tried to extricate his men off Old Nan's Hill and down the lane, Prince Maurice attacked. His men tore down on the Parliamentarians from the front and both flanks, seizing the initiative of the high ground. The fury of the assault, coming out of the sun and from three directions, completely panicked the Parliamentary troops at the head of the lane and they retreated in complete disorder. Haselrig's heavily armoured cavalry, the 'lobsters', tried to stem the retreat but were said to have lost fifty men out of their total strength of seventy. To try to slow down the charging Royalists, an old gate was hastily thrown across Coach Road as a temporary barricade. Reinforcements under Colonel Massie arrived at this point but were beaten back by the Royalists. The day was only saved for Waller by the timely arrival of yet more reinforcements and he was finally able to extricate himself and retreat back to Tewkesbury. The Royalists claimed that eighty of Waller's army were killed, and an equal number drowned in trying to swim back over the River Severn. By the following week they had inflated the death toll to over 500 men! The Royalists were said to have lost only two men.

from September 1643) until it was destroyed at Tewkesbury on 4 June 1644. The costs of Beaumont's regiment were added to the charges expected to be paid out of the monthly Assessment during 1643. Not surprisingly, there were local objections and one of Russell's counter-charges against Clare in their dispute was that the latter had opposed the King's command to pay Beaumont's regiment out of the Assessment 'whereby one half of this regiment was lost', i.e. they had deserted.[42] The survivors after June 1644 remained in the garrison. The experienced professional soldier Henry Washington (1615–64: brother-in-law to Sir John Packington of Westwood, Droitwich, and who eventually married the widow of Samuel Sandys), was appointed as the new governor of Evesham in December 1643 and he brought his regiment of dragoons with him. Washington had served in the Thirty Years War (1633–39) and had then fought at Edgehill, Lichfield, Bristol and

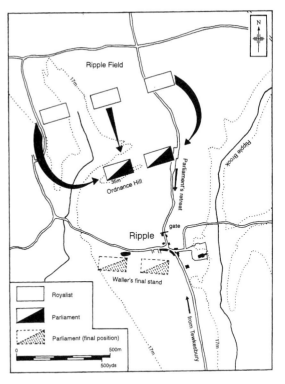

Plan of the battle at Ripple, 1643.
(Worcestershire Historic Environment and Archaeology Service)

Gloucester, but in February 1644, Washington left to join the field army and was replaced by the Warwickshire gentleman, John Knotsford. The garrison was also reinforced around this time by some of Sandys' regiment, placed under Knotsford's command. Being on the main routeway of the armies, the garrison was always prone to troops being drawn off for service elsewhere. In May 1644, 50–60 men were sent from Godfrey's regiment to Leveson at Dudley. In 1645 the garrison was disastrously depleted as men were drawn off into the field army for the Naseby campaign. This led to the town's capture by Parliament: a key stage in the collapse of Royalist control of the county (see below, p. 113). Other garrisons are less well documented. The defences of the medieval moated manor house at Strensham were strengthened in February 1645 using impressed labour from the parish of Queenhill. At Pershore, Sir Walter Pye's men from Herefordshire garrisoned the town in the early part of 1644 and a regiment of Horse was also quartered there in November 1644. There is no evidence of any defences being constructed although a careful guard would certainly have been put on the bridge.

The above units formed a regular Royalist presence in the county, but other outside regiments were also based in the county on a more temporary basis.[43] The

The Civil War encouraged the production of atlases to assist officers as they moved across the country. This book of maps by Wenceslas Hollar was reputed to have been left at Inkberrow Church by Charles I in 1644.

(Courtesy of Vicar of Inkberrow Church and Worcestershire Record Office)

county was responsible throughout the war for feeding and housing other regiments as they simply passed through the county, including the regular hurly-burly of feeding and billeting troops protecting the armaments convoys as they passed to and from Oxford. Russell spent £1,813 of the badly-needed Assessments on assisting the passage of outside troops through the county in 1643. The people of Kidderminster were obliged to make a contribution of £28 8s 2d to re-supply Sir Thomas Aston's regiment, infamous for its looting, as it passed through north Worcestershire in January 1643.[44] Units of the field army were regular visitors. In September 1643, following the disastrous failure of the siege at Gloucester, the King sent 700 of his Lifeguard to help protect Worcester as the county regiments were still with the field army. For a time, the whole of the defeated Royalist army of 30,000 men – tired, hungry, sick and quarrelsome – was camped in the Vale of Evesham around Evesham and Pershore and down to the River Severn. The parishes in which they were quartered were 'miserably vexed' by the looting that went on, over and above the costs of providing daily official rations to them.[45] Law and order broke down: at Sheriffs Lench on 15 September, Colonel Richard Crispe quarrelled with another officer, James Enyon, and killed him in a duel. Crispe was reprimanded but was cleared of murder on the grounds of self-defence. It was a mammoth task to feed such a large body of men. On 12 September, the King (then staying at Hinton, near Evesham) ordered the county to bring in 50lb of bread and 50lb of cheese daily to either Worcester or Evesham and carts, horses and oxen were impressed to carry the food to the troops. The parishes of the Vale of Evesham were spared from this order, being already under the control of the commissary of the army in providing daily food and shelter for the troops quartered upon them.[46] All of this was on top of the county being expected to pay £7,000 towards a week's pay of the army and the continued demands of free-quarter. Not surprisingly both Worcester and the county made excuses as to why they could not afford this additional burden, but it was to no avail and in June 1644 Charles I quartered 3,000 of his field army on the city for a week. At the time, Worcester had a population of only 7,000, already squeezed within the area of the city walls following the demolition of the suburbs as part of the defence works and suffering under the presence of its regular garrison. It is probable that most households had fresh soldiers quartered upon them and the city must have been bursting at the seams.

The difficulties in providing regular pay to the regiments or prioritising the funds that were available created fierce tensions between the different military factions. The men of Sandys' and Russell's regiments were bitter rivals. This may reflect a division of local loyalties between north and south Worcestershire, with Samuel Sandys of Ombersley supporting Sir Francis Clare of nearby Kidderminster against the Russell family from south Worcestershire. They first clashed over who received preference in being paid by Russell (as the then governor of Worcester) out of the monthly Assessment and this led to a long-running dispute during 1643 over the management of the finances of the war effort between Russell and the rest of the Commissioners. In March 1643 Russell complained to Charles I of the 'mutinous and seditious carriage of some officers and soldiers of Colonel Sandys' Regiment of Foot'. Taking his part, the King gave Russell the authority to proceed with court martial proceedings 'to the terror of others and for the prevention of future disorders'.[47] Sandys' men were also accused of beating up the engineer Mr Pratley and workmen sent by Russell to Bewdley to collect building materials for the drawbridges at Worcester.[48] This conflict continued throughout the war and during the 1646 siege, the men of the two regiments actually began fighting with each other![49] In return, the governor (Sir Henry Washington) railed against Russell and Roman Catholics – 'Papists … That will set all by the ears and will do nothing themselves'. Washington attacked a Captain Massey (one of the reformadoes) with the flat of his sword and Russell himself was beaten up by a 'Mr Welsh'.[50] Despite the early royal support, Russell spent much of the war from late 1643 under a cloud after Sandys' attacks on his financial management of the county, but his name continued to appear on documents of the Commission of Safety.

It was to try to overcome such damaging local tensions and to provide a more professional military government that the King replaced Russell as governor of Worcester in November 1643 by an outsider, the Lancashire gentleman and former mercenary in the Low Countries, Sir Gilbert Gerrard. It was probably no coincidence that this was followed shortly after by Russell's regiments leaving the county to temporarily join the field army. With Russell's replacement at Worcester soon mirrored by the replacement of Samuel Sandys at Evesham by Henry Washington it was clear that the intention was to supplant local magnates and gentry by the professional 'swordsmen' who owed their allegiance only to the King and not to any local faction. Such men would probably also be less bothered by local concerns and be more ruthless in raising the regular Assessments. Gerrard's appointment was, not surprisingly, deeply resented by the local gentry establishment and by February 1644, there were increasing complaints from the county as to the scale of the garrisons, their management and behaviour. Equally, Gerrard was not impressed by the state of his new command. Many of the Worcester citizens were now unwilling to serve in the Town Regiment which had been described by the new governor in December 1643 as being 'slovenly and inefficient'. Gerrard believed that 'the citizens kept but poor guards' and that 'many of the citizens are very base'. By the end of January 1644 he was in a state of 'frustration and fury' at the state of the city's fortifications and attitude of the citizens.[51] The tensions in the city were reflected in the fact that by February the disheartened Town Regiment had been reduced by desertion to only 200 men. Some men may have left to join the Parliamentary army; others went into hiding. Large numbers of Worcestershire deserters hid in Shrawley Wood, to the north of Worcester, during the war. The Assessments were also heavily in arrears (by January 1644 only one tenth was being collected), and created a vicious circle forcing soldiers to loot to support themselves and therefore reducing the resources that allowed the inhabitants to find the money for the Assessments!

The Royalist government was desperate to restore confidence in the administration and maintain the army. Gerrard's chaplain, Oliver Whitby, preached a vehement sermon urging the citizens to go beyond their present neutrality and was already seeking to create a spurious mythology of loyalty to the Crown in the first months of the Civil War.[52] Prince Rupert, as the new Lieutenant General of Worcestershire, held a council of war at Worcester Town Hall on 10 February 1644 with the governors of the county's garrisons (Samuel Sandys now at Hartlebury, Gilbert Gerrard from Worcester and Henry Washington from Evesham) along with Sir William Russell and the civilian Commissioner Henry Townshend in order to resolve how to deal with the problem. Prince Rupert demanded a new establishment of 2,000 Foot and 500 Horse for the county in the local regiments. The Foot were presumably based on Sandys' regiment and the garrison troops of Evesham. This establishment could only be achieved by a new monthly Assessment of £4,000 for a period of three months.

In return, a number of concessions had to be made to try to win support from the local community. The Assessments were to be made only on the basis of weekly muster returns, which was to prevent false claims of spurious numbers of troops (as suspected in 1643). The county was also to be freed from the detested burden of free-quarter (the practice of providing goods and services in return for a promissory note for future payment by the local garrison or village constable – the origin of the modern banknote) and rates for billeting troops were set (8s per week for a cavalry trooper and 2s 6d per week for a foot soldier). The Grand Jury of the county even tried to revive the principle of the parochial Trained Bands with an obviously desperate Prince Rupert agreeing that volunteers who armed themselves should not be obliged to serve outside the county. It is not clear how this would have been operated in practice. The volunteers could also choose in which company to serve. Gerrard had little time for the civilian Commissioners, moaning to Prince Rupert 'I confess myself altogether ignorant of the Commissioners powers, but if nothing can be done without them, I believe His Majesty's business will not be much advanced'.[53] The reforms did lead to some temporary success and Gerrard managed to clear north Worcestershire from Parliamentary troops, defeating Colonel 'Tinker' Fox on 24 March. Fox had his revenge and in April managed to capture Sir Thomas Lyttleton at Bewdley in a daring, and for the Royalists embarrassing, night-time raid whilst pretending to be a unit of Prince Rupert's Horse.

Neither the financial target or the concessions of the military could be maintained. The situation would not have been helped by the King's efforts in March 1644 to conscript a further 6,000 men across the country for the field army, with quotas from each county. With no end in sight to the problem of raising sufficient funds from the county, in May the Council of War was obliged to bow again to civilian pressure that the Assessment was not to be diverted for the maintenance of any new troops. Then in late July 1644, following the disastrous defeat at Marston Moor on the 2nd, and a renewed Parliamentary offensive on north-east and south Worcestershire, there was a major re-organisation of the core regiments in the county. They were combined to provide one Foot regiment of 1,000 men placed under Sir Gilbert Gerrard (the Governor's regiment) and a regiment of 400 Horse (divided into seven troops) under Samuel Sandys.[54] The latter seems now to have formed the main garrison of Worcester. There was also a train of artillery in the city. By this stage in the war, Sandys' regiment of Foot had first been transferred to the Evesham garrison under John Knotsford (much to Sandys' displeasure) and was now absorbed into Gerrard's regiment with the other units of Foot. To tighten military control over the collection of the Assessment, in August each parish in the county was allocated to fund a particular troop or company. The amalgamation of units avoided the common problem in the Royalist army of the proliferation of part-recruited regiments under rival local gentry and hoped to improve local discipline by centralising control. It did, however, further the growing antagonism between the military government and

Sandys who had been transferred as governor from the town of Evesham to the lesser outpost at Hartlebury and had lost control of his regiment of Foot.

Russell's troops managed to preserve their independence in this re-organisation. His regiment of Foot was probably out of the county with the field army at the time, although he continued to have an important local role himself and his regiment of Horse was 'about the citty' in June 1644.[55] By August, the main body of Russell's troops were clearly back in the county. Sir William Russell and Gerrard were reported as launching a series of attacks on Gloucestershire to support Colonel Mynne's Irish troops from Hereford. The Hereford and Worcester troops were to rendezvous to make a combined assault on Gloucester but the Worcestershire men under a Lieutenant Colonel Passey (150 Horse and 500 Foot) arrived too late on 4 August to prevent Mynne's troops being defeated at Redmarley although they became caught up in the aftermath. Mynne and 150 men were killed, and another 300 were taken prisoner. Passey was himself mortally wounded and was carried back to Worcester. On 23 August the city agreed to pay the wounded Passey £5 'towardes the supply of his wantes', but it was to no avail and he died.[56]

The Royalists did not give up in trying to raise the number of troops. By the time that Prince Maurice took overall command of the forces in Worcestershire in January 1645 the county had managed to raise an establishment of 1,600 Foot in a regiment of 16 companies, a regiment of 400 Horse, 16 cannoneers and 16 matrosses (gun crew). But these were primarily tied up in local defence and despite frequent attempts to draw the local troops into service on a broader front, they could not help the Royalists in their primary problem of how to maintain a powerful and well-equipped field army on a regular basis. By contrast, Parliament at this stage was planning the creation of a novel centralised and professional army – the New Model Army.

Nonetheless, the full-time regiments raised in Worcestershire during the war were regularly involved in periodic campaigns outside the county. Sir James Hamilton's regiment of Foot served in the Forest of Dean before joining the field army for the rest of the war. Hamilton's Horse and Dragoons, along with Sandys' Horse under Major Savage and Captain Hanbury (also listed in Appendix 2 as officers in Russell's Foot) served at the siege of Bristol. Hamilton's regiments suffered heavy casualties and by 1644 his regiment of Horse had been reduced to just 50 men. For a short time, Russell was Governor of Tewkesbury, after his dragoons captured it in February 1643 and they remained there as a temporary garrison. In April 1643, part of Russell's regiment of Foot was sent to join Lord Capel in Shrewsbury and large parts of the garrison troops were involved in the unsuccessful Royalist siege of Gloucester in August–September 1643. Troops from both Russell's and Sandys' regiments of Horse and Foot were camped in fields at Kingsholm on the east side of Gloucester.[57] Beaumont's regiment from the Evesham garrison was also present at the siege – Sir John Beaumont was amongst the fatalities. In all, it has been suggested that c.800 Foot and a regiment of Horse from the Worcester garrison was present at Gloucester.[58] The huge Royalist army of c.30,000 found little food in the surrounding countryside, and soon began to starve and became riddled with disease. Twelve bargeloads of supplies were sent down the Severn from Worcester to support them.[59] Showing local enterprise, the Worcestershire soldiers stole cattle which were later ransomed back to their owners for £29.[60] On Saturday 12 August their camp was attacked by a determined sally of 150 musketeers from Stamford's regiment of blue coats. Captain Rumney (from Sir William Russell's regiment of Foot) was killed along with eight or nine common soldiers. One other Worcestershire casualty at the siege was John Freeman, a Royalist captain of Horse from Bushley who was killed on 9 August 'pierced through by the stroke of a gunner's bullet at the siege of Gloucester, in the camp of the King'.[61] His memorial in the graveyard of Hempsted church (behind the Royalist camp at Llanthony) is one of the few contemporary memorials to the dead of the Civil War.

Sandys' Foot subsequently accompanied the Queen to Oxford and served with the field army for the rest of the summer of 1643, taking part in the first battle of Newbury on 20 September in Vavasour's Brigade before returning to the county. Sandys' Horse served widely across the country. They were ordered into the Forest of Dean under Sir John Wintour in March 1644 and in May 1645, 150 men from the regiment served within Howard's brigade at the siege of Leicester.[62] They survived the battle of Naseby and in July they were at Stokesay in Shropshire; in August they were at Huntingdon within Vaughan's brigade and in November were in Wales at the defeat at Denbigh. Russell's regiment of Foot was also at Naseby, in Sir Henry Bard's

Tomb of John Freeman from Bushley, Worcestershire, killed at the siege of Gloucester in August 1643 and buried in Hempsted church, Gloucestershire. One of the few contemporary memorials to the dead of the Civil Wars

(Author Collection)

Tertio. One worry for the commanders was that if contingents were detached from local regiments for outside service, there was always the possibility that they might never return. Out of Captain Francis Blunt's troop of Horse that was sent to Bridgnorth in the spring of 1643, 10 men were killed but another 30 were described as 'none returned' and another 20 were 'lost in the pursuit of the enemy and transferred to other command'.[63] The Troop ceased to exist. But temporary deployments could not properly remedy the weaknesses of the Royalists in maintaining a permanent, mobile, field army and this was to prove their undoing.

Appendix 4 lists the known officers that served in the locally-raised regiments, mostly local men, but an unknown number of Worcestershire Royalists also served in other regiments within the Royalist field army, recruited during its frequent forays into the county. William Sheldon of Bromsgrove commanded a troop in Prince Maurice's Horse which also included John Sheldon as his cornet. Thomas Sandys is also listed as a lieutenant in the regiment. For thousands of Worcestershire men service in the Royalist armies brought the excitement of travel beyond their county boundaries, but the romanticism would soon have been tempered by lack of food and shelter and many hundreds fell as casualties in the campaigns of the south and west.

Chapter Four
Maintaining an army

The funding of the Royalist garrison troops via a monthly Assessment has already been referred to in passing in Chapter 3. A large part of the cost of raising the local regiments during the initial stages of the war was personally borne by Sir William Russell and Samuel Sandys, with other voluntary contributions from sympathetic gentry. From 10 December 1642 to 15 May 1643, Russell claimed that the Worcestershire gentry had provided £31,018 0s 9d to maintain the Royalist army. In the same period, the citizens of Worcester could only claim to have raised a mere £700. By early 1644, the military establishment in the county was c.4,000 men according to Richard Symonds.[1]

The Royalists could not rely on the generosity of sympathetic gentry to fund the war effort for long and, as soon as it was clear that the war was not going to be settled

The financing of the army remained a critical problem for the Royalists throughout the war. A contemporary cartoon shows how far they failed. The soldier's equipment has been replaced by plundered cooking implements and food.

(The National Archives)

by a single battle, plans were put in place for a more organised system of funding. On 17 December, the King authorised Russell (as both High Sheriff and Governor of Worcester) to arrange local contributions to pay for the county regiments. As a result, a system of monthly Assessments was introduced from January 1643 and the county was obliged to provide £3,000 per month. John Baker, gentleman, was appointed as tax collector. Worcester City Council conveniently described itself as being confused by the propositions of Russell which 'are not cleerlie by us understood'.[2] It then tried to negotiate its own terms in a fresh attempt to assert itself against the County Committee. The Commissioners were not fooled by this ploy and Worcester was reluctantly forced to pay a levy of £180 per month 'towards the fortification and other publique uses of the Cittie as the governor shall appoint'.[3] Before the war, the responsibility for such works would have rested with the City Council and therefore reflects a serious loss of control to the new military authorities. Those of the citizens who volunteered for the militia were initially to be completely excused this contribution. The Royalists could not, however, afford to be so generous for long. In June 1643, an angry Charles I was told that without pay the Worcester(shire) troops would not fight and that 'our soldiers for want of pay both horse and foot are many times in great disorders and discontent and for that cause some of them go abroad and commit great spoil and robbery'.[4] The Hundred and Parish Constables were accused of not making enough effort to collect the Assessments – not surprising given the unpopularity of the tax. The seriousness of the situation is shown by the fact that at times it appears that it was even impossible to muster the men of a regiment together in case they were roused to collective mutiny through lack of pay. The Commissioners wrote in their Inquiry into Russell's administration:

> We cannot according to your honoured command give answer what numbers of horse or foot officers the said William Russell hath in his said Regiments in that the officers of the said foot Regiments refuse to muster until their soldiers may have their full pay which for the present we are not able to make (alleging) they cannot draw them together for fear of mutinying.[5]

This was no idle threat as 400 of Russell's regiment of Foot did indeed desert during the summer of 1643 through lack of pay. The pay of his Horse and Dragoons was

The Parliamentarians had seized the main mint at the Tower of London. The Royalists established a number of small mints during the First Civil War. One of these was probably at Hartlebury. This half-crown shows the three pears of Worcestershire on the reverse and has the mintmark HC for Hartlebury Castle.

(Worcestershire Museums Service)

over £1,700 in arrears during this period.[6] Such men were not only deserting the army but were also, as a consequence, forced to leave their homes and family for fear of being quickly re-captured by their regiment. Many local deserters took refuge in Shrawley Wood, north of Worcester. It was supposed to be the duty of local villages to round up such men and they could be fined for harbouring deserters. The deserters theoretically faced a death sentence if recaptured but the King, increasingly desperate for manpower, offered pardons in 1644 and 1645 in an attempt to encourage them to return to their regiments.[7]

Payment for wages aside, the funds were also insufficient to properly equip the men with necessities of warfare. The county was also expected to cover the costs of casting shot, making gunpowder and match and sundry equipment out of any surplus from the Assessments. In practice, this resulted in additional charges. In June 1644 Droitwich was expected to provide six tanned hides and five 'white' hides to the collarmaker of the Train of Artillery (white hides are those tanned in alum).[8] Funds were always limited and therefore ammunition and equipment was likely to be in permanent short supply. At this time, muskets cost 10s–15s each, lead musket balls were £17 a ton and cavalry mounts cost £7 10s. Of the 151 Foot that Russell sent to Lord Capel at Shrewsbury in April, only 80 were described as being well-armed and the rest simply carried wooden clubs.[9] There was a particular problem in supplying mounts for the Horse and Dragoons: horses cost £4–£10, or perhaps £3 for a dragoon's 'nag', and might be purchased, levied from local districts or simply confiscated from those suspected of supporting the opposing side. Hamilton's regiment of Dragoons eventually reached an establishment of 370 men in 1643 but not all could be mounted. Sergeant Major Henderson's troop consisted of 20 mounted and 50 unmounted men, whilst Hamilton's troop consisted of 20 mounted and 50 unmounted men. Separate rates of pay had to be established for the two classes of soldier. When Washington lost his mounts at Marston Moor in 1644 they could not be replaced and so his regiment of Dragoons at Evesham were converted to a Foot regiment. The Horse and Dragoons also required daily supplies of fodder if they were not simply to strip local meadows.

The payment of the Assessments was always in arrears, reflecting both a lack of resources and a local unwillingness to pay, when faced with an ever-increasing range of demands from new taxes to the ever-present threat of free-quarter. In Worcester, additional constables were appointed to collect the monthly Assessment but from March 1643 troops had to be used to enforce payment from the citizens. The county was clearly under military rule and one of the charges against Russell in 1643 was that 'he hath lately endeavoured to set his soldiers upon the Commissioners about their pay in a mutinous manner'.[10] Similar charges of partiality by the governor towards the military were made against Sandys in 1645. Payment of the regular regiments took priority over the Worcester Town Regiment and this may help to explain the scant references to the militia during the war. On 11 March 1643 Martin Sandys was instructed to deliver invoices for his expenses, and Lieutenant Webb, Sergeants Thomas Allen and John Baker and three drummers should be paid 'as the said captaine Mr Mayor and mr Aldermen shall think fitt', with the money raised by fifteenths.[11]

Musket and pistol balls found at Greenhill, Evesham (probably from the 1651 camp). Some of these were evidently cast on site, as seen from the casting sprue still joining two of the pistol balls.

(Worcestershire Historic Environment and Archaeology Service)

Civil War cavalry sword, found adjacent to Powick Bridge.

(Worcester City Museum)

Pay of the Worcester garrison (per day), June 1643[12]

Foot

	Old pay	New pay
Colonel	£2 – 00 – 0d	7s 6d
Lieutenant Colonel	£1 – 10 – 0d	7s 6d
Sergeant Major	£1 – 05 – 0d	7s 6d
Captain	15s 0d	7s 6d
Lieutenant	4s 0d	4s 0d
Sergeant	1s 6d	1s 6d
Corporal	1s 0d	1s 0d
Common soldier (per week)	4s 0d	4s 0d

Horse

Colonel	15s
Captain	15s
Lieutenant	10s
Cornet	8s
Quartermaster	5s
Corporal	3s
Trumpeter	2s 6d
Surgeon	2s 6d
Smith	2s 6d
Common Trooper (per week)	12s

In order to save money, the Commission of Safety tried to limit expenditure on the army by only agreeing to pay costs when the local regiments were actually within the county boundaries (a throwback to the principles of the pre-war Trained Bands). This was of little comfort for the troops or for the unfortunate inhabitants of the territories through which the unpaid men passed. The failure to provide for their needs inevitably led to a breakdown in law and order as the soldiers turned to plunder and the continuing practice of free-quarter. For the soldier, free-quarter had another advantage in that it probably provided a better diet than their basic army rations of bread and cheese. Sir James Hamilton's regiment received no pay for the three weeks that it operated in the Forest of Dean during April 1643, neither did the large number of Worcestershire troops that were present at the siege of Gloucester in August. The county was evidently bedevilled by administrative problems and squabbles amongst the Commissioners, both between civilian and military and between the various gentry factions. The complaints of the King in 1643 as to the behaviour of the Worcestershire troops continued throughout the war. Few details survive as any action that was taken came before military courts rather than the Quarter Sessions, although there was supposed to be an appeal system to the

Commissioners (which would also result in action against any officer who had failed to act on a complaint against one of his men).[13] The local gentry also wanted to be provided with more details as to how the monthly Assessments were spent, as there were suspicions that officers were being overpaid and were also claiming the pay of non-existent soldiers. Many of the complaints in 1643 were directed against the Governor, Sir William Russell, who was accused of mis-appropriation of funds by his fellow Commissioners. He was accused of acting out of control in raising troops without consultation and paying them at too high a rate. As an example of the absence of proper auditing, it was said:

> That Captain William Walsh hath received from Sir William Russell from the 12th of July until September the 8th £131 10s od for the pay of a troop of horse by him raised, but the number of the said troop we know not, never having seen the said troop, nor yet the muster roll, the said Captain with his said troop leaving this County in September last.[14]

In an effort to reduce costs, the pay of the officers was cut throughout the war but it may be presumed that they found other ways to make up their wages which no doubt rebounded on the local populace. The wages of the common soldiers in the garrison in 1643 were then only *c.*7d per day – less than for a farm labourer. A cavalry trooper earned over 20d per day, but had to find expenses for his horse out of this. The cost of fodder might be 12d per day. The men of the part-time Worcester Town Regiment could maintain their normal livelihood in the city but this was not the case for the men of the other full-time regiments whose pay was irregular and almost invariably in arrears. The impact on their home lives as families struggled to maintain themselves against a decrease in both income and availability of labour can now only be imagined. For some, the answer may have been for the families to accompany the men into the garrison although this brought its own dangers. In July 1645 one camp follower of the army – 'a strainge woman wounded at the battel in Leicestershire' – was buried in Kidderminster. The presence of such camp followers brought an added burden to the garrison towns, fearful that the women and any children might be left behind as paupers to become a burden on the parish. A graphic illustration of this is provided by an incident during Charles II's escape from Worcester whilst staying in the George Inn in Broadwindsor, Sussex. The inn was also occupied by around 40 soldiers and their families who were on their way to embarkation ports for Jersey. A pregnant woman went into labour, leading to fierce arguments between the soldiers and the officers of the parish as to who would be responsible for maintaining the mother and child when the soldiers moved on.[15] Repeated efforts from February 1644 to prevent families of soldiers being billeted with their menfolk without the consent of the householder suggested that the practice remained a serious problem throughout the war. (Lots were later drawn for a limited number of wives to follow their husbands in the New Model Army to Ireland but Cromwell encouraged wives to accompany soldiers to Scotland in 1650 so that they could serve as nurses.)

Local soldiers with families that remained at home would have been well aware of the likely effect that the Assessments, ruthlessly collected to provide their own wages,

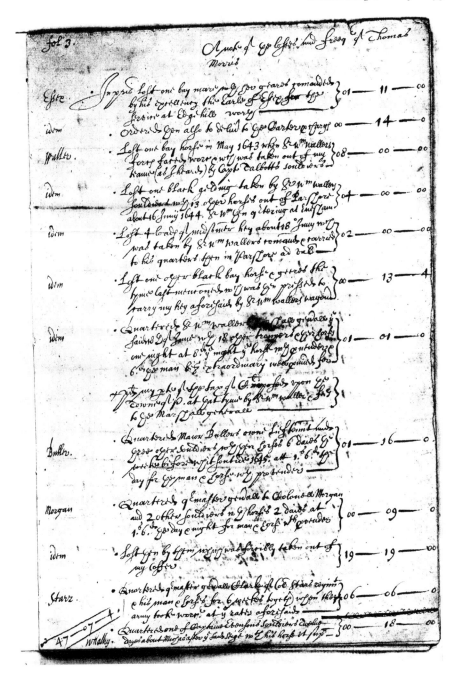

Extract from the Commonwealth Exchequer Papers for Pershore, detailing the losses suffered by Thomas Morris, particularly from the army of Sir William Waller. Plundering by Royalist troops was probably no less extensive, but is less well documented.

(The National Archives)

would be having in their own parishes and on their own families. For this reason, units were attached to parishes for Assessment outside of their recruiting areas, but local soldiers who were permanently based in the county could not fail to see the depressing effect that the war was having on their communities. The large-scale desertions were therefore not surprising, even from the part-time Worcester Town Regiment from which 100 men deserted in 1643–4 along with over half of the strength of Russell's regiment.

The county was required to supply the garrisons with more than simply money and the depletion of staple goods caused considerable strain to the local economy. Despite the importance of the manufacturing and metal-working industries this was still primarily an agricultural county with *c.*67 percent of the population engaged in agriculture.[16] Food that would have been stored for home consumption or sold at market in order to buy other goods was extracted out of the local economic equation in order to support an economically non-productive army. Meadows were stripped of fodder that was required for the farmer's own animals. Thus, in one instance, the people of Doddingtree hundred were ordered to supply thirty loads of hay, thirty quarters of oats or peas, bread and cheese to supply the Worcester garrison.[17] In 1643, prior to the abortive siege of the city by Sir William Waller, the constable of Elmley Lovett was ordered to provide 'one load of Hay, one quarter of oats, six cheeses, six loaves of bread and two bushels of meal, and deliver the same at the Foregate for the relief of His Majesty's garrison within the City of Worcester'.[18] In June 1644, an order was made to the constable of Kempsey, 'to will and require you and either of you in his Majesty's name to charge you that you presently provide and bring to the Pied Bull in Sidbury by ten of the clock, two quarters of oats or peese, one fat veal, one fat mutton, one fat lamb, one dozen of poultry, three or four young geese, one dozen of pigeons, one fat pig, one flitch of bacon, and 5s. worth of cheese, two dozen of boulted bread'. Temporary requisitions of men and equipment would also be made. In May 1643 the King commanded Worcestershire to provide 100 draught horses for 20 days for his field army and in June orders were circulated to impress further horses, carts and carters from Worcestershire and the adjoining counties to carry ordnance from Worcester to Oxford.[19]

From 1644, the military tried to tighten control of the collection of Assessments. Every parish was allocated to support one of the main garrisons. The collection was to be made weekly by the Parish Constable and paid to the Treasurer of the Committee of Safety. Ominously, however, any arrears would be collected by the troops of the garrison. The parishioners faced men like Sir Henry Bard of Chipping Campden who, in November 1645, demanded unpaid taxes from south Worcestershire with the threat: 'Know you that unless you bring unto me (at a day and hour in Worcester) the monthly contribution for six months, you are to expect an unsanctified troop of horse among you, from whom if you hide yourselves ... they shall fire your houses without mercy, hang up your bodies wherever they find them, and scare your ghosts'. His men were unflatteringly, but probably entirely accurately, described as 'cormorants' or 'shirt-stealers'.[20] In an effort to reduce the threat of violence, it was eventually agreed the Constable would be in attendance when the soldiers arrived to collect their unpaid dues.

As one important concession, half of the monthly Assessment from the county was allowed to be provided in kind rather than in cash, although this caused no less serious problems in the medium to long term. Those parishes assigned to supply the Horse had to bring in hay, oats, peas, beans and straw as well as provisions for the men. The daily fodder for a horse was supposed to be 14lb of hay, 7lb of straw, 1 peck of oats and half a peck of peas.[21] At the time the basic ration for the men was 1lb of bread or biscuit and ½lb of cheese per day, together with two pints of beer or a bottle of wine. Civil War soldiers were normally expected to pay for any additions to this, but the Worcestershire garrisons did rather better. The men had to be provided with cheese, butter, dry bacon, bacon and beef. The county was, therefore, a relatively comfortable posting for the Royalist troops. The supplies were to be delivered weekly to Worcester on Saturdays and on Mondays to the garrisons at Evesham and Hartlebury. If this was not enough, both the Royalists and Parliamentarians tried to raise taxes from the same areas, collecting whenever the opportunity arose as control of territory shifted. Strensham, on the west bank of the River Avon (five miles north of Tewkesbury), was assessed at £12 10s 0d by both sides in 1644. Assessments were backdated to take into account the periods under the opposition's control so that, after Massey's troops took increasing command in 1645, the Assessment of £10 per month for Elmley Lovett (four miles east of Stourport) was backdated for twelve months! A fresh burden came in May 1644 with the creation of the Excise Committee to collect a tax on merchandise that was sent to Oxford.

Pershore Bridge, partially demolished by the Royalist army in 1644.

(Author Collection)

Key Events: 1644 – Waller's passage through the county

The English Civil War was not a war of fixed front lines. Although Worcestershire was under Royalist control for much of the period from 1642 – 1645, this did not stop frequent raids into the county by Parliamentary forces from Gloucestershire and Warwickshire and in the summer of 1644, General Waller's army of 10,000 men from the Southern Association passed through in a game of cat and mouse with the King's army.

Waller was shadowing the King's army on its retreat from Oxford in May. Waller's men followed the Royalists through Broadway in early June and then occupied much of the Vale of Evesham until 12 June and stripped it bare. The Earl of Essex described them as living at 'free quarter,

Sir William Waller (1597–1668), Parliamentary general whose army looted east Worcestershire in 1644.

free plunder … without control'.[22] They then moved on to Bromsgrove with the Horse pushing on to Kidderminster which was attacked by nine troops of Horse on 15 June. Disappointed in their hope of plunder, they found it little better than 'an empty farm'. They then attacked Bewdley but were thwarted by the Royalist demolition of the bridge. Waller's men remained on the opposite side of the river for two days until 16 June, planning to repair the bridge, before giving up thought of any attack against what Waller optimistically described as the Royalist army in its 'discouraged, broken condition'. They then moved on to Droitwich which they entered on Sunday 17 June, where the troops were billeted in the salt cellars. With hardly a pause, the army then made a token appearance in front of Worcester before the Horse rode on to Evesham on 18 June. Here Waller levelled the defences and then moved through Gloucestershire and then back into Oxfordshire, where he was defeated in battle at Cropredy Bridge on 29 June.

It is difficult to imagine how the people of the county coped with imposition piled upon imposition – month after month and year after year. A dismal Richard Baxter, writing from Rous Lench, summed up the situation across the nation in his *Saints Everlasting Rest* of 1649: 'Nothing appears to our sight but ruins. Families ruined; congregations ruined; sumptuous structures ruined; cities ruined; country ruined; court ruined; kingdom ruined; who weeps not when all these bleed'.[24] It became impossible for the farmers to hold anything back in reserve from the regular monthly

Assessments. Any surplus was likely to be seized by the additional demands imposed by the garrisons, the periodic visits of the field army or by raiding parties by Parliament. Normal work was impeded by the seizure of draught animals, fodder and equipment. If they did manage to harvest a crop then it provided an even easier target. In some cases the farmer might try to bribe soldiers to leave them alone – as

Key Events: 1644 – Rebellion in Evesham

Waller's army found a county already exhausted by war. In June, the people of Evesham took action. On 5 June, the King retreated across the River Avon into Evesham with an army of *c*.5,000 Horse and 2,500 musketeers. The fast-approaching Waller had *c*.10,000 men and Colonel Knotsford was ordered to slight the Evesham defences and then remain in the town with his men as a rearguard until he saw the enemy approach. As he retreated, he demolished part of Evesham Bridge as a standard tactic to slow down the pursuers. In this case, however, the rebellious citizens of Evesham showed their Parliamentary leanings and rushed to repair their bridge so as to allow the army of William Waller to pass over it. Clarendon described how 'the evil inhabitants received him [Waller] with willingness'.[23]

In the fluid nature of the war in Worcestershire, the King was soon back. On 16 June a furious Charles headed back with his army to an apprehensive Evesham. Pausing there only an hour or so, he forced the town to pay a fine of £200 and provide 1,000 pairs of shoes for his soldiers (at approximately 1s 4d–2s a pair) for their action in repairing their so recently-demolished bridge on Waller's behalf. He also broke down the bridge once again. The connivance of the town council in the act of rebellion was evidently suspected and the then mayor, George Kempe, and a number of aldermen were taken as prisoners to the Royalist capital at Oxford.

Engraving of Evesham Bridge, now demolished. In an effort to support the approaching Parliamentary Army, the citizens of Evesham repaired the bridge after the Royalists had tried to destroy it, in order to cut the route across the River Avon.

(Almonry Museum, Evesham)

Old Evesham Bridge in 1854.
FROM A SKETCH MADE SHORTLY BEFORE ITS DEMOLITION.

T. Pearse from Powick did by offering the soldiers of Captain Devereux 4s not to steal his horses![25] In June 1644 Waller's Parliamentary army, made up of men from the southern counties and London Trained Bands, imposed their own free-quarter and stripped much of the Vale of horses, fodder, foodstuffs, bedding and clothing. The parish accounts presented to the Exchequer in 1647 divide their unpaid expenses into the costs of assessments, free-quarter, other expenses and plunder. Although directed towards Parliament, the accounts offer a sample as to what was taken by both sides during the war. On one occasion in 1644 the Parliamentary troops requisitioned 30 bushels of wheat, 30 bushels of barley, 50 bushels of pulses, 24 bushels of malt, 30 bushels of mill corn and 12 bushels of oats worth in all £25 11s from William Saye at Fladbury. They also seized from him a roan gelding worth £6.[26] At Pershore, fourteen horses and four loads of hay to a total value of £6 were requisitioned from Thomas Morris whilst Thomas Aynsworth claimed £2 for the cost of two hogshead of strong beer.[27]

The distinction between what was officially seized on behalf of the army and what was simply individual plunder quickly became blurred. Not for nothing were soldiers accused of using their swords primarily to terrorise civilians.[28] Apart from one 'black nagge' worth £3 5s 8d., Thomas Saunders from Hill and Moor also lost a cloak, two hats and linings worth £2 6s 8d whilst Mary Daye had a doublet, two pairs of

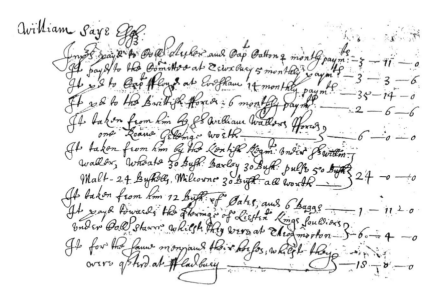

Extract from the Commonwealth Exchequer Papers for Fladbury detailing William Saye's losses of £120 11s during the Civil Wars. They include the costs of quartering troops, seizure of horses and foodstuffs. Although they relate only to Parliamentary troops, they may be taken as representing losses to both sides during the wars.

(The National Archives)

Fladbury Church. The village was looted wholesale by the Parliamentary troops as they camped here in 1644.

stockings and a blanket taken, worth in all £1.[29] The ill-disciplined Kentish Horse under Liversay seemed particularly enthusiastic in stripping the Pershore area. There were less good pickings at Kidderminster which Waller described as having been reduced to 'an empty farm', and the inhabitants of Chaddesley Corbett complained particularly of the violence of Waller's men in stripping their houses and farms. Both sides tried to cure the problem of plundering by threatening the death penalty and although isolated instances are indeed recorded of this throughout the country, the problem was too widespread to control effectively without their officers being able to offer regular pay.

By the time the Royalist field army returned to the Vale of Evesham after Waller had withdrawn, the countryside had been stripped bare of food and they were obliged to bring in supplies from as far away as Shropshire. The governor of Bridgnorth supplied ten tons of cheese to the army at Evesham, at a cost of £150.[30] The exactions went on year after year. On 4 April 1645, the Royalists demanded 3,000 bushels of wheat (of which 500 quarters were to be baked as biscuit, the rest baked as bread), 500 pickaxes, shovels and spades, 20 tons of hay, 20 quarters of oats and 10 quarters of beans to be delivered to the Cross Inn when the army arrived at Worcester. The county was also to supply twenty-eight teams of horses with carts and carters for each team, supplied with three days rations, to be brought to College Green on 11 April.[31] £500 worth of cheese was also to be supplied. The situation worsened when

Parliament began to re-assert its authority in the county from the summer of 1645 as now both sides were competing for ever-limited resources. The new garrisons at Evesham and Strensham scoured the countryside for supplies and furnishings. Beds seemed to be in particularly short supply. Dormston was targeted by the Evesham garrison, who seized beds from a number of claimants, varying in worth from a mere 7d to one from the parsonage worth 5s 6d – most were in the order of 2s 6d. Eckington was also obliged to provide beds for Evesham and Strensham at a total cost of £5.[32]

What could happen if a parish tried to resist the demands of the army is illustrated by the experience of Amscote and Blackwell in the parish of Tredington (now in Warwickshire). In June 1643 they complained to the King that Royalist troops of Sir Thomas Aston's regiment had stolen forty of their horses, beaten up the owners, and then 140–160 cavalry deliberately rode through their fields of beans and peas simply to spoil the crop![33] The Worcestershire Committee was obliged to write to the King to complain of their 'plunderings and abuses' across Droitwich, Bromsgrove, King's Norton, Alvechurch and Abbotts Morton to the point where those parishes could no longer afford to pay their monthly contributions.[34] The Northern Horse gained a particularly bad reputation in the summer of 1644. Gerrard did his best to control them and, as a result, was accused of offering them only meagre hospitality.[35] Their officers complained 'many having deserted the service and those that remain so dejected it doth much prejudice the public service, and in earnest the common soldier so generally unfurnished that we can make no great promise of success'.[36] The defeated soldiers of the Royalist field army who retreated into the county in October 1645 brought new problems for local garrisons. Vaughan's Horse, including local units, drifted through the Marches and Worcestershire after their defeat at Denbigh on 31 October, taking money and supplies intended for local regiments and insulting those officers who attempted to control them. They even held Sir Ralph Clare and the ironmaster Richard Foley to ransom![37]

The worst reputation of any army was held by the Scots when they passed through the county in 1645 as allies of Parliament. From the various parish claims to the Exchequer it appears that they drove off all the sheep that they could find. Thomas Hornblower from Kidderminster Foreign lost 240 sheep to them at a cost of £80.[38] In Hartlebury, Emanuel Ives had 20 'good sheep' taken at a cost of £6 13s 4d; Emanuel Smith lost six oxen to them, worth £27. In all, 497 sheep were taken by the Scots from Hartlebury parish. In Mathon, William Hall claimed losses of £30 'by the Scottish armies, in plundering all our apparel, beef, bacon, cheese and all kinds of household stuff, out of my house'.[39] They also took food, wagons, blankets, sheets, napkins, hand wipes, suits, petticoats, aprons, stockings, brooches, kettles, flagons, dishes – i.e. anything they could possibly remove! What they could not take, they destroyed. The local people made repeated claims that the Scots trampled fields of corn as they passed by. It is not surprising that they received so little support from the area when they returned, this time on the side of the King, in 1651.

Known enemies could expect little mercy. The house of the royalist Rowland Bartlett was plundered twice by the Gloucester troops in 1642 and three times in 1643.[40] Following their capture of Evesham in 1645, the Parliamentary troops went on a plundering spree which included burning the crops, barns and buildings of Thomas Savage of Elmley Castle. The most intense plundering, however, followed the Battle of Worcester in September 1651. The citizens of Worcester had infuriated the approaching Parliamentary army by so readily surrendering to the Scots (now on the side of King Charles II). They took their revenge in the immediate aftermath of the battle. Nicholas Lechmere of Hanley Castle wrote in his diary, 'The city of Worcester was taken by storm and all the wealth in it became booty to the soldier'. Sir Rowland Berkeley of Cotheridge wrote of 'all houses being ransacked from top to bottom, the very persons of men and women not excepted' and the ruin of many families.[41] Private houses, shops, and warehouses may all be expected to have been looted.

With so many of their menfolk in the army from 1642–6, the burden of carrying on a normal life in order to pay taxes and provide supplies therefore fell more heavily on those that remained. All this led to a considerable redistribution of wealth towards the benefit of a military structure whose appetite seemed insatiable.[42] Collapse was inevitable. By the end of the war the system of apprenticeship in Evesham and Kidderminster had broken down and the proportion of Worcester citizens on poor relief rose in 1645 to 23 percent from a peace-time average of only 4–5 percent.[43] Many tenant farmers failed in the task and simply stopped paying rent. They hid what money they could. One such hoard from south Worcestershire, probably hidden in a roof beam, comprised eighteen coins dating from 1560–1 to 1646, including a Royalist issue shilling.[44] Other hoards are known from Cradley and Tenbury. It was even necessary to consider the possible effects of the war in drawing up one's will. In 1644, John George of Eckington wrote:

Coin hoard from South Worcestershire, with 18 coins dating from 1560–1 to 1646. Probably hidden in a house roof during the Civil War.

(Worcester City Museum)

I give also unto my said wife Anne George Tenne Pounds of like lawfull money to be paide unto her within two years next after my decease out of all my stock of goods cattells and chattels, provided that if my stock be plundered or receive overmuch loss by quartering of souldiers, then my will is that the saide tenne pounds shall be paid unto her within ffower years next after my decease.[45]

The women of these beleaguered communities played as valuable a contribution to the war effort in maintaining a semblance of ordinary life as did the better-publicised, but more isolated, instances of direct participation by women in the fighting. To report the grinding effect on local communities, however, served no political purpose for the chroniclers of the time. A considerable number of widows had been called upon to fund the arms of the Trained Bands. Now, the wives of the gentry were left to run estates, whilst others ran businesses supplying the army. Poorer women were already well known as farm labourers – the wages for those in Essex was fixed by 1651 at 1s 2d per day for work in the harvest field and 10d per day for work in the hay field.[46] Nonetheless, it may be expected that normal maintenance of the land deteriorated, as ditches became clogged, hedges and coppices were neglected and trees were cut down. Transport to markets became more difficult as the roads and bridges, already in a poor state of repair at the start of the war, deteriorated further through lack of maintenance. There must have been a widespread shortage of horses as draught animals were regularly requisitioned by both sides. Harvests were redirected towards the garrisons rather than to local families and seed stocks were threatened. By the autumn of 1645, Townshend starkly summed up the state of the county as follows: 'The country is fallen into such want and extremity through the number and oppression of the Horse lying upon free quarter that the people are necessitated (their hay being spent) to feed their Horses with corn, whilst their children are ready to starve for want of bread'. But there was no respite and in the early stages of the siege of Worcester in 1646 Townshend described how the garrison plundered the farms out to Kempsey and Pirton 'and take all sorts of cattle from off the grounds, fat or lean, and as soon as they have them knock them down and kill some, sell others, though they be not fit man's meat nor they necessitated … and so a poor honest man ruined in one night what he hath laboured for all his days'.[47]

The wealth of the countryside was an impossible temptation for the soldiers to resist. It was an uncomfortable life on campaign: if they could not find billets in town or village they were expected to make what shelter they could in the fields and woods. The distribution of the diagnostic powder flask tops and musket balls found to the east of Evesham and in Spetchley Park indicate the site of the huge temporary camps of Cromwell's army in 1651.[48] They probably followed the example of the Earl of Essex's army when it marched into Worcestershire in 1642 and made do with the cover provided by hedgerows or by making rough shelters. Nehemiah Wharton complained that 'our beds, the earth; our canopy, the clouds'. They scavenged what they could to make temporary shelters and left a desolate landscape, with Wharton admitting 'we pulled up the hedges, pales, and gates, and made good fires'.[49] Tents were not generally supplied to armies in England although Parliament ordered 1,000 at the start of the conflict, and when the Royalist army descended on Worcester in June 1644 they brought tents for around 1,000 foot who were camped in the fields around the city. But another 3,000 Foot were billeted in houses within the city (which at the time only housed *c.*7,000 inhabitants) and 3,000 Horse were scattered in surrounding villages 2–3 miles away.[50] The most detailed description of an army tent comes from the New Model Army Contracts for 3 April 1645 when an order was placed with John Snow, tentmaker, for 'Tents for the Trayne 200 of John Snow Tentmaker the Tents 7 foote long 7 foote broad and 6 foote high of good Lockeram according to … the best Trench Tents at 20s per Tent'. The lockram was a lightweight cloth, also used to make shirts. In 1650, the women of Edinburgh were persuaded to donate coarse linen bed sheets to make tents. The soldiers preferred to scavenge locally and make more substantial wooden huts for longer stays and for the army, this avoided the need to arrange large baggage trains to carry the canvas. Huts were built by the Parliamentary besiegers on Wheeler's Hill on the east side of Worcester during the siege of 1646.[51] From contemporary descriptions on the continent, these were probably makeshift shelters built of branches and planks on the plan of a ridge tent.[52] Unfortunately, they were burnt down during the night of 28 May during some drunken revels![53] One of the most unusual accommodations came when Waller's army temporarily occupied Droitwich in June 1644. The soldiers were billeted in the salt cellars of the town and as a consequence they 'grew so drie, that we drank the town drie'.

Wherever possible, the troops were billeted in the houses of the local population and soon outstayed any welcome, the overcrowding and the poor conditions on campaign increasing the ever present 17th – century risk of disease and epidemic in

The Civil War armies were not generally issued with tents. Instead the soldiers were expected to make their own shelter or billet themselves on the local populace.

(Author Collection, with thanks to the Fairfax Battalia of the English Civil War Society)

the towns, especially from typhus (camp fever) and bubonic plague. The situation in Worcester and Evesham was probably not dissimilar from that in the garrison at Newport Pagnell, where the soldiers slept three to a bed.[54] There were continual pleas from Worcester to reduce the numbers of the soldiers in the garrison although they actually increased during the war. The situation was exacerbated by the large numbers of the civilian population who were probably also living in temporary accommodation following the demolition of the suburbs. In an effort to lessen the strain, the garrison troops might be scattered over wide areas, especially the Horse (making it easier for them to forage), but equally making it harder for the authorities to control their actions. From October 1644, civilian pressure, presumably led by self-interested local county gentry, made the army agree to contain the troops within the garrisons or other towns rather than billet them on farms and villages where it was more difficult to control free-quarter or general plunder.[55] This would have been of no comfort to the citizens of Worcester or Evesham! In addition it was agreed that any 'strange forces' of Royalists could be removed by the county troops if they tried to billet themselves for more than one night whilst on the march.[56] This was an army beginning to wage war upon itself within a hostile environment, but the agreement was not honoured and it is clear that many of the troops continued to be quartered across the county.[57] The Worcester garrison was scattered over a radius of four miles in 1645. Townshend described how 'the parishes within 4 miles of the city are by freequarter of the Horse eaten up, undone, destroyed'. It proved impossible to replace the detested free-quarter by regular rates for billeting. Complaints against free-quarter had begun as early as April 1643 but as the war clearly began to turn against the Royalists there were increasing fears in occupied areas such as Worcestershire that they would never be paid back.

The soldiers took great advantage of their hosts. The troops garrisoning the county were, in the main, local men, possibly relations and former friends, but once they became soldiers they were regarded as thieving parasites, a constant reminder of the disruption to ordinary lives that the war had brought. Many had brought their families as the only way to maintain them and insisted that householders also billet these camp followers. Promises of payment via free-quarter were not honoured and the men demanded the best accommodation and food that the household could provide. Prince Rupert tried to resolve the complaints in his reform of the army in February 1644 in order to try to win back support from the county. He agreed that families of the soldiers could not be billeted without the consent of the householder and tried to abolish all free-quarter and free billeting.[58] If anyone failed to pay for his billet then the Treasurer was meant to deduct the sum out of the man's pay. The soldier was not to expect to live at any higher standard than his host and not to take up more space or use any more fire, candles and salt than the family used themselves. The soldiers seem to have spent much of their time simply hanging around which no doubt further irritated the local population who were not only expected to feed and house them but also to work on the fortifications on their behalf. The boredom of the troops was also a problem for their officers in trying to maintain discipline. As a consequence, Prince Rupert agreed to make unarmed soldiers work on the fortifications rather than be idle and so relieve some of this burden from the citizens.[59] But Sir Gilbert Gerrard was still obliged at the same time to introduce a system by which all householders, including the cathedral clergy, had to undertake one day's labour a week on the city defences. This lasted until the siege of 1646. There were similar problems in forcing local people to construct the defences at Evesham. John Twyning (a Fladbury man then living in Evesham) claimed that he was twice thrown into prison for refusing to oversee the works.[60] The ineffective nature of such measures to protect the civilian populations can be measured by the frequency of their repetition.

If dealing with the basic needs of the army were not enough, the cost of entertaining the garrison commanders and visiting officers was considerable. Worcester was obliged to provide £16 17s 10d worth of claret, sack, white wine and other delicacies to Prince Maurice's staff for the celebrations that followed the battle of Ripple on 13 April 1643, when his army was camped around Claines. The city also had to pay Prince Maurice's living expenses, amounting to £3 15s 6d per day, during his time as Lieutenant General of the region from 1645, which consisted of a daily supply of mutton, lamb, veal, beef, pullets, pigeon, chickens, white and brown bread, and strong and small beer.[61] The officers could behave as badly as the common soldiers. In Worcester, early in the occupation at New Year 1643, Lieutenant Colonel David Hide, a former mercenary and one of those 'cavaliers' that Worcester had so rightly feared, complained at a banquet that he expected a New Year gift from the mayor and pay for his men. This was too much and after a disturbance he was arrested but on the way back to his quarters he assaulted two women. He then tried to pick a fight with Sir James Hamilton and Captain Dennis and eventually was restrained and sent to Oxford for court martial, although the charges were eventually dropped. In another incident in March 1644, Martin Sandys and his servant, Augustine Irans, were accused of murdering Captain Robert Stayner of Worcester.[62]

The local population would also be expected to care for any wounded soldiers – and to bury the dead! The Guildhall at Worcester was turned into a temporary hospital after the battles there in 1642 and 1651 but the usual practice was to leave them in private houses. Although the army surgeons might visit them, the day to day care would have been in the hands of the household. In Newlands, probably during the sieges of Madresfield and Worcester in 1646, James Cooke found himself spending 7s 6d on the care of Parliamentary soldiers from the regiments of Captain Cannon and Colonel Whalley whilst they were 'under the Churgions [surgeons] hands'.[63] They were not always successful: it cost the city 4s to bury a dead Royalist soldier in Worcester in 1644. After the siege of Worcester in 1646 it cost the city 12s to tend wounded soldiers from Colonel Rainsborough's regiment and a further £1 to then carry them to London. The costs of nursing, food, rudimentary medicines, heating and bedding must therefore be added to the everyday costs of free-quarter. They might also have to bear the cost of transporting recovering soldiers back to their garrison, and on one occasion Worcester had to provide horses to carry wounded soldiers to Chester. Many of the fatalities were buried anonymously. For Bewdley, there was a problem of dealing with the corpses of soldiers that drifted down the river.

During the course of the war, accommodation in Worcester was put under even greater pressure due to the loss of a considerable number of houses in the suburbs that were deliberately burnt down by the garrison in order to create a clear field of fire from the defences. Following the unsuccessful siege by Waller in June 1643, houses and other buildings in the suburbs along with trees, hedges, mounds and fences were all levelled on the orders of the governor. The destruction was so complete that after the war the Cathedral authorities found it difficult to re-establish the historic boundaries of their properties.[64] This is remarkable given that such boundaries tend to survive in the topography of English towns from the 12th century to the present day. The inhabitants from these homes also had to be re-housed within the city. It is unlikely that this was achieved by any new building work but rather by the subdivision of the existing housing stock causing families to live in ever-more cramped conditions, first as refugees and then with the garrison troops billeted upon them. With the city teeming with unpaid, but armed, soldiers, there was an uneasy atmosphere and farmers were afraid to come to market in case their produce was seized to pay for arrears in the monthly Assessments. During the siege of Worcester in 1646, further damage was done by the troops tearing down outhouses and fences ostensibly to provide fuel but in reality to purchase alcohol!

There were similar pressures in Evesham with its population of *c*.2,000. When the field army paused here in 1644 the baggage train included thirty carriages carrying the ladies of the court and their luggage. No doubt they were billeted amongst the finest houses and inns of the town. In September 1643 there were complaints that the presence of the Royalist field army, quartered in villages and farms of the Vale after retreating from the unsuccessful siege of Gloucester, had frightened people away from Evesham Fair. As in Worcester, disorder extended to the officers. In 1645 a Royalist officer, John Watson (Commissary to the then governor), tried to attack a local man, Mr Pitway, with his sword for 'refusing to drink to the confusion of Parliament'.[65]

Of the smaller outposts, the 160-strong garrison at the moated manor house at Hartlebury under Captain William Sandys (described, mistakenly, by the contemporary Richard Symonds as being uncle to Samuel Sandys) became notorious for their behaviour. The troops were based around a company of Sir Gilbert Gerrard's regiment of Foot detached for duty to this small outpost which was important as the site of a possible Royalist mint during the war. Making themselves as comfortable as possible, in July 1645 they plundered the house of Thomas Brooke, amongst others, seizing his 'linens, apparell, bedding, pewter and other necessaries' at a cost of £10. Townshend described William Sandys' men as having drained the countryside around to fortify the place. In his words, the governor 'had so sharked the County thereabouts, that for beef, malt, Hay and bacon he lived in free cost'.[66] As the lawless reputation of this garrison spread, even the Royalist high command became concerned at the appalling reputation that the troops were gaining at a time when they were increasingly desperate to retain support amongst the local community. Three times the treasurer of the Hartlebury garrison was summoned to give an account of the huge cost of the work undertaken on the defences by local parishes.[67]

Aerial view of Hartlebury Castle. This moated manor house became a notorious Royalist garrison.

But not all contact with the garrisons was unwelcome. We can only speculate on other effects of the presence of the garrisons and passing troops on the social life of town and village. The presence of large numbers of young single men, telling tales of life in far-off places (i.e. beyond the county boundary) or of daring deeds of war must have raised a spark of interest in many a local girl. The situation may not have been much different in Worcestershire from that recorded by a despairing Sir Samuel Luke over his (Parliamentary) garrison at Newport Pagnell. This was described by

Charges for billeting in Worcester (per week) 1645

Captain	10s
Lieutenant	7s
Troopers	3s 6d
Foot	2s 4d

him as being akin to Sodom and Gomorrah, where it seems his men tried to persuade local girls that adultery was excusable in wartime![168] However, there was considerable social pressure against this – mixing morality and practicality in seeking to avoid any offspring of an illicit relationship becoming a charge on the parish! There could be more permanent attachments, and in Scotland the Parliamentary army was obliged to regulate the number of marriages between the garrison troops and local lasses.[69] Unfortunately, the normal records of the passage of life, death, and social order in a community largely broke down as parishes found it increasingly difficult to maintain their parish registers.

Some people were able to make a profit out of the war. Much of the money raised by the assessments would ultimately have been spent in local markets. The war could also bring new employment for carpenters and masons. Townshend complained bitterly that 'workmen, carpenters and masons expect money now for their work' during the siege of 1646. The carpenter, Henry Baldwin, made a considerable fortune out of his work on the Worcester defences for both Royalists and Parliamentarians. In 1651 he was paid to rebuild the defences first for Parliament and then for the Scots – and subsequently to level them for Parliament. Accounts from December 1642 – October 1643 also detail payment of £152 to William Richardson for the making of saltpetre, £55 11s 5d to William and Jane Baber and to James Powell for making powder and to others for casting ammunition, boring cannon and making cartridges.[70] It is also likely that the war boosted the cap industry of Bewdley. The manufacture of knitted Monmouth caps was the main industry of Bewdley and these were the standard headgear of the common soldiers. They were knitted for 2d each but sold for 2s – 4s. The main problem was, however, getting the payment for any work done on behalf of the military. Some bills were unpaid for many years! In June 1645 the King ordered Worcester to provide £84 14s 4d worth of cloth to make uniforms for Prince Rupert's army. George Heming was one of the suppliers.[71] He was to be paid out of the residue of the June Assessment – after the militia officers had taken their wages first! But the

Langstone House, Evesham. King Charles I stayed here whilst deciding the fate of Evesham after they had supported the Parliamentary Army in June 1644.

(Author Collection)

Assessments were now well in arrears and the bill remained unpaid in July when it was agreed to pay Heming and the other clothiers out of the arrears of the January, February and May assessments. It is not known if this was ever paid as the Assessments were still in arrears in October.[72] Another unfortunate creditor was Christopher Gardner who applied in July 1643 for payment of £86 9s for three brass cannon that he had made for the city.[73] He was still claiming payment in April 1646.

Meanwhile, from Warwickshire and Gloucestershire, Parliament was steadily building up its own forces from the area. In February 1643, 45-year-old Sir William Waller had been appointed Major General of the Western Association including Worcestershire and was ordered to raise five regiments of Horse and five of Foot. This evidently encouraged local resistance in occupied Worcestershire and in June 1644 the people of Evesham felt confident enough to make a stand of defiance by helping the army of Sir William Waller cross the bridge at Evesham that had just been part-demolished by the Royalists. In August, 'divers of Worcestershire offered to raise forces for the Parliament, and an ordinance was passed to enable them to do so'.[74] By the autumn, the Royalist war effort at both a national and local level was beginning to show signs of disintegration and on 23 September 1644 a Parliamentary Committee was established for Worcestershire under the Earl of Denbigh. On 25 September an ordinance authorised the raising of new Foot and Horse from Worcestershire. By the end of 1644 Parliament was recruiting on a large scale within east Worcestershire and Edward Rous and William Lygon were commissioned to raise regiments there. At the same time, Parliament also tried to collect its own tax assessments. The wolf-pack of the Parliamentary armies gathering on the borders of Worcestershire now had the scent of victory, although the Royalists had a satisfying victory at a skirmish at Pinvin on 11 November, when a regiment of Horse stationed at Pershore managed to ambush a raiding party and capture three troop colours.[75] A new determination on the Parliamentary side came in 1645 with the creation of the New Model Army under General

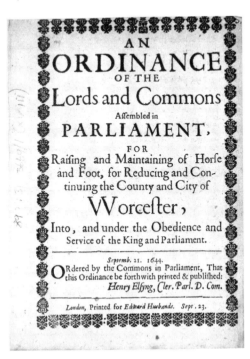

Ordinance of September 1644 authorising the raising of Parliamentary troops from Worcestershire. This signals a rising confidence in the Parliamentary forces to the east and south of Worcestershire

(Worcestershire Record Office)

Thomas Fairfax. Richard Baxter rejoined the army as a chaplain after the battle of Naseby and commented on the changes that had occurred. It was now, he believed, driven by a small number of religious fanatics influencing the rest to believe that the King was a tyrant and that they were now entitled to kill or conquer him. But as Parliamentary resolve hardened, that on the Royalist side began to crumble.

Chapter Five
Losing an army 1645–6

Sir Gilbert Gerrard, Governor of Worcester, was killed at Ludlow in mid January 1645 and, in a conciliatory move towards local interests, was replaced as Governor by Samuel Sandys.[1] A re-assertion of the influence of local gentry was to be a feature of the coming year although it did not lead to a greater harmony in the Royalist ranks. Worcester had already left its marker of discontent by appointing a new mayor in 1644 against the wishes of the King. Prince Maurice was appointed Lieutenant General of Worcestershire in January 1645 and raised the army establishment again to 1,600 Foot and 400 Horse. This was organised in a Foot regiment of 16 companies and a regiment of Horse comprising 5 troops of 80 men. The intention once again was to centralise control and constrain local rivalries, but the increase in numbers could only be financed by reducing the pay of the soldiers – a fact not likely to have improved their conduct. The pay of the common soldiers was reduced by 6d to only 3s 6d per week and the troopers' pay was reduced by 2s to 10s per week.[2] In addition, by March 1645 a total of 1,800 part-time soldiers (including gentlemen volunteers) was reported to have been raised to defend Worcester as part of the city militia. They were said to perform their duties on a rota basis 'in turn'. This was probably a renewed attempt to mobilise the *Posse Comitatus* and only a

Cover of a pamphlet describing the Parliamentary seizure of Evesham in May 1645. This was a crucial event in the collapse of Royalist control of the county.

(Worcestershire Record Office)

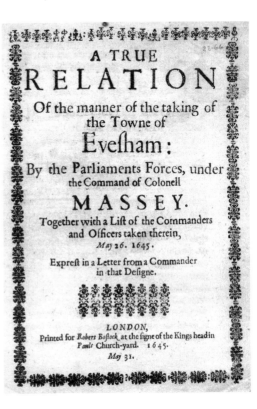

A TRUE
RELATION
Of the manner of the taking of
the Towne of
Evesham:
By the Parliaments Forces, under
the Command of Colonell
MASSEY.
Together with a Lift of the Commanders
and Officers taken therein,
May 26. 1645.

Expreſt in a Letter from a Commander
in that Deſigne.

LONDON,
Printed for *Robert Boſtock* at the ſigne of the Kings head in
Pauls Church-yard. 1645.
May 31.

nominal establishment on the strength of the Town Regiment. There may have been ulterior motives to join the muster roll of the Town Regiment as service still brought a reduction in taxes. The citizen-soldiers therefore claimed that they could not pay their full share of the taxes by virtue of their service.[3]

There was a new urgency in the need to recruit fresh troops. Parliament was increasing its pressure on the east side of the county and a new assault on the garrisons by the newly-formed New Model Army seemed inevitable. Defeat at Marston Moor in July 1644 and subsequent reverses, and then seeing the shattered remains of the army drift back through the area, had convinced many in the county that the Royalists could no longer win the war. In January, Strensham was garrisoned by 16 troops of Parliamentary Horse under Captain Dormer; in March 1645, Colonel Edward Massie's men from Gloucester rode into Pershore and burnt down a house next to the Abbey.[4] It is not clear why one property should be so targeted except as a warning to the rest not to support a more permanent Royalist garrison. The garrison regiments were over-stretched and were finding it difficult to manoeuvre outside their bases due both to the widespread incursion of raiding parties from Gloucestershire and Warwickshire and also by financial restrictions on their movements agreed to appease the local communities. Many troops were also taken into the field army, including 150 men of Sandys' Horse and some of what had been Gerrard's regiment of Foot at Evesham. This left the Evesham garrison, under its new garrison commander, Lieutenant Colonel Robert Legge, with only *c.*700 men. Parliament soon learned of this and, urged on by exiled Worcestershire Parliamentarians in Warwickshire, decided that the time was finally right to launch a major assault on the county.[5] In May, Evesham was captured and in July a new threat came to the local garrisons with the approach of the Scottish army (then allies

of Parliament). Locust-like, the passage of the Scottish army caused considerable damage in the north part of the county and down through Hartlebury parish, just 10 miles north of Worcester. The presence of the Parliamentary army nearby was enough encouragement for Droitwich to provide it with supplies although the town was nominally still under Royalist control. The Constable of Droitwich provided £6 worth of bread and cheese for the Scots whilst based at

Colonel Edward Massie (1620–74). Commander of the Parliamentary garrison of Gloucester, he led the assault on Evesham in May 1645. A Presbyterian, he later joined the Royalists and was wounded in the preliminary stage of the battle of Worcester in 1651.

(Gloucester City Museum)

Key Events: 1645 – Battle of Evesham 26 May

The river crossing on the Avon at Evesham controlled the strategic route from the Royalist capital at Oxford to the recruiting grounds of Wales and the arms manufactures of the Midlands. In May 1645 Parliament felt strong enough to try to capture the town and use it as bridgehead to plan the reconquest of Worcestershire. Colonel Massie from Gloucester advanced on the town with an army of *c*.2,000 men. The Royalist garrison had only 700 men, reduced in order to provide reinforcements to the King's Army. They managed to get a message to Worcester appealing for help – but the town was abandoned to its fate.

On 26 May, Massie crossed the Avon at Twyford Bridge and engaged the Royalists on the east defences. A second contingent tried to storm Evesham Bridge from across the river at Bengeworth. Given the odds, the battle was fiercer than expected. Time and time again, attacking at three points, the Parliamentarians were thrown back from the east defences by withering musket fire. The concentration of the attacking forces on specific points can be noted by the fact that excavation of the Civil War defences on their south side contained no musket balls or other recognisable military artefacts. Eventually Massie's men managed to effect a breach on the north side of the defences (probably where the ditch was narrower against the river) and crossed using ladders commandeered from local villages. Dragoons were now able to pour into the Royalist flank. Legge retreated back into Evesham, still determined to rally his men, but then the troops attacking Evesham Bridge managed to force their way across to attack Legge in the rear. As the Parliamentary cavalry charged down Broad Street, Legge's courageous troops were surrounded and had no choice but to surrender. In this fierce battle of only an hour, Massie took over 500 prisoners.

The town was then garrisoned by Parliament under the local man, Colonel Edward Rous. As Massie had hoped, this cut the critical line of communication from Oxford, Worcester and South Wales. Evesham now also provided a secure base for the Parliamentary Committee for Worcestershire to recruit men, collect intelligence and try to collect taxes. Its capture marked the start of a Parliamentary ascendancy in the county.

Alcester, and the bailiff, John Wheeler, supplied 24 dozen loaves of bread at £1 4s and 1cwt of cheese at 18s.[6] On 7 July Prince Maurice ordered labourers to Worcester to prepare the defences in case of a siege, although much to everyone's relief, the Scots moved on into Herefordshire.[7]

The Royalist leaders were frustrated in their attempts to combat these new threats. Charles simply did not have enough men in the field and therefore sought to channel the local fears as to the maintenance of law and order into creating a new, more mobile, local defence force as part of a regional Association of Worcestershire, Herefordshire, Shropshire and Staffordshire. This was to be based on the principal

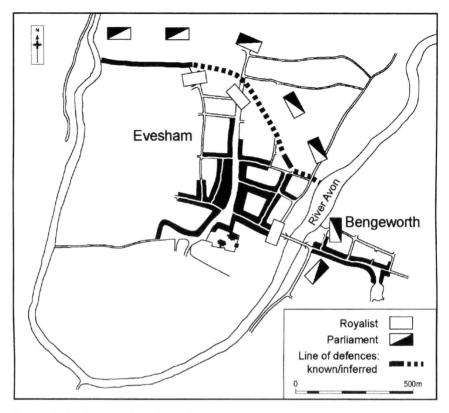

Plan of the Battle of Evesham, May 1645.

(Worcestershire Historic Environment and Archaeology Service)

Excavation of the Civil War defences off Swan Lane, Evesham. The ditch was 5.5m wide. INSET: Clay pipe dating to the 1640s, found in the Civil War defence ditch at Evesham.

(Birmingham University Field Archaeology Unit)

16th century Abbey belltower, Evesham, showing (inset) the damage caused by musket fire during the battle of Evesham in May 1645.

(Author Collection)

of the traditional *Posse Comitatus*, but allowed for service in neighbouring counties. Hopefully, this would free garrison troops for service elsewhere. Carlton has estimated that up to 48 percent of Royalist troops may have been contained within garrisons by June 1645.[8] But the Royalists in the county were divided and demoralised and two very different and conflicting agendas came to promote the Association. The local agenda was to provide a means of maintaining local law and order and provide parochial defence for their communities. The King, however, saw the new force as acting much more on a regional and strategic basis. In view of the failure on a number of occasions of trying to raise the *Posse Comitatus* during the war, this new attempt could be seen as a naïve, or at best desperate, manoeuvre. Even if raised, it is difficult to imagine that the Royalists had the resources to equip it and make it any sort of serious threat.

Local gentry saw the development as a means of wresting back the traditional control of local forces from the military and the Propositions of the Association offered serious criticisms of the latter: 'For the soldier assumes a liberty to rapine and violence … our fortifications neglected, our frontiers laid waste, And in the most inward parts of the County no man's person secured'.[9] Harsh terms were offered in return for their support. The men were to assemble on the summons of the Sheriff, not the governor, and were entitled to choose their own officers. They were not to be subject to martial law and members had the right to resist, by force if necessary, plundering by soldiers. The Grand Jury asserted the right of the people of the county, if threatened by robbery or violence from the soldiers, to 'rise upon them and bring them to justice'.[10] The Association made yet another demand to ban free-quarter and to confine the garrison troops to the towns; it sought the right to check for fraudulent muster rolls from the garrisons (to control the level of payments), and demanded a ban on garrison commanders making additional levies on the surrounding countryside. Continuing the increasingly bitter battle between civilian and soldier, the civilian Commissioner Henry Townshend was made muster-master to assist the sheriff in taking a monthly muster of the troops to ensure that accurate accounts were being presented by the officers. He was also assigned the duty of reporting on the contents of the Worcester magazine to the Quarter Sessions.[11] In return, the Proposals for the Association agreed that the monthly Assessments should continue – but only as long as their conditions were fulfilled. This was clear blackmail but the King agreed in principle to the demands, only insisting on the right to choose the general officers under the command of Prince Maurice and that troops could be drawn out of the county with the consent of three of the Commissioners. He did, however, attempt one last concession from the county and called for 600 men to be impressed into the field army by 21 March. Rather than create a new common purpose amongst the Royalists, the Association heightened still further the tensions between the professional officers, gentry

Cavalry troopers on patrol in north Worcestershire. Such men became the terror of the local population as they enforced tax collection and plundered homes. The Horse of both Royalists and Parliamentarians would have been similarly equipped and dressed. The idea of Parliamentary troops in buff coats and lobster pot helmets, as opposed to Royalists in floppy hats, feathers and lace is a piece of Victorian romance.

(Susanne Atkin, with thanks to The Troop)

and local communities; and nothing came of it. In particular, the garrison commanders feared that the Association would draw off the already decreasing funding that they relied on to support their own regiments.

If the Association was by no means a force borne of outright enthusiasm for the Royalist cause, it was quickly to serve as a dangerous precedent for more overt opposition. The attempt to create more of a locally-accountable movement – at least as far as the local gentry was concerned – ostensibly to preserve law and order, raised the expectations of the general population who feared yet more taxes and the increased risk of impressment. This encouraged the rise in the county of the more popularly-based Clubmen Movement, also initially designed to defend law and order, and which harked back to the militant neutrality of the last few months of peace. Worcestershire had had enough of the war and the watchword of the Clubmen was

'If you offer to plunder, or take our cattle,
Rest assured we will give you battle'.

The message of resistance had spread into Worcestershire from adjacent Shropshire and Herefordshire in early 1645, and was part of a wider, albeit disparate, movement that encompassed Wiltshire, Dorset, Somerset, Berkshire, Sussex, Hampshire and parts of South Wales as frustration with the war mounted. There was an early meeting of the Worcestershire Clubmen at Pershore but at this stage most of the documented activity concerns the west side of the county. In north-west Worcestershire they met 'several times in very great bodies for their own protection'.[12] Colonel Barnabas Scudamore described the movement as a 'disease' spreading through the Marches into the county.[13] On 27 February, a scout informed Sir Samuel Luke that three troops of Royalist Horse had arrived to plunder the home of Sir Walter Devereux at Leigh Court but that '1,000 of the country rose against them. And said that if they took one pennyworth of goods from there, they would kill them'. The tactic worked as the soldiers' desisted and marched quietly away'.[14] The movement became more formally established when on 5 March, 1,000 Clubmen of north Worcestershire trudged to the summit of Woodbury Hill, near Great Witley, to declare 'We have long groaned under many illegal taxations and unjust pressures and that contrary to orders presented to his Majesty … And nevertheless finding no redress of our grievances, but that we, our wives and children, have been exposed to utter ruin by the outrages and violence of the soldier; threatening to fire our houses; endeavouring to ravish our wives and daughters, and menacing our persons. We are now enforced to associate ourselves in a mutual league for each other's defence …'. This statement came from an area beyond the range of the Parliamentary raiding parties and in a period of relative calm but their complaints were clearly directed against the oppressive, but ineffective, Royalist government, which was increasingly reliant on threat and military force yet was unable to control its own soldiery.

At the heart of the aims of the Clubmen was 'To retain the property of the subject by protecting and safeguarding our persons and estates by the mutual aid and assistance of each other against all murders, rapines, plunder, robberies, or violences which shall be offered by the soldier or any oppressor whatsoever …'.[15] Yet these soldiers who were the subject of such bitter complaint were in the main local men from the county who had been put beyond the pale by their service and their need to support themselves by any means. A second Declaration from the Malvern area (Malvern, Mathon, Cradley, Leigh Sinton, Suckley and Powick) later in March took up the terms of the Woodbury Declaration and refused membership to anyone who was listed for recruitment into the army. The movement brought together all classes of local society, with people worth more than £10 p. a. expected to provide 'a musket, fowling piece or other sufficient arms'. Gone were the niceties of more 'gentlemanly' pikes as expected in the pre-war Trained Bands.[16] In their refusal to take orders from papist recusants there was clear criticism of what was seen as an undue Roman Catholic influence in the proposed Royalist Association which was led by the Earl of Shrewsbury (who had property in Worcestershire).

Nonetheless, at this stage the movement still focused on trying to maintain law and order within the existing framework of the Royalist government of occupation. They therefore resisted the calls from an irritated Colonel Massie of Gloucester (who had even supplied them with weapons) to declare themselves for Parliament or be considered traitorous rebels, whilst his chaplain, John Corbet, described them as 'foolish neuters' who 'could not declare for either side'.[17] Massie and Corbet were to

Aerial view of Woodbury Hill in 1960s. 1000 Clubmen met here in March 1645 to launch a self-defence force and demand a return to law and order.

(National Monument Record)

The Woodbury Declaration of the Clubmen 5 March 1645

We having long groaned under many illegal taxations and unjust pressures and that contrary to orders presented to his Majesty by advice of the Lords and Commons assembled at Oxford And ratified and published by his Majesty's gracious proclamation. And nevertheless finding no redress of our grievances, but that we, our wives and children, have been exposed to utter ruin by the outrages and violence of the soldier; threatening to fire our houses; endeavouring to ravish our wives and daughters, and menacing our persons. We are now enforced to associate ourselves in a mutual league for each other's defence, and do declare to the world that our meetings have been, are, and shall be to no other intention or purpose than as followeth.

1. To maintain the true Reformed Protestant Religion contained in the Doctrine of the Church of England against all Popery and Popish superstitions and all other Heresies and schisms whatsoever.
2. To defend the King's Majesty's person, honour, and estate against all those that shall oppose the same.
3. To preserve and uphold the ancient and just privileges of Parliament and known laws of this kingdom against all arbitrary Government which shall be endeavoured to be introduced and put upon us under what pretence soever.
4. To retain the property of the subject by protecting and safeguarding our persons and estates by the mutual aid and assistance of each other against all murders, rapines, plunder, robberies, or violences which shall be offered by the soldier or any oppressor whatsoever, as is allowed by those orders lately signed by his Highness Prince Maurice as appeareth by the 5th Article of the said orders.
5. To quicken the execution of those wholesome orders abovesaid ratified by his Majesty's proclamations as also those other orders which at several times since have been agreed upon and signed by his Highness Prince Rupert, Prince Maurice, and also consented unto by the Honourable the Governor and Commissioners for the safeguarding of this county and the great Inquest at several Sessions of the peace held for the body of the same.
6. Our resolution is not to submit to the execution of any commission intrusted upon any pretence whatsoever in the hands of any Papist, or Papists, Recusant or Recusants or any other joined in commission with any Papist, or Papist Recusant for that by the known laws of this kingdom no Papist, nor Papist-recusants ought to be intrusted in any office of state, justice, or judicature: neither to keep any arms in their houses that may be or prove offensive to any of His Majesty's Loyal subjects.
7. Our desire is that this our Declaration and resolution may be presented to the High Sheriff of this County to whom alone as his Majesty's Vicegerent we conceive we are bound to render an account of these our doings. And

> further our petition is that he would be pleased to endeavour that all Popish
> Recusants within this County may be pressed to take the oaths of Allegiance
> and supremacy as by law is provided. And upon refusal they may be disarmed
> as by law they ought.
> 8. That it is our request that the Grand Inquest now intrusted for the body of
> this County may be moved seriously to weigh and consider how they do
> consent to the illegancy of such Commissions as shall be committed to the
> hands of Papist, or Popish Recusants lest they betray our trust and so expose
> both themselves and us to utter ruin.

be proved right when the Herefordshire Clubmen (joined by comrades from
Worcestershire) were ruthlessly crushed by the Royalists. In March or April, Leigh
Court and Madresfield (both homes of absent Parliamentarians) just east of the
Malverns, were provided with garrisons to try to keep such local disorder in check.[18]

By April, Parliament propaganda inflated claims that other groups of Clubmen
on the east side of the county were ready to ally themselves with their forces and took
every opportunity to fan the seeds of revolt. The *Kingdom's Weekly Intelligencer* of
April 1645 claimed that grateful local people were ready to rise and join the
Parliamentary troops in adjacent Warwickshire after the latter had rescued some of
their cattle taken by Royalists in the aftermath of a skirmish. The newsletter claimed
'Divers of the inhabitants of Worcestershire and Warwickshire, by the reason of the
restoring of their cattel to them, are ready to rise upon all occasions to join with the
Warwickshire forces'.[19] This may, however, have been a vain hope and there is no
evidence that such an alliance actually took place.

The new Royalist Association failed to live up to the hopes of the King and despite
Prince Rupert's commitment that local troops would not serve outside the county,
local regiments continued to serve with the field army. The latter rendezvoused at
Evesham on 9 May with *c.* 11,000 men and were joined by part of the late Gerrard's
regiment of Foot, 150 Horse under Sandys and part of the Evesham garrison.[20] The
county was urged to provide supplies to the army as speedily as possible so that they
would depart sooner! They did indeed march out of the county and many of the men
were later killed or captured at the battle of Naseby on 14 June. It is quite likely that
captured local men joined the New Model Army along with many of their comrades.
Following that disastrous defeat, the King was again in urgent need of fresh troops.
Despite the recent loss of Evesham (see above, p. 113) and the collapse of control
over a large part of east Worcestershire, Prince Maurice ordered a further 2,000 Foot
and 50 Horse to be raised immediately from the county for the field army, and an
additional £3,000, above and beyond the monthly Assessment, to be paid within ten
days. This was an unavoidable risk for the Royalists who needed to maintain the local
garrisons upon which they relied to secure local political power and raise taxes, but
at the same time urgently needed to rebuild the defeated field army. The County

agreed to try to raise this sum, subject to plaintively repeating their demand yet again that freequarter be ended.[21]

It became more and more difficult to raise the monthly Assessments and order rapidly broke down; army officers took the law into their own hands in increasing desperation to feed their men. In June, Prince Maurice and Samuel Sandys quarrelled.[22] Fearing the effects of any local loss of confidence, the King tried to re-assure Sandys of his confidence and friendship. On 30 September he wrote to Sandys to say 'there is no gentleman in England upon whose faithfulness and entire affections to my person and cause I do more confidently rely' and urged him to ignore any rumours spread by 'malicious' parties.[23] Proving, however, that local leadership did not necessarily mean a more understanding attitude (and reflecting the earlier charges against Sir William Russell in 1643), Anthony Langston (a younger son of the Sedgeberrow family, a captain in Sandys' Horse and also Prince Maurice's secretary) wrote to Lord Digby in September complaining of the administration of the county under Sandys saying 'The hands it is in and their assistants are men of very little care, and their reproaches are great upon all those that have any'.[24] Confirming this opinion, there were other complaints of 'daily robberies of all market people, killing and wounding men who resist and stand on their own defence'.[25] As a consequence, in October 1645 Prince Maurice published an order 'regulating governors and soldiers against seizing on men's persons, imprisoning them, seizing on their cattle'.[26] With many of the parishes assigned to fund them on the east side of Worcestershire now under parliamentary control, the county regiment of 400 Horse had been reduced once again to living on free-quarter, many of the officers had quit and the troops were described as 'shattered'.[27] The situation was made worse by the broken remains of Vaughan's brigade of Horse, including Sandys' regiment, drifting back through the county after their defeat at the battle of Denbigh. No-one was safe. Even the leading Royalist, Sir Ralph Clare, was assaulted by a Major Fisher and his men (possibly from Sandys' Horse). In the autumn of 1645 the state of the county was summarised:

Edward Dingley (1600–46). A former Royalist, he became leader of the Clubmen movement on east Worcestershire during 1645. His monument is in Cropthorne church.

(Susanne Atkin)

That the Insolencies, oppressions, and Cruelties have already so disaffected and disheartened the people; that they are grown desperate, and are already upon the point of rising everywhere, and do not stick to say that they can find more justice, and more money, in the Enemy's quarters than in the King's.[28]

The fear of rebellion was not an idle threat. Parliamentary recruitment to its army in the area was increasing, spurred on by the establishment of a bridgehead within the county at Evesham. By the end of 1645, over 3,000 men had also joined the Clubmen, the character of which had changed under the new circumstances. Those on the west side of the county, still within an area of firm Royalist control but antagonised by the plundering of Vaughan's Horse and others, continued in the main to proclaim nominal allegiance to the framework of the Royalist government. They re-formed in December 1645 and maintained watches against plundering soldiers, parish by parish and developed an elaborate early warning system.[29] Nonetheless, 100 men from Rock parish, from north Worcestershire close to Woodbury Hill, were reported as having openly declared for Parliament as early as May.[30] Those on the more exposed east side of the county now decided to commit their fate to the rising fortunes of Parliament in the hope of a speedy resolution to the conflict. On 11 November 3,000 Clubmen met on Bredon Hill for a conference with Colonel Liggen and Captain Patman of the Parliamentary garrison at Evesham. Now in open opposition, the Clubmen agreed to pay no further taxes to the Royalists and to reform as a Parliamentary militia with the 45-year-old Edward Dingley of Charlton (a former Royalist Commissioner of Safety) as their leader. The new participation of disaffected Royalist gentry as leaders of the Clubmen movement is a clear sign of the collapse of Royalist confidence in the county as well as a desire to ensure that any popular movement developed under the control of the traditional county leadership. In a fit of enthusiasm this poorly trained and ill-equipped militia attacked part of Rupert and Maurice's Horse on its way to Oxford in early December at Charlton, between Evesham and Pershore, but were easily dispersed. They recovered, and on 14 December the Committee for Salop wrote that the Evesham garrison was 'joined with the country who rise so freely that Worcester is already much straitened for provision'.[31] East Worcestershire was rapidly slipping out of Royalist control and in early 1646 the Clubmen militia participated first in the siege of Madresfield and then that of Worcester.[32]

The Royalist war effort staggered towards its final desperate stages. In north Worcestershire there was fighting around Kidderminster in November when Sir Thomas Aston was captured at a skirmish at Trimpley. In December there was fighting within Kidderminster and a Royalist force was defeated by Gloucester troops at Abberley, adjacent to the focal point of the Clubmen movement on Woodbury Hill. The garrisons became increasingly isolated. Nonetheless, at the end of 1645 Lord Jacob Astley came into the county to try to raise yet a new field army. His commission was to command 'His forces, horse, foot, dragoons, trained bands, volunteers and others raised or to be raised in our counties of Worcester, Stafford, Hereford and Salop, and in our cities there, with power to impress men and levy forces'.[33] There can have been few eligible men left in the county by this stage but having scoured the garrisons and recruited whatever fresh men from the region that

By Tho: Browne

Taken away by 2 of Capt. ffletchers men
when they came to ... Dowlife for Contribucon } 0:18:0
one horfmans Coat worth —

ffor quartering ... horfe & men 2 dayes &
nights under Capt Badger wth the bagg } 0:10:0
Lay agt Madresfield —

Due to me from the ... & promifed me
by Geo: Hill Con... for the quartering } 0:10:0
of Capt ffoote ... agt Madresfield —

Loft in goods provifion & beare wth Madresfield } 8:0:0
was ... to the value of —

Suffered by quartering while the frigo lay } 0:12:6
agt Madresfield ... Worcester by ... forces
& others to the value of —

10 : 10 : 0

Extract from the Commonwealth Exchequer Papers for Powick, detailing the losses suffered by Thomas Browne to the sum of £10 10s, including at the siege of Madresfield in 1646.

(The National Archives)

he could, by whatever means available, he finally marched out of Worcestershire with *c.*3,000 men. He was obliged to travel a roundabout route to avoid Evesham, going from Worcester via Droitwich, Feckenham, Inkberrow to Bidford and then on to Honeybourne. His army, the last Royalist one in the field, was, however, destroyed at Stow on the Wold on 21 March 1646. Many of the local men would have been killed or captured, adding to the mounting tally of previous losses. This time there could be no replacement and Parliament could turn its attention to mopping up the last remaining Royalist garrisons in the county. The minor garrisons in

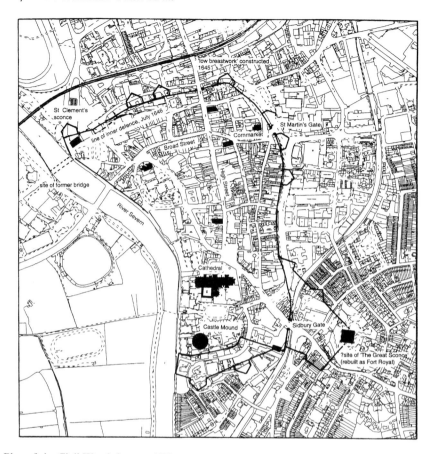

Plan of the Civil War defences of Worcester at the time of the siege in 1646.

(Worcestershire Historic Environment and Archaeology Service based on the Ordnance Survey
1:1250 digital mapping. Crown Copyright.)

Worcestershire fell like a pack of cards, Townshend being particularly bitter over the loss of Madresfield and Hartlebury which surrendered with some ignominy.

Samuel Sandys' efforts throughout the war had apparently come to nothing and, feeling slighted by Astley's commission in the county, in February 1646 he resigned as Governor of Worcester — to be immediately replaced by his adversary. The King wrote to Samuel urging him to continue to fulfil his other commissions and responsibilities and, following the defeat at Stow on the Wold and the initial phase of the siege of Worcester, the family decided to make their own last stand within the command of their kinsman, William Sandys, at Hartlebury.[34] But the 160-strong garrison of Hartlebury (120 Foot and 40 Horse) surrendered to Gloucester troops without a fight on 16 May after a siege of only two days and without a shot having been fired, despite having ammunition and stores for a year: it was rumoured to have been in return for secret terms being given to Captain William Sandys.[35] Looking pragmatically to the future, he

Key Events: 1646 – Siege of Worcester

Charles I surrendered to the Scots on 5 May. Colonel Whalley, fresh from the siege of Banbury, was ordered by Parliament to 'straiten the garrison of Worcester until such time as the army was at liberty to march against it'. The new governor, Henry Washington, had a garrison of 1,507 men, including the Governor's regiment, and the depleted ranks of the local regiments of Sir William Russell, Colonel Samuel Sandys, reformadoes and 224 cavalry plus the city militia regiment, now lacking their captain, Martin Sandys. Many of the troops were Irish. The garrison also had twenty-eight cannon and six lighter drakes, together with other 'sling-pieces', manned by fifty-eight cannoneers and matrosses (assistant gunners). This was to be against a force of around 2,500–5,000 of the New Model Army, and new militias which continued to be raised from the county. On 21 May, the Parliamentary army under Colonel Whalley began to encamp on the high ground on the north-east side of the city. He formally demanded that the city surrender on 25 May, and the army began to build a line of ditches and emplacements (sconces) defending their camp on Roger's Hill and towards Rainbow Hill (Wheelers Hill). By 3 June, the siege lines that were designed to enclose the city on the east side stretched from Windmill Hill (Green Hill, Bath Road) on the south side to Barbourne on the north and then through fields to the river. Washington tried to disrupt this work as best he could by mounting raiding parties against the workmen. Yet another call to surrender had been made on 30 May, and Whalley pointed out that Worcester was now 'the only Troublers of this Kingdom'. Some took heed. Townshend tells how, around the 4 June, 'Many foot have run out of the City to the enemy for want of pay, and some servants have stole their Master's Horses, clothes and money and gone away to them or to their own country'. Whalley continued his steady progress to tighten his grip on the city. On 9 June, the besiegers had pressed forward with 1,500 men to Henwick and St Johns.

On 10 June, King Charles (now a prisoner of the Scots) issued a general order to surrender to those garrisons, including Worcester, still holding out. Unfortunately, there was a considerable delay before the garrison became aware of this order and on 11 June the bombardment began in earnest from both east and west sides. The city needed to relieve the mounting pressure and on 12 June a sally of around 700 men (nearly half the garrison) managed to drive the besiegers out from St Johns , but the respite for the city was only temporary. On 14 June the besiegers completed a bridge of boats to cross the river to the north of the city at the upper end of Pitchcroft.

Discipline was rapidly breaking down within the city. Henry Townshend, who was in the city, offered this advice to insert in one's prayers: 'From the plundering of soldiers, their Insolency, Cruelty, Atheism, Blasphemy and Rule over us, *Libera nos Domine* (God deliver us)'.

By 22 June the city were preparing last ditch defences in case the medieval fortifications might fall to an assault on that side. A second line of defence on which to fall back was built next to The Butts, between Foregate Street and St Clement's Church, but Washington still refused offers to surrender. On 25 June, however, the citizens finally received confirmation that Oxford had indeed fallen and that another Parliamentary army of 10,000 Foot and 5,000 Horse was marching on the city. Washington still wanted to fight on but the pressure from the citizens was now overwhelming and a committee was formed to negotiate peace terms. A truce was agreed on 27 June but this collapsed on 30 June with Whalley becoming impatient for a quick decision. A more aggressive new commander was appointed – Major General Thomas Rainsborough – soon to be a hero of the Leveller movement. Further siege lines were constructed between Perry Wood and Red Hill and a new artillery barrage was launched. A further truce was agreed and the atmosphere relaxed with fraternisation between the two sides. But it was made clear that if the city did not surrender it would be taken by storm. On 18 July Rainsborough offered what he insisted were his final terms. The city only had powder for one day's further fighting: three barrels of powder for cannon, five for muskets and one for pistols. There was food only for a further two weeks. Many of the garrison had already deserted; the mayor and corporation therefore finally decided to accept terms. The city felt keenly that they had been let down by the King: 'Never poor Gentlemen and City held out more loyal and never any so ill-rewarded as being neither remembered, by the king or the Council at Oxford in the Treaty'. The garrison finally marched out on the 23rd, following a service in the Cathedral, and held a ceremony of surrender on Rainbow Hill. Rainsborough finally marched into the city at 5pm. The First Civil War was finally over.

A literal 'last ditch' defence dug behind the main defences on The Butts in July 1646, during the siege of Worcester. It was 6 metres wide and 1.6 metres deep, associated with a rampart that still survived to a height of 1.7 metres.

(Worcestershire Historic Environment and Archaeology Service)

was said to have accepted a bribe of £3,000 and a promise to protect the family estates from sequestration (in the event unsuccessful). No family had done more for the Royalist cause within the county but Townshend was scathing over the surrender, declaring Sandys and Captain Aston, the governor of Madresfield, as like Judas! Here, however, was a family recognising that with the capture of the King (on 5 May), the war was over, honour was served, and they had to focus on the protection of their family interests. There was less comfort for the surrounding population of Hartlebury who, it may be imagined, had supplies stripped from them by the garrison in anticipation of the siege, and then were systematically plundered by the besieging troops. At Madresfield, the garrison were actually being besieged by the owner of the house, Colonell Lygon, who bribed the garrison to surrender on 20/21 June with an offer of £200 to Captain Aston, 30s to the cavalry troopers and 10s to each foot soldier. He was also reported to have bought the garrison cannon!

Meanwhile, Worcester had been summoned to surrender on 26 March as a preparation for being placed under siege. The new governor was Henry Washington (former governor of Evesham). With only isolated pockets of resistance remaining, Parliament could now confidently recover the arrears of taxes owed by the county and, as in the case of Captain Millward's men at Droitwich, pay the expenses of the soldiers whilst they did it![36] Five days after the fall of Hartlebury, the siege proper began on 21 May and lasted until 23 July.[37] The first stage of the siege was one of containment as Colonel Whalley's men dug in, waited for heavy siege artillery and more Foot to arrive, and offered the city a number of opportunities to surrender. The besieging army was not kept in the siege lines continuously. The Horse was dispersed between Worcester and Evesham, and from Kempsey to Droitwich, in order to spread the burden of supply – ready to be called back to the siege lines when required. At least thirty parishes in the county had troops billeted upon them during the siege. A regiment of 400 dragoons, under Colonel Betsworth, was quartered at Kempsey. Fladbury, 10.5 miles east of Worcester, quartered both Horse and Foot at intervals for over a month, including men from the regiments of Colonels Whalley and Starr, and Sir Thomas Fairfax (Lord General of the Army). William Saye billeted three of Fairfax's soldiers for five weeks at a cost of £3 15s whilst the unfortunate Thomas Barnes had men of the regiment billeted upon him for 70 days at a cost of £4 13s 4d. The troops and companies of individual regiments could be widely scattered. Another Fladbury man, William Jewkes, billeted two of Colonel Starr's Horse for 31 days at a cost of £4 2s 6d but others from Starr's regiment were quartered at Pershore, Throckmorton and at Flyford Flavell.[38] Many of the Parliamentary regiments included exiled Worcestershire men, including a troop of Whalley's Horse and no doubt eager for the war to be over so that they could return to their now liberated homes. Even where troops were not billeted, the towns and villages were called upon to provide supplies for the army. Droitwich regularly sent food to the camps at Ombersley and Worcester. They sent carpenters to help construct the siegeworks, and tended the wounded. Saltpetre to make gunpowder was also collected from Wickhamford.[39] It would have been gathered from dovecotes, dung heaps and middens – or even from under the floorboards of the church!

The strength of the Royalist garrison at the time of the siege was recorded by Townshend as 1,507 men, although the City collected its assessment on the basis of 1,600 men.[40] This total excludes the Worcester Town Regiment which may have numbered up to *c*.400 but who were by now considered a doubtful asset. The three principal regiments of Foot listed are the Governor's regiment, Samuel Sandys regiment (commanded during the siege by Major Moore) and William Russell's regiment. These were all long-standing local regiments, although greatly changed and reduced from their original composition. Sandys' regiment of Foot, once comprising 1,000 men, was now reduced to 272 men including officers. There was a high percentage of officers within the reduced companies which deteriorated to as low as 24 men and with one officer per six soldiers – a clear measure of the desertions that had occurred. They were supported by smaller bodies of Horse and men from broken regiments ('reformadoes') that had sought refuge in the city, including men from the former Royalist garrison at Evesham and some Irish troops. The preponderance of gentry officers prepared to fight on to the bitter end in the garrison seemed final proof of the fears of the city at the beginning of the war that 'cavaliers' would pursue the war to their own ends (see above, p. 50). With a population of 5,676 (according to Washington), every household was assessed for a sum to support the troops, but from the start of the siege the city struggled to support such a garrison and it was reported that 'Many foot have run out of the city for want of pay'.[41] These deserters included Taylor from Bransford 'a notorious rogue' who joined the Parliamentary army but was then captured and sentenced to hang.[42] There was particular resentment towards the foreign Irish troops and the ill-disciplined reformadoes who were seen as having no interest in the fate of the city. The sum of £20 was paid to the reformadoes in February 1646 in the hope of keeping the peace.[43] The Town Regiment had already disintegrated as an effective force and were only being used for guard duties. Their loyalties were possibly seen as being too close to the rest of the civilian population and were therefore not prepared to sacrifice their city further for a cause that was already lost. A disheartened Martin Sandys decided to abandon them early in the siege and make his last stand with his family at Hartlebury. The desertion of the city by Martin and Samuel Sandys cannot have improved morale in the beleaguered garrison.

Some means had to be found to buy the continued loyalty of the troops. A new tax was introduced to pay them although in order to spin out the money there soon became no option other than to progressively cut their pay. The rates of pay for a common soldier fell

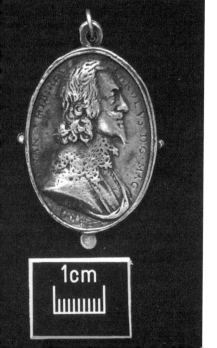

Charles I medal given as a reward for good service. Made of silver, it was found at Severn Stoke. In private possession.
(Worcestershire Historic Environment and Archaeology Service)

Prices of food in the Worcester garrison			
	1644	**25 June 1646**	**5 July 1646**
Beef	2d per lb		8d per lb
wheat	4s per strike	3s per strike	4s per strike
rye	3s per strike	3s per strike	2s 8d per strike
peas	2s per strike	2s per strike	2s 8d per strike
biscuit	?	10s per cwt	?
bacon	4d per lb	4d per lb	6d per lb
cheese	2d per lb	3d per lb	5d per lb
butter	4d per lb	4d per lb	?

again to 3s per week on 26 May, and there was a further reduction just a few days later on 29 May to just 2s 6d (to be paid 12d in cash and the rest in food). By 16 July it had been reduced dramatically to just 8d.[44] Inventive new ways were found to raise additional resources: the families of those men who had deserted the city had to provide for additional soldiers, and if their menfolk were found to have joined the Parliamentary army they would be turned out of their homes.

The siege was hard on the local population. They had to house, feed and pay the garrison and faced physical danger themselves. Many were forced to work on the defences and risk being shot there. No-one was safe: on June 11 a boy of the city was shot dead whilst collecting peascods at the Butts.[45] No-one could relax: on June 13 a man and wife were killed in their bed in the Trinity by cannon ball. Food prices in the city inevitably rose. By 11 July, Sir John Knotsford (the former governor of Evesham) was paying over 30s for a piece of good roasting beef, with fresh meat selling at an 'extreme' rate of 8d per lb.[46] The price of grain, however, was held stable to ensure a cheap supply of bread. This was not easy and the bakers sought to take advantage of the situation by threatening to strike for more pay. The response was firm. Smith the baker was whipped for not baking bread and was then threatened with being hung over the city walls.[47] Abandoned property was searched to bring any additional food to the magazine. There was also a severe shortage of fuel which meant that many of the city's outhouses were demolished and burnt and even the carriages of the gentry were chopped up for firewood. The besiegers exploited the situation and refused to allow children to leave the town in the worsening conditions so as to encourage their parents to surrender. When the governor had to allow the final reserves of food in the magazine to be opened up then all knew that it was only a matter of time before surrender was inevitable, under whatever terms the besiegers allowed.

As the siege became ever tighter, the garrison was increasingly dependent on the co-operation of the civilians but at the same time there was a growing gulf between them. The majority of the citizens no longer saw this as their war but according to Townshend, himself a civilian member of the Commission of Safety, were naïve if they thought that this would save them from the wrath of Parliament if the city fell

18th century Engraving of Worcester Bridge (now demolished). It was on the drawbridge that someone scrawled the slogan 'Civitas Fidelis Deo et Rege' and began the legend of the 'Faithful City'.

(Worcester City Library)

by storm. He described them as being 'besotted and stupid concerning their own preservation'. Thus, civilian workers on the defences struck for more wages and a large party within the city were reported to be ready to support Parliament if the city were actually attacked. Informants had already told Rainsborough, the Parliamentary commanding officer from late June, the exact strength of the depleted stores in the city. Discipline broke down: even Townshend complained 'Other soldiers take the insolency to pull down men's back houses upon pretence of fuel, and to sell it for liquor that most part of the suburbs of St Peter's in Sidbury is defaced ... So wicked are the Irish soldiery chiefly and given to spoil and ruin ... From the plundering of soldiers, their Insolency, Cruelty, Aetheism, Blasphemy and Rule over us, *Libera nos Domine*'.[48] The division between soldier and civilian was now absolute and the mayor, corporation and a deputation of wives therefore called upon the Governor to seek terms of surrender.

In such circumstances, the governor and loyalist gentry feared that if they tried to hold out further, the city might well withdraw the militia from the guard, refuse to provide provisions or even deliver the city up behind their backs. Some citizens had already broken the lock on the postern gate at the Foregate. Townshend describes how 'the city began to grow so mutinous that many gave out, they will throw the soldiers over the wall or club them if they should oppose this treaty, being now as all quiet people are weary of war, desiring their trading may go on'.[49] This open conflict between soldier and civilian contrasts sharply with the bravado exemplified in the painting by some unknown fanatic of the slogan *Civitas Fidelis Deo et Rege* ('City Faithful To God and King') on the drawbridge of Severn Gate.[50] This was not a popular sentiment and in fact, the city felt keenly that they had been let down by the king: 'Never poor Gentlemen and City held out more loyal and never any so ill-rewarded as being neither remembered, by the king or the Council at Oxford in the Treaty'.[51]

Under the terms of surrender finally agreed on 20 July, the garrison was to disband and promise never to take up arms against Parliament again and all arms and ammunition were to be surrendered. In return, there was to be no plundering of the city. The local militia organisation had collapsed and the Town Regiment are not reported as marching out with the regiments of the garrison to the place of formal surrender on Rainbow Hill on 26 July. Edward Solley, as Lieutenant Colonel of the militia was, however, excepted from the general term preventing the citizens to be questioned as to how far they had taken up arms against Parliament during the siege.[52] The terms were generally respected by the local members of the garrison who, with considerable relief, now returned to their farms and workshops. Only a few of their number supported the Royalists in either the Second or Third Civil Wars. One officer was executed for supporting the rising in Wales in 1648 and this may have served as a warning to the rest. Nonetheless, none of those few local gentry and their adherents who did renege on their agreement in 1646 and fought for Charles II at the battle of Worcester in 1651 were executed.

It is impossible to assess how many men from local regiments were killed during the First Civil War. Baxter was not an impartial witness but his commentary on the small number of surviving Royalist volunteers who returned to Kidderminster (see above, p. 68) suggests a high casualty rate. This is also supported by the considerable changes that took place in the structure of regiments raised in the county during the course of the war and the repeated need to raise fresh armies (Appendix 4). Charles Carlton has estimated that 3.7 percent of

Extract from Bewdley Parish Accounts recording the burial of soldiers, some unknown, in 1645.

(Worcestershire Record Office)

the population in England was killed as a result of the wars (6 percent in Scotland and 41 percent in Ireland). By comparison, the death toll in the British Isles as a result of World War I has been put at 2.61 percent and only 0.6 percent during World War II.[53] On such statistics, Worcestershire may have lost over 2,000 men during the war (the equivalent of the population of Evesham). Sobering statistics indeed for anyone who thinks this a romantic interlude in British history! The death toll in Worcestershire, excepting the later Battle of Worcester, was largely as a result of small skirmishes and most of the casualties from Kidderminster that Baxter gloated over probably met their fate beyond the borders of their home county. Worcestershire men fought at Edgehill, Bristol, Gloucester, Marston Moor, Naseby, and Denbigh (battles at which their presence was documented). Hamilton's regiments – recruited in the county during the winter/spring of 1642/3 – suffered particularly heavy casualties. By 1644 his regiment of Horse had been reduced to just 50 men. The dead would have been buried anonymously on the battlefield or in nearby churchyards, their families relying on returning comrades to tell them of their loss. Thus, ten men of Francis Blunt's troop of Horse that was sent to Bridgnorth in the spring of 1643 were identified as having been killed, but another 30 were described simply as 'none returned' (see above, p. 86).

Chapter Six
A Parliamentary Militia 1647–60

The Royalist establishment in Worcestershire was disarmed in 1646, but large numbers of the New Model Army remained in the county and, like the Royalists before them, there was no relief in the demand for money to maintain the soldiers. This was a continuing frustration for a country not used to the costs of maintaining a standing army during peacetime.

Engraving of Worcester Cathedral in 1672, still showing the belltower demolished in 1647. The Cathedral itself was only narrowly spared from demolition in the aftermath of the First Civil War.

(Author Collection)

Whalley's regiment was billeted in the Evesham district for months after the siege was over, and part of the regiment was quartered in the Lenches. Part of General Fairfax's own regiment of Horse remained in Fladbury until October 1646.[1] In June 1647, the county was assessed at £704 18s ¹/₂d and the city at £43 5s 6³/₄d to support the regiments of Fairfax's army that were still quartered in the county and also to contribute to the costs of transporting troops to Ireland. The continuing burden of maintaining a standing army caused considerable resentment both with the general population and Parliament. The presence of so many soldiers idling around Worcester evidently caused some problems of discipline – in 1647 the city paid 9s to make a 'wooden horse' on which punishments would be carried out. Attempts to either disband the army or send it to Ireland increased the rancour between the army and Parliament and also caused divisions between the senior officers and the common soldiers, leading to the rise of the Leveller movement. In late April 1647, 520 men of Colonel Lilburne's regiment of Foot under Lieutenant Colonel Kempson were quartered at Evesham and were being made ready to be sent to Ireland, but they claimed they had been tricked by Kempson, later joined the army mutiny and were at the centre of the Leveller revolts.

On 28 November 1646, a naïve Charles I claimed that 'most of the eastern, western and southern countries [sic] are resolved to rise in arms, and declare for me, with putting a great body of men into the field, and possessing all the important places'.[2] Divisions in the Parliamentary ranks between Presbyterians and Independents, and attempts at mutiny by some troops, had indeed provided the opportunity for a series of risings by Royalists and discontented Parliamentarians, allied with the disenchanted Scots, that together formed the Second Civil War of 1648–9.

In this atmosphere of suspicion and only two years after the siege of 1646, Worcestershire men were again mobilised (June 1648) in a return to the pre-war system of the Trained Bands – now acting as a police force against its former allies. Under new officers, they were summoned to defend the state in the name of the House of Commons alone without any suggestion of royal authority. The new militia was again under the authority of the County Committee, although diplomatically, the City Council was invited to name the officers of its company. The city was a step nearer its pre-war demands for autonomy. On 4 August Major Foulke Estopp was appointed the commanding officer of the Worcester company. Son of a Worcester clothier (b.1613), he had been a member of the Chamber and an officer in the Parliamentary Army during the First Civil War.

Not for the first or last time, the Royalists had greatly inflated the scale of popular support for their cause, and the machinations of Charles I proved to be his final downfall. The involvement of Worcestershire in the Second Civil War was somewhat peripheral, although one of those who took part was Charles Lyttleton, the younger son of the now elderly Sir Thomas (who died in 1650). Charles Lyttleton resolutely took up the mantle of Royalist support from his father. He was captured at the siege of Colchester and, not for the last time, was briefly imprisoned. One of the main leaders in Wales, Sir Thomas Nott also owned land in Worcestershire. There were clearly some plans for local Royalist involvement that came to nothing. In July 1648

Colonel Dud Dudley was arrested whilst drilling 200 Royalists in Boscobel Woods and another local Royalist, Edward Broade of Dunclent, employed a local joiner, John Brancill of Kidderminster, to make stocks for muskets to be used in the rebellion.[3]

But locally, the main driving force was not ardent Royalists but officers of the Parliamentary Army who resented the disbanding of their units after the end of the First Civil War and their consequent lack of employment. Around eighty discontented army officers met at Broadway, at the foot of the Cotswolds, in January 1648 to plot a rising. Their main targets were said to be Gloucester and the small garrison at Hartlebury. They also hoped for the support of 2,000 'capmen' from Bewdley (the manufacturers of the famous 'Monmouth' caps), possibly harking back to the Royalist tendencies of the Kidderminster journeymen before the First Civil War. Significantly, there was evidently no hope of support from Worcester, despite there being riots against the Excise in that month thought to be engineered by 'divers souldiers that had been Cavaliers'. As a precaution, the City company of the new Trained Bands was mobilised against 'any tumult or uproare that shall arise'.[4] This, therefore, was a return to the traditional role of the Trained Bands to protect the county from disorder from whatever faction it might arise.

Nothing actually came of the plot, although in one embarrassing incident in early 1648 a supernumerary troop of dragoons from Okey's regiment (due for disbandment) under Captain Edward Wogan, produced forged orders to ride north and then promptly joined the Royalist Scots![5] As a precaution, troops of the New Model Army guarding the Welsh border were billeted on Worcester to stiffen local resolve. On 12 May it was agreed to collect the sum of £70 to pay the innkeepers of Worcester for billeting the men of Captain Saunders from Thornhagh's Horse. Another 80 troops were expected that night. In all, a brigade of Horse was stationed in Worcester over the year.

The execution of Charles I in January 1649 by an exacerbated army and its supporters in Parliament seemed to bring the wars to a final conclusion and the country started to rebuild a normal life. His son, now Charles II, was, however in exile on the continent and, like his father in 1648, was persuaded by attending courtiers that the country was ready to rise in his support. He was no doubt encouraged in this both by the widespread grumbles about the costs of maintaining the standing army and by the discontent within the army itself over arrears of pay and the continuing threat of service in Ireland. He landed in Scotland in June 1650 and joined in an uneasy alliance with the Scottish covenanters. Many of the English

In July 1648, Colonel Turton at Hartlebury received intelligence of Royalist plotting in Shropshire. One of the leaders, Major Harcot, was arrested and taken to Hartlebury where he was tortured by having lighted musket fuses placed on the soles of his feet in order to make him confess and identify his confederates.

army officers were not prepared to invade the country of their former ally and fellow presbyterians to defeat this new threat to peace. Even the Lord General of the army, Thomas Fairfax, resigned his command. His second-in-command, Oliver Cromwell, became commander of the Parliamentary army and marched into Scotland. Despite winning a notable victory at Dunbar in September 1650, the campaign did not go well for Cromwell and after a winter wracked with illness he decided on a radical new tactic. The plan was to entice the Scottish Army of 13,000 men into England and thereby unite the divided country against what would then be seen as an invading foreign power. They could be destroyed by overwhelming forces away from their main power base.[6]

The campaign was well planned. Nationwide, the re-formed militias were mobilised from March 1651 to provide a solid defence in depth to support of the regular troops of the New Model Army against the triple threats of the Scottish Army, internal rebellion and invasion from the continent. Cromwell and General Harrison shared concerns as to the traditional value of such troops and the latter had to be stiffened with regular officers.[7] But many of the militia were by now experienced veterans, and in action they were later described as performing 'with singular good service'.[8] The long-standing antipathy to the Royalist cause in Worcester and tensions between the city and gentry were again important factors in considering the failure of Worcester to provide active support to the Royalists in 1651. Instead, the Worcestershire militia was to play a crucial role in Cromwell's plans to defeat Charles II in his invasion of England.

The Council of State appointed Colonel John James of Astley as garrison commander of Worcester on 31 March 1651 and to raise and command the Horse and Dragoons of the Worcestershire militia.[9] No mention was made of the Foot at this time. He evidently suffered the recurring problem during the Civil Wars of finding enough mounts for his men. On 23 May he had to return some horses supplied by Gloucester as being 'of stature too little and quality so bad'.[10] To add to his problems, at the end of June he was also instructed to list fresh volunteers from the county for service in the New Model Army. A levy of troops from Gloucester was also put under his command.[11] Their first task was to isolate any potential support for the King within the county and prominent Royalists were arrested or prevented from returning to Worcestershire. The former commander of the Royalist Town Regiment, Martin Sandys, was already under arrest on suspicion of a murder carried out in Worcester.[12] In May, his brother Samuel (the former governor of Worcester), was refused entry to the county from London. Other prominent local Royalists, Sir John Packington and Shropshire-based Lord Talbot, were also imprisoned in Worcester (from where they were later rescued by the Scottish Army). For less notable individuals, there was always the danger that careless talk of support for the Royalists would be reported to the authorities. Edward Powys, a bookbinder of Worcester, was immediately reported to the Quarter Sessions in March 1651 for reputedly drinking a toast in Bridgnorth to the King's Army in Scotland.[13] A more difficult task was to come. If the Scottish Army invaded Worcestershire then the militia would be in the forefront of the battle. The Horse and Dragoons would have to slow down the advance, allowing the 500-

Oliver Cromwell (1599–1658). Although popularly regarded as the leader of the Parliamentary Army throughout the Civil Wars he only became Commander in Chief in 1650. Prior to that he served as second-in-command to Sir Thomas Fairfax.

(19th century engraving after Robert Walker. Author Collection) strong Worcester garrison to prepare their defences and giving the rest of the Parliamentary Army time to rendezvous for the final battle.

As the Scottish Army began its long march southwards along the west coast of England, the Worcestershire militia obeyed Parliament's orders and rallied on Pitchcroft field, Worcester, in considerable numbers under Colonel John James and Captain Andrew Yarranton (the iron-master from Astley, who had raised a troop of Horse).[14] These were confusing times. Thomas Soley fought with the militia whilst at the same time his goods were being confiscated in London as a suspected Royalist![15] No details survive of any uniforms, beyond the fact that they wore coloured ribbons in their hats. The defences of Worcester were ordered to be repaired once again with the hope of denying the King and his increasingly dispirited army any shelter until Cromwell was ready to engage the enemy. It may be that the original plan was to force them to march on to Gloucester where another army was being readied to form an anvil against which the Scots would be crushed. On 15 August the Council of State praised the Worcestershire Militia Commissioners for their efforts in assuring 'the good posture' of the county and encouraged them to be ready for the impending contact with the Scots, who were on their way from Wolverhampton.[16] The Scots finally arrived in the county near Kidderminster on 21 August. Events then moved very quickly.

The local militia rose to the challenge of the invasion. The Horse and Dragoons were sent forward to harry the enemy, whilst newly-raised Foot remained in Worcester. Yarranton first tried to demolish the stone bridge at Bewdley in order to block any river crossing across the Severn and hinder any support arriving from Wales — this first attempt failed. The Scottish columns fanned out through the fields beside Kidderminster and passed through Hartlebury; they were only 10 miles north of Worcester. As the forward units of the Scots approached, Whitelock says that 'the country forces [i.e. the militia] made a gallant resistance and beat back the enemy several times'.[17]

Initially it seemed as though the citizens of Worcester might try to resist a Scottish siege. Volunteers from the city had set-to with the garrison in order to repair quickly the so-recently levelled city defences, probably by patching the city walls, cleaning out some of the wide ditches that fronted them (although apparently not on the east side) and blocking the gates with banks of earth and stone. General Harrison wrote three letters within the space of twelve hours on 21 August urging them on and promising reinforcements. At least a part of the city therefore decided to 'hazard our lives in the keeping of the City and did what we could to strengthen the walls, and the well-affected in the City and County came in to us willingly engaging themselves and in the expectation of assistance from the Major General [Harrison] according to his promises'. The Parliamentary faction was centred on the County Committee and the members of the clothing industry. It was led by the former governor, George Milward (a wealthy clothier), Simon Moore (vicar of St Peter's, rector of St Michael's Bedwardine, Master of St Oswald's Hospital and one of the county magistrates), Edward Elvins (another clothier and former Sheriff), Gervase Buck (a

Justice of the Peace from near Kempsey), former army officers William Collins and Richard Inett, and Andrew Yarranton.

But as night fell on Thursday 21 August, resolve crumbled within the city at the prospect of a battle being fought on their doorsteps. There would still have been stark memories of the long siege of 1646 and the citizens were anxious to persuade the troops of both sides to move off elsewhere and finally leave them in peace. With the King having passed through Kidderminster, the Mayor and Sheriff requested a meeting between the City Council, Colonel James and the County Committee to discuss 'the peaceful entry of the enemy into the city'.[18] There was a heated debate but eventually those advocating armed resistance until the arrival of Cromwell's army (a faction led by Edward Elvins, and militia officers Major Fowlke Estopp and Captain Theophilus Alie) were outvoted by the rest of the more nervous Chamber. Instead, with the sound of gunfire coming ever closer, the citizens prepared to surrender and thereby avoid the destruction that would inevitably accompany an assault. The Scots were evidently coming prepared for a siege: sixteen cartloads of ladders were brought up with the rear of the army.[19] The city's hope now was that the Royalist army would only rest in Worcester temporarily and then continue its march elsewhere.

The militia were made of sterner stuff and ignored the decision of the city to surrender. They fought on throughout Friday 22 August, still hoping for reinforcements and determined to buy further time for Cromwell to gather together his forces, but not even the last minute arrival of five troops of Welsh Horse from Harrison could restore the confidence of the city. Other Foot requested from Hereford had not yet arrived and it was clear that there would be no further reinforcements before the now-imminent arrival of the Scots. Yarranton's troop of Horse fought a skirmish with the Scots at Ombersley, 5 miles outside the city. With the help of the Welsh Horse there was further skirmishing up to the outskirts of the city, probably in the area approaching St Martin's Gate which was now the main access point into the city from the north. Fore Gate on the more obvious approach route of the Scots had already been blocked, or 'mured up', by the garrison. The garrison seem at this stage to have been scattered into small units to harry the advance as best they could. With the Scots at the very gates of Worcester, the Horse were reportedly again sent to Bewdley to raid the quarters of the Scots in the rear, taking advantage of the fact that the Scots had not occupied the west side of the Severn. They reported some success, killing two quartermasters and taking some prisoners.

The odds were, however, hopeless for the Worcestershire and Welsh troops fighting with their backs to the walls of Worcester. With the Scottish advance guard now at the gates of the city, the regrouped garrison had little option but to withdraw. The leading civilian Parliamentarians also prudently decided to retreat to Gloucester with them. In order to impress the fast-gathering Scottish army, some amongst the citizens began to fire on the thirty-strong rearguard of the retreating garrison. With great presence of mind, troops under Captain Boyleston were quickly ordered to load up the contents of the ammunition magazine (seven firkins of powder) and take this to safety in Gloucester. It might also be presumed that they had tried to 'spike' the

The Worcestershire Militia fought a skirmish through Ombersley as they attempted to slow the advance of the Scottish Army, thereby buying extra time for Cromwell to organise the rendezvous of his army at Evesham.

(Author Collection)

heavy artillery in the city although this is not certain. The advance guard of the Scots entered the city on the night of 22 August, whilst King Charles delayed his arrival to make a grand entrance in the daylight. Looking around at the preparations that had been made to resist his army, it is doubtful if the King was really convinced by the protestations of loyalty of the Council but his army was too exhausted to travel further. The city was occupied by up to 16,000 men. Although small garrisons were established at Upton on Severn and at Powick, most were probably billeted in the city and on Pitchcroft.

The Scots spent the next two weeks feverishly refurbishing the defences, including the rebuilding of Fort Royal beside London Road. With less than 24 hours notice, the parish of Salwarpe was ordered to provide 30 men, equipped with spades, shovels and pickaxes to begin work at 5am on 25 August.[20] No doubt, they also stockpiled food from the surrounding countryside and the city spent a small fortune in feeding them! They also tried to re-equip their ragged army as best they could. Henry Wright, draper, provided £453 1s 5d of red and grey cloth to the army on 2 and 3 September. Not surprisingly, given the dramatic events of 3 September, he did not get paid and his widow was still trying to claim payment in 1675. Cromwell's army of *c.*30,000 men (one-third made up from militias raised from across the country) was getting closer and on 27 August the Council of State warned the militia committees of Warwickshire, Shropshire, Gloucestershire, Herefordshire and Worcestershire to prepare provisions for the imminent arrival of the Parliamentary

Army (for which they would be reimbursed). The irritation aroused by the rapid, and undignified, collapse of Worcester is evident in the addition to the order sent to Worcestershire to collect supplies 'and thereby show how little you approve of what your revolting city hath done'.[21]

Few local people appear to have joined the Royalists. If they did have leanings towards the Royalists the reputation of the battle-hardened New Model Army was probably enough to dissuade most from any action. None of the City Council who had surrendered to the King, and very few other Worcester men, are documented as having played any role in the battle, with what support there was mainly coming from the county gentry and their tenants or labourers. Two citizens who did join the muster were the Worcester clothiers Walter Heming and William Clarke who had recently deserted the Worcestershire militia for the Scots.[22] One other recruit was the impressionable 18-year-old orphan, John Romney of Knightwick, who was living with his uncle in Worcester at the time of the arrival of the Scots; some of them had been billeted on the house. He claimed he had been forced to join the muster because he was 'terrified by their threats'.[23] Another was Walter Morice, a Worcester clothier. He had been a soldier in the Bishop's War, had also served in Ireland and fought in the battle of Worcester as a lieutenant in the Royalist army. He was taken prisoner and was due to be transported to the colonies – having been sold to a shipping merchant for 14s 6d. He had a fortunate escape as a friend followed him to Bristol and bought him back for £5. By 1675 he was described as having 'grown old and in prison for debt'.[24] In all, only 23 of the local gentry and 140 men were listed as being present at the muster.[25]

They included:

Francis Lord Talbot now Earl of Shrewsbury, with about 60 Horse
Mr Mervin Touchet, his Lieutenant Colonel
Sir John Packington [of Westwood, Hampton Lovett]
Sir Walter Blount [of Sodington]
Sir Ralph Clare
Sir Rowland Berkeley [of Cotheridge]
Sir John Winford [of Astley]
Mr. Ralph Sheldon of Beoly
Mr. John Washburn of Witchinford with 40 Horse
Mr. Thomas Hornyold of Blackmore Park with 40 Horse
Mr William S[h]eldon of Finstall
Mr. Thomas Acton [of Burton]
Captain Benbow
Mr Robert Blount of Kenswick
Mr Robert Wigmore of Lucton
Mr Edward Pennel the Elder [of Woodston in Lindridge]
Captain John Kingston
Mr Peter Blount
Mr Edward Blount

Mr. Walter Walsh [of Abberley]
Mr Charles Wash (sic)
Mr William Dansey [of Stoke Prior]
Mr Francis Knotsford

Francis Lord Talbot, Sir John Packington, Sir Ralph Clare, Sir Walter Blount and
Thomas and Ralph Sheldon had all been members of the Royalist Committee of
Safety for Worcestershire during the First Civil War. At least one quarter of the

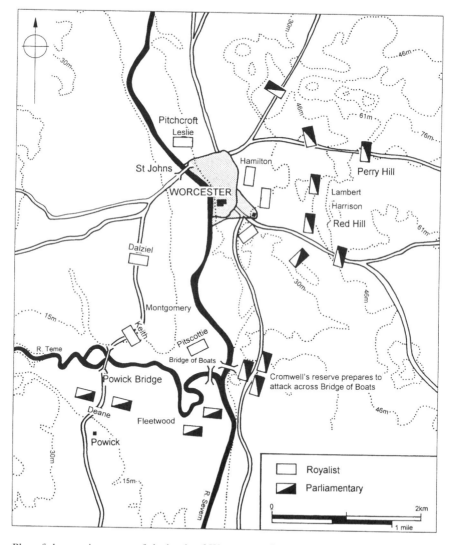

Plan of the opening stages of the battle of Worcester, 3 September 1651.

(Worcestershire Historic Environment and Archaeology Service)

named individuals had been present at the siege of Worcester in 1646; many were also Catholic. Some of those listed were able to bring a retinue with them: John Washburn and Thomas Hornyold each brought forty men. Lord Talbot, newly released from prison, summoned 60 men under his lieutenant, Mervin Touchet; they included Colonel William Carlis, a Staffordshire man (who later took up residence

Powick Church. Prior to the Battle of Worcester on 3 September 1651, this was used as a forward observation post by the Scots. INSET: Marks left by musket shot on the wall of Powick Church.

(Author Collection)

Key Events: 1651 – the Battle of Worcester

On 3 September 1651 the final battle of the English Civil Wars was fought at Worcester. An exhausted Scottish Army of 13,000 – 16,000 men (including a paltry *c*.2,000 Englishmen) had been trapped inside the city after their long march from Scotland. Against them, Oliver Cromwell had amassed an army of 30,000 men comprising battled-hardened New Model Army troops and members of militias that had flocked to the battle from all over the country.

Having seized the river crossing at Upton upon Severn some days earlier, part of the Parliamentary Army advanced on the ridge at Powick at dawn and drove the Scottish defenders from the church. Another column advanced up the river bank of the Severn, dragging pontoons with them to make two bridges of boats with which to cross the rivers Severn and Teme. There was bitter hand-to-hand fighting and the battle became bogged down as the parliamentary troops found it impossible to cross the Teme. At *c*.3pm Cromwell stormed across the bridge of boats on the Severn with his reserve of New Model Army Horse. The Scots, taken in the flank, were forced to retreat and were pushed back into St Johns.

King Charles II had believed that the main attack (as in 1646) would come from the east and had not, therefore, provided a sufficient reserve on the west side of the Severn. He now tried to relieve the pressure on his men by launching a pincer-movement on the Parliamentary troops on the east side of the city at *c*.4pm. He possibly hoped to punch a hole through the Parliamentary lines and make a break-out for London. But, again reinforced by Cromwell's mobile reserve, the line held and the Essex and Cheshire militias poured down from the high ground to seize first Fort Royal and then to force an entry into the city through Sidbury Gate. Meanwhile, Fleetwood's cavalry had pushed across the Severn Bridge from St Johns. Isolated pockets of resistance remained until 10pm but most of the Scots were pushed back onto the Quay where they surrendered. Charles II managed to escape at *c*.6pm, covered by a small party of Horse from the troop of local gentry under Lord Talbot. Around 10,000 prisoners were taken with accounts of the Scottish death toll being up to *c*.4,000. Many of the prisoners were transported to the New World or were forced to work on the Fens drainage schemes. Charles II's attempt to win back his throne by military means was crushed – but he was restored to his throne in 1660 by popular consent and with the aid of the same New Model Army that had defeated him at Worcester.

---

at Hallow, Worcs.), who was described as being Major to Lord Talbot, and Richard Kemble who was his Captain Lieutenant. William Penn of Belbroughton was also later accused of being a captain in the troop.[26] Although not mentioned in the muster, the troop also included Charles Giffard and his servant Francis Yates from Boscobel, Richard Lane from Bentley Hall in the West Midlands and a Worcestershire man, Richard Walker, the 'scout-master' (intelligence officer). Although small in numbers, these men were later to play a critical role in assisting the escape of the King from Worcester.

Cromwell's Army of 30,000 men gathered at Evesham on 27 August and were rejoined by the men of the Worcestershire militia. The first stage of the battle to surround the Scots began without delay on the next day when General Lambert seized the crossing over the River Severn at Upton upon Severn, preventing any Scottish breakout southwards. Using local guides, a mixed mounted column of elements of the Worcestershire militia, together with New Model Army Horse and militia under Colonels Twistleton and Kendrick, was sent westwards to Bransford Bridge on the Teme in order to prevent any escape of the now encircled Scots into Herefordshire and Wales. Five troops of Worcestershire Dragoons and Horse, with two troops of Rich's regiment of Horse, were sent north to Bewdley to block any escape into Wales or northwards, and probably included Yarranton's troop as they were later involved in pursuing the Scots into Shropshire.

At the same time, the rest of Cromwell's Army moved to occupy the high ground on the east side of the city and began to pound the city with artillery. The Scots were surrounded and the pressures to feed the vast number of people now trapped in the city would have rapidly worsened. Cromwell made his final preparations for the battle that commenced on 3 September. More local people flocked to join the militia so that 'the country came in freely to the Parliament's army' whether by conviction or simply in a desire to be seen to have supported the winning side, they probably joined the main Parliamentary Army upon Red Hill as reserves behind the front lines of the Essex and Cheshire brigades of militia.[27] The battle lasted approximately ten hours. Between 2,000 – 4,000 Scots were killed at a loss to Parliament of only *c*.200 men. There was no mention of the Worcester troops during the actual battle. The Worcestershire Horse and Dragoons did, however, take part in the pursuit of the Scots into Shropshire. It is likely that Cromwell decided not to risk the loyalty of the local militia in giving them a leading role in attacking their own city. The hours following the storming of the city were probably the most fearful suffered by Worcester during the war. Under the contemporary rules of war they could have expected little mercy – with lives and property considered fair game by the men who had been forced to take the risk in mounting a frontal assault. Colonel Stapleton, for one, decided not to enter the city until 'the soldiers fury was over'. 'Lords, knights and gentlemen were there plucked out of holes by the soldiers'. The bodies of men and horses were piled in the streets and houses were indeed ransacked but the citizens fared perhaps better than they hoped. Even Cromwell felt it necessary to write to Parliament that supporters in the town had suffered alongside the Royalists: 'The town being entered by storm, some honest men, promiscuously and without distinction, suffered by your Soldier – which could not at that time possibly be prevented, in the fury and heat of the battle'.[28] The city later estimated the total cost of plundering after the battle at £80,000 and some of the debts were not repaid until 1675. There was evidently considerable sympathy around the country for the plight of the inhabitants. In March 1652, the sum of £91 was raised by the citizens and Common Council of Gloucester 'for the relief of the poor inhabitants of Worcester that were plundered when the Scotts army was beaten

Charles II's lodgings during the Scottish occupation were on New Street / Cornmarket, from where he made his final escape from the city at 6pm on 3rd September.

(Susanne Atkin)

out of Worcester'.[29] Stolen goods included the Civic Sword and there was even an attempt to steal city records. Five shillings had to be paid to a soldier by Stephen Field to return some civic documents to the Treasury. A new sword had to be purchased in 1652 at a cost of £5 8s 6d.[30] Wine glasses, bottles, butter pots and pewter dishes were all lost from the Deanery.

After the battle, local people joined in taking revenge on the hated Scots. Richard Baxter was woken up at Kidderminster by the sound of the fleeing Horse on the cobbles. He described the scene when 'many hundreds of the flying army' were ambushed in the market-place by about thirty troopers sent the few miles from Bewdley: 'And till midnight the bullets flying towards my door and windows, and the sorrowful fugitives hasting by for their lives, did tell me the calamitousness of war'.[31] Local people, resentful of this new attempt to bring the country to Civil War, were eager to show their loyalty to the victorious Commonwealth. Cromwell reported that 'the country riseth upon them everywhere' and Clarendon later wrote 'very many of those who ran away were every day knocked in the head by the country people, and used with barbarity'.[32] Villagers from Chaddesley Corbett were reputed to have killed a number of Scots and buried them close to a local cross-roads in Broome, south of Hackman's Gate.[33] The reported discovery of a skeleton at Huddington with the remains of a purse on his thigh, containing 32 copper coins, almost entirely Scottish issues of Charles I, suggests that one survivor of the battle may have crawled away to die as surely his purse would otherwise have been removed prior to burial.[34]

It is clear that Worcestershire had raised considerable numbers of men, particularly Horse and Dragoons, to join the Parliamentary army in 1651, but in all, only twenty-three of the local gentry and 140 other men were listed as being present at the Royalist muster. Although few in numbers, this troop of local men under Lord Talbot were to play a key role in the final stages of the battle, mounting a brave rearguard action to allow the escape of the king. Fortunately, it also contained members of the Giffard household who were to play a major role in leading the King through the Catholic escape route in Staffordshire and Shropshire. Clarendon complained that few of the gentry who had previously written letters of support actually joined the army at Worcester although 'some common men' who had previously served in the Royalist armies loyally rejoined the colours.[35] Particular anger was directed against the 45-year-old Lord Coventry at Croome who, upon the approach of the King's Army, conveniently retired to bed with an unspecified illness. Charles II ordered him to be pulled 'out of his house by his ears' and sent troops to steal his horses!

Having won the war, Parliament and the army found it impossible to find a stable form of government to replace the monarchy. In 1655 the country was divided into eleven military districts each under an experienced Major General. Their principal task was to round up suspected Royalist activists assisted by a small, newly-raised, 'select' militia of Horse (which would complement the existing 'general' militia). The sixty-six troops of 'select militia', totalling originally 6,250 men (largely veterans of the New Model Army and loyal to the Protectorate), were to be funded out of a new 'decimation tax' consisting of a 10 percent levy on all Royalist estates worth

A contemporary impression of the fighting at the Battle of Worcester. Extract from 1660 plan of Worcester.

above £100 p.a. Seemingly in contravention of the 1652 Act of Oblivion, it was not simply those who had taken up arms in the recent risings that were to suffer but any that had supported the Crown in the past. In September 1655 the 46-year-old Major General James Berry (1610–91) was sent into Worcestershire to oversee a large district including Shropshire, Herefordshire and Wales. Berry was of lowly origins, having been a clerk in a Shropshire ironworks before the War, when he had become a friend of Richard Baxter (although Baxter was later to criticise him for his increasing religious radicalism). He had served during the war as a troop commander in Cromwell's cavalry regiment and was promoted to colonel in 1651. His headquarters were in Shrewsbury, with Captain Talbot Badger of the Worcestershire militia acting as his deputy in Worcestershire. Worcestershire had just one troop of the new militia, originally being 100 men.

But the system was chronically short of money and, at first reduced to 80 men, the troop was short-lived and was paid off at the end of the year after being given a full year's pay. Berry was a lenient governor seeking reconciliation and he listed only 11 Royalists in the county (as opposed to the 322 listed by his counterpart in Gloucestershire). It was clearly a token selection with only one person listed for each

Annual Pay of 'Select Militia'[36]	
Captain	£100
Lieutenant	£50
Cornet	£25
Trumpeter	£13 6 8d
Corporals	£10
Trooper	£8 (+ pay of New Model Army trooper whilst on active service)

place. Although it includes some familiar names from Royalist county gentry, such as Sir Ralph Clare, Thomas Savage and William Sheldon, Worcester City was represented only by James Abrell, a pewterer. Berry was also tolerant of Fifth Monarchists and released a number of Quakers from Evesham prison, ordering Worcestershire magistrates to allow them to worship freely.[37]

There were renewed fears of war in 1659 with an abortive rising in Cheshire. As a response, in the summer of 1659 a new Act of Parliament sought to revive the general Trained Bands. Anyone with property valued at over £15 p.a. or with a personal income of over £200 p.a. was liable to serve. Former Royalists were not excluded and in Worcestershire this included the former Royalist muster-master Henry Townshend and his son. New Foot soldiers were raised from the county in July and three troops of Horse on 15 August, along with a troop of Dragoons under the command of Captain Boyleston (who had commanded the Parliamentary rearguard at Worcester in August 1651), but the rising did not directly affect the county.[38] The revolt was only thinly supported nationally and was routed by General Lambert at Hartford Green, near Northwich, on 19 August. Exaggerating slightly, the County Committee for Worcestershire proudly told the Committee for Compounding that locally, only the Lyttleton family had joined the revolt. Charles Lyttleton had returned from exile on the continent

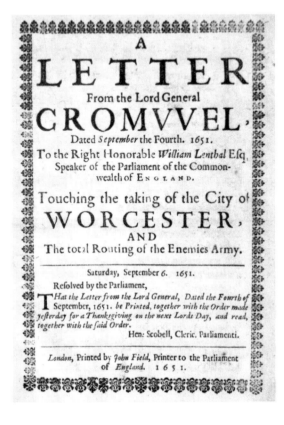

Title page of letter from Oliver Cromwell, 4 September 1651, announcing the victory at Worcester.

(Worcestershire Record Office)

to join Booth's revolt. He was captured, briefly imprisoned and then rejoined Charles II on the continent. The local militia was stood down in September once the initial crisis was over but there remained a rising sense of unease in the county and indeed in the country as a whole. From 14 September until they marched north in late 1659 to meet General Monck at York, Worcester was garrisoned by three companies of regular troops from Samuel Clark's regiment, newly returned from Flanders 'for the preservation of the peace'.[39] The Governor of Worcester in 1660, William Collins, wrote to the Commissioners for the Government of the Army on 4 January that his garrison had been on 'hard duty' for eight weeks because of the threat posed by roving bands of highway robbers composed of former soldiers. He had been obliged to pay their wages himself as 'their necessities for want of pay are very great, having been on hard duty for eight weeks, to preserve the peace of this country, which was much disturbed by highway robbers, being considerable parties, and supposed to be of the old enemy, they riding in the posture of soldiers; for this time they have had no money but what I have borrowed, and lent them, besides three years arrears formerly due to them'.[40] In such circumstance of a breakdown in law and order, the various intrigues of the Royalists were to prove to be irrelevant. The Protectorate of Richard Cromwell was already in its final death throes and the Interregnum was about to grind to a sorry end. The Restoration would be achieved not by military might – but by the consent of the general populace, Parliament and the army.

Chapter Seven
The Militia at the Restoration

On 25 May 1660, Charles II landed in England, not in another attempt to win his crown by force but in answer to an invitation by Parliament and the army under General Monck. No other constitutional experiment had succeeded in finding a stable replacement and the Restoration was generally met with relief. In Worcester, news of the King's arrival was greeted with the lighting of bonfires in the streets and the ringing of the church bells. The officers of the former Royalist Worcester Town Regiment of 1642–6 (Edward Solley and Frances Hughes) were restored to their places on the City Council and the Trained Bands showed once again that they were ready to act in support of the government of the day.

Surprisingly perhaps to modern eyes, and despite all of the tumult of the past eighteen years, the Restoration was not taken as a time to settle old scores or as a time for vengeance and retaliation, with the exception of the regicides who had signed the death warrant of Charles I. It was with great relief that Evelyn wrote that the Restoration had been won without a drop of blood being shed.[1] The former Lord General of the Parliamentary armies, Thomas Fairfax, who had not signed the Royal death warrant, retired to his estates. On a more local scale, in Worcestershire the nobles and gentry delivered a declaration to General Monck promising not to 'harbour any such thought of Ransom or Revenge … but willing to lay aside all animosity and return to all mutual Christian love'.[2] The survivors of the original protagonists were fourteen years older from the time that the

Charles ii (1630–85). Restored to his throne in 1660.

Illustration from the Seal of the
Committee for Maimed Soldiers
(Partizan Press Picture Library)

First Civil War had ended: Sir Thomas Lyttleton was dead, Samuel Sandys was 45 and Sir William Russell was 58. Their principal opponents had not, in the main, been local men – Archer from Warwickshire, Massie from Gloucestershire or the army led by Waller. Massie was himself now a leading Royalist. There was no rancour against the local Parliamentary gentry led by Edward Rous, Nicholas Lechmere and William Lygon who had been militarily active but had not taken a decisive role in the campaigns, or been pitted against each other in the same way that the opposing garrisons in Shropshire had been. The feeling might have been different against the 'turncoat', Edward Dingley, but he had died in 1646. Overwhelmingly, the concern was, as in 1651, to restore normal economic and social life as soon as possible.

The county did, however, continue to pay the economic and social costs of war for many years to come. Pensions for service in the Royalist armies continued to be claimed as late as 1681 in the county. From early in the war, both Parliament and the King tried to provide for pensions to maimed soldiers, as an obvious effort to maintain morale. The King even tried to arrange preferential treatment for former soldiers for accommodation in almshouses, but the responsibility devolved to the county via the Quarter Sessions and simply became another burden on the local economy. Only limited funds were available via the local taxes levied for maimed soldiers although in 1662 an Act of Parliament was passed for the 'reliefe of poore maimed officers and soldiers who have faithfully served His Majesty and His Late Father in the late wars' (having been barred from claiming relief during the Interregnum). The Act provided for a measure of temporary relief until a pension could be granted through the Quarter Sessions. By the end of that year Worcestershire was paying £240 p. a. for the relief of maimed soldiers. The small number of surviving petitions for relief in the records of the Quarter Sessions provide a rare connection with the experiences of the common soldiers during the wars. In 1661 Richard Powell, described as a disabled soldier with four children, could be given a pension only because the former pension holder had died.[3] Richard Hall of Kempsey had to wait until 1677 at the age of 60 for his pension, having been wounded in the war.[4] In 1676, 10s was given to that 'poor cavalier', Captain Underhill, but new claims continued to be made until as late as 1681 (20 years after the battle of Worcester). The survivors frequently claimed that they had borne their wounds without complaint until old age and their disability made it impossible for them to work. In accord with the 1662 Act, they invariably professed their faithfulness to Charles I and Charles II in the 'unhappy wars'. Whether this was a genuine expression of loyalty to their monarch or a mere convention cannot now be judged but there was clearly no magnanimity extended to former Parliamentary common soldiers. For some petitioners, simply having served their King and survived to great age seemed good enough reason to be provided with a pension. In 1681, Roger Bundy of St John's, Worcester, maintained that he had kept himself in honest labour since the wars without having to make any charge on the parish but now he was suffering failing eye sight and old age and had been brought 'very low and poor'.[5] The 'very aged and decayed' petitioner Arthur Bagshawe of Feckenham, however, claimed on the basis that he had been shot in the arm and the throat which now made him unfit to work.[6] Henry Dyson of Arley Kings similarly claimed 'many wounds and hurts' for which he had not previously made a claim. But now he and his wife had been sick for a year, during which time they had relied on the charity of their neighbours and therefore he begged for the sympathy of the justices of the peace.[7]

Petition of Henry Dyson of Arley Kings who claimed a pension for injuries received in the Civil Wars as late as 1681.

(Worcestershire Record Office)

At the Proclamation of the Restoration on 11 May 1660, there was a grand procession, led by 100 of the city company of the Trained Bands under their new captain, Alderman Vernon, followed by two companies of Samuel Clark's regiment. This was, of course, part of the same New Model Army that had defeated Charles I, crushed the attempt of his son to win back the throne by military force at Worcester in 1651 and had defeated Booth's Rising in 1659! Not surprisingly, the King tried to disband most of the New Model Army. Some regiments were sent overseas but Monck's regiment was retained as a new guards regiment (the republican origin of the Coldstream Guards!) alongside other new regiments of guards created from units that had served him in exile. Thus, in August Lord Windsor's troop of the King's Regiment, under a no doubt triumphant Captain-Lieutenant Charles Lyttleton, arrived to take up winter quarters in Worcester.[9] Lyttleton was the same younger son of Sir Thomas who had taken part in the siege of Colchester and Booth's Rising. He eventually became governor of Jamaica and Colonel of the Lord High Admiral's regiment. To

Key Events: 1660 – the day of Thanksgiving in Worcester for the Restoration, 11 May 1660

'The scaffold at the Cross was encompassed with green, white, and purple colours, the two first are his own colours, being prince, the third as King.

Mr Ashby, the Mayor, a mercer and all Aldermen in scarlet, the Sheriff of the City, the 24 and 48 in their Liveries, each Trade and freemen marching with their colours.

First went 100 trained city band men after their Capt Alderman Vernon, then came the Sheriff Thomas Coventry, Esq., the Lord Coventry's eldest son, Servants, then the two Army Companies, then the several livery companies with their showmen or banners, then the City officers, then the maces and sword bearer, then the Mayor with Mr High Sheriff and some gents., then all the 24 and 48, then part of a troop of Horse of the Army.

The Mayor, mounting the scaffold with the gents. and Aldermen, Mr Joseph Astley reading softly by degrees the Proclamation of Charles the Second to be King of England, Scotland, France, Ireland. The Mayor himself spoke it aloud to all the people which then all with a shout said, "God save the King." Then all guns went off, swords drawn and flourishing over their heads, drums beating, and trumpets blowing, loud music playing before the Mayor and Company to every scaffold, which was done in the same manner throughout, and all finished the Mayor and City gave wine and biscuits in the Chamber liberally. Bonfires made at night throughout the City, and the King's good health with store of wine was drunk freely, never such a concourse of people seen upon so short a notice with high rejoicings and acclamations for the prosperity of the King, God guard him from his enemies as he ever hath done most miraculously and send him a prosperous peaceable reign and long healthful life for the happiness of his subjects who is their delight'.[8]

celebrate the Restoration, on 14 September 1660 the Foot of the county militia were mustered and processed into the Cathedral. A second muster for the Horse followed on 18 September.[10] But not everyone in the city was pleased with the outcome of events. In January 1661, after Venner's rising in London, the Horse and Foot of the Worcestershire militia were called upon to guard the bridge at Worcester against any disturbance.[11] They were again put on guard across the city for the Coronation on 23 April 1661 against the possibility of further rising by Fifth Monarchists. In the event, the worst that they had to deal with was some 'fly-posting' by a disgruntled Presbyterian who nailed up the following rhyme around the city:

This day it is said the King shall swear once more,

Just contrary to what he swore before,

Great God, O can they potent eyes behold

This height of sin and can thy vengeance holds?
Nip thou the Bud before the Bloom begins,
And save the Sovereign from presumptuous sins.
Let him remember Lord; in mercy grand
That solemnly he swore the Covenant.[12]

A reward of £20 was offered for the identification of the author who proved justified in his cynicism. On 1 June Charles II ordered the Covenant that he had sworn to uphold in return for receiving Scottish support in the Third Civil War to be burnt in every town in England!

Parliament now gave up any claim to control the militia. A new county muster-master was appointed in January 1661, Major Thomas Muckley (Muclow) from Arley Kings. He was described as a gentleman of the county and 'an old soldier' who had served in the King's Army since 1642 when a member of the Lifeguard of Foot. Muckley had been captured at Marston Moor and then served at Naseby as a captain in Colonel Anthony Eyre's Horse. His Provost Marshall was a Captain Pitt, possibly that Richard Pitt who had led one of the original companies of Worcester Trained Bands in 1642. A Richard Pitt served in Lord Goring's Horse and was present in Worcester in 1660 and so may well have been the same man. Muckley was paid £60 p. a and Pitt £20 p. a. Muckley was ordered in July to make good the magazines at Worcester, Bromsgrove, Evesham and elsewhere in the county, to attend musters and to certify the readiness of the militia.[13] Muckley took his duties seriously. In Worcester, £2 2s 0d was spent in 1661 in initially recruiting 42 trained soldiers and over £2 at each of their first two musters up to November 1660 (possibly part of the ceremonial parades, see below). They mustered again in December for two days (at a cost of £4 12s 0d). Meanwhile, they had mended one of their drums and made another (at a cost of 4s) and been supplied with 4lb of lead musket balls (at a cost of 1s 6d).

The militia continued its ceremonial duties and the old order was finally restored with the re-introduction of the clergy company of Trained Bands. On 12 September 1661, the Bishop of Worcester was escorted into the city by the Lord Lieutenant (Lord Windsor), the County Horse and city and clergy companies of the Trained Bands.[14] The clergy Trained Bands then regularly paraded at the Cathedral for important ceremonies throughout 1662. The tumultuous days of the Civil War were finally over.

The Civil Wars had seen the traditional role of the amateur Trained Bands supplanted by a professional standing army. The Restoration Parliament wished to dispense with the latter completely, although the King manoeuvred to keep a small standing army in the form of Foot and Horse Guards. Thus responsibility for defence was once again handed back to part-time county militias under local control – although the Militia Act of 1662 made it clear that allegiance was firmly owed to the Crown not to Parliament. Now by force of statute it declared that 'sole supreme power, government, command, and disposition of the militia ... is, and by the laws of England ever was, the undoubted right of his Majesty' and that 'both or either of the Houses of Parliament cannot nor ought to pretend to the same'.[15] This authority was exercised through the Lords Lieutenant who appointed the officers from the local gentry. The Lords Lieutenants were ordered to 'be very vigilant over those of the republican party, there being too much reason to believe that there is a design among men of desperate fortune to make some sudden insurrection'.[16] The local establishment was back in control.

Appendix 1

A muster of the Trained Bands was held at Worcester in 1641. One document lists 136 soldiers drawn from south-west Worcestershire (82 musket and 54 pike). A second return (in the same ink, style and handwriting) lists the company of Captain John Clent from North Worcestershire.[1] Clent was a captain of the new volunteer regiment in 1642, training in the Bewdley area and it would appear that this was the successor to the company of Trained Bands from 1640, then led by Captain Boys.

The documents detail the soldiers supplied per township (parish) and lists those who were responsible for providing armour and weapons which consisted of either corslett (armour) and pike, or a musket. The cost of the equipment was approximately 4s 10d per pike, 10s per pikeman's back and breast plate with 5s for tassets, together with 4s 6d per helmet and 10s per musket.[2] The costs are frequently shared. In only a few cases do we have details of the occupation of those supplying the soldiers, including widows, farmers and gentlemen. In only a few cases do the serving soldiers appear to be supplying themselves (as they were supposed to do). This may be an indication of the falling status of the Trained Band soldier or a concern to ensure that the arms were considered as communal property.

Extract from the Muster Roll of 1641, showing part of the company of Captain John Clent.

(Worcestershire Record Office)

Abbreviations

c or cors = corslett = armour
p = pike
m or musk = musket
f or fur = furnished
The names of the townships have been modernised.

Township	Souldiers	Men charged with armour	Armour
White Ladies Aston	Thomas Bradford	Edmund Giles	
		******** Soley	One corslett
		John Lett	and pike
		James Bateman	furnished
		Thomas Bradford	
	Thomas Kings	George Symonds, gent	one musket f.
Broadwas	William Fir* ard	Mr Cratford	1 musk f.
	Thomas Fir* ard	Richard Marshall alias Willard	1 musk f.
	William Branfield	Thomas Chumbleyn gent	
		William Nores	1 musk f.
		John Pitt	
		Humfrey Fissher	
Wick Episcopi	Anthony Sm*all	Gyles Blunt gent	1 cors. p. fur
	Richard Hawkins	Thomas Gyles for Wick farmer	1 cors p. fur
	Thomas Saunders	Anthony Barnes gent	1 musk fur
	Edward Wiggfold	Henry Best	
		Thomas Farmer	1 cors p. fur
		John Unwyn	
	Thomas Callowhill	Widdow Wiggfold	1 cors p. fur
		Henry Best	
Birtsmorrton and Staunton	John Steward	William Cale	
		Thomas Tomkins for Mr Thackwell's Land	1 cors p. fur
		Edward Thackwell	
		Robert Jakeman	
	Thomas ?Duttfield	Thomas Cowper	1 musk fur
		Thomas White	
	Michell Bosley	George Pirton	
		Christopher Borne	
		Thomas Baldwin	1 musk fur
		Richard Cooke	
		John Ward	
	Thomas Jakeman	Thomas Bowle	
		Widdow mann	
		Mathew Drake	1 musk fur
		Thomas Jakeman	
	William Bridges	The townshipps	1 musk fur
Berrow and Leyshend	Edmund Teynton	Widdow Teynton	1 c. lp. fur
		John Teynton, John Berrow	
	John Clarke	Edmund Tomley	1 m. f.
		William Burward	

	John Morley	William Morley	
		Thomas B* oule	} 1 m f
	William South	Anne Cox widdow	
		Thomas Clarke tenant to the	} 1 c. 1p. f
		heirs of John Cox	
Bushley. Poole and Queenshill	Thomas ?Bebbe	John Cl** gent	
		William Tirrett	} 1 c. 1p. f
		Edward Biddle	
	Philippe Lane	Margaret Berrow	
		Edward Biddle	} 1m. f.
		George Jeffes	
	Thomas Garland	Mr Ludford	
		Rowland Bradstocke	} 1c. 1p. F.
		Philipp Batchler	
	Joseph Hambury	Richard Dowdswell	
		Anthony Stratford	} 1 c 1p f
	William Ocheridge	Thomas Jones	
		Richard Towne	} 1m. f.
		& Ann Hay**ten	
	William Biddle	Thomas Marks gent	
		John Biddle &	} 1 c 1p f
		Elizabeth Harard	
	Anthony Hall	The Townshippe	1m. f.
Claynes	Richard Y*ternoll	Mrs Jones Mr Deakes,	
		Richard Buttler	} 1 c. 1p. F.
		Walter Gittoes	
	Anthony Mawlton	Mr Cratford	
		Anthony Attwood	} 1c. 1p. f.
		Jervase Bearley	
		Thomas Mawlton	
	John Twittys	William Throgmore	
		Mrs Grace Attwood	} 1 c. 1p. f.
	John Williams	John Smyth gent	
		Mr Robert Pitt	} 1c. 1p. f
		Jasper Wigges	
		William Amphlett	
	Thomas Colles	Gilbert Norton	
		Anne Coxe	} 1 c 1p f
		Widdow Bennett and	
		Rowland Gardner	
	Jerram Soley	John Attwood sen. gent,	} 1 m f
		Mr Walter Gittoes	
	Anthony Brodhurste	William Norton	} 1 m f
		Widdow Baker	
	John Norton	The townshippe with Hinlippe	} 1 m f.
		& Martin Hussingtree	
Churchill and Bredicot	Robert Paroyt	William King	
		Marten Gibbons	} 1m. f
		John Knight	
		Widdow Soley	

Chatisley	Henry Little	Archer Helmes gent	1 c. 1p f.
	Thomas Hyes	Henry Browne gent	1m. f.
	John Tirrett	Richard Tirrett	1c 1p f
Part of Crowle	John Gettus	Jane Daniell, widow,	1m. f
	Richard Tollye	John Kings	1m. f.
Eldresfield	William Pitt	Th Hallsey & Jerram Prior for Sir John Franklin's land	1c. 1p. f
	Edmund Chattfield	Th Beale David Griffin & ?Paper Saving equally	1c 1p f
	Thomas Tovey	William Holmes John Jones Th Halford	1m. f.
	Walter Underhill	Mr Bray	1m. f.
	Thomas Clark	Walter Underhill Widow Weaver William Cooke Th Hayward	1c. 1p. f.
	William Carter	William Blunt & Widdow Symonds	1m. f.
Longdon	Thomas Clarke	William Parsons Widdow Gilbert & Richard Buckle	1c. 1p. f
	John Michell	John Wrenford & Guy Whittington	1c 1p. f
	Richard Grindle	Thomas Cook gent	1m. f.
	Michell Hobbs	The Townshippe with Chatisley	1m. f.
Hallow & Grimley	William Wormington	Townshipp of Grimley	1m. f
	John Bolt	Widow Hall & Henry Hill	1c. 1p. f
	William Turner	Samuel Powell Thomas Else William Nott Thomas Evett	1c. p. f.
	John Else	Skidmore Pitt gent Widdow Brewer & William Nott of Greenstreet	1m. f.
	Thomas Bromfield	Mr Chetleford & Henry Symes	1 m. f.
	Richard Wiggfold	Townshipps of Hallow & Grimley	1m. f.
Hanley Castle	Francis Richmond	Thomas Grainger William Mason Richard Cowrle Mr Thomas Young	1c. p. f
	George Chandler	Edmund Leachmere gent	1m. f.
	Charles Dyer	John Cholmley gent	1m. f.
	John Mattys	Edmund Barnes Th . Suffield Francis Richmond	1m. f.
	Thomas Barnes	William Langston gent	1m. f.
	Richard ?Pace	The Townshipp	1m. f.

Kemsey cum membris	William Rea	Edmund Kings Thomas Birt Edmund Rea	1m f
	John Lircock jun	Richard Hardman William Hall John Nash	1c p f
	Thomas Knight	Thomas Gourrle William Porter Widdow Bullock Widdow ?Prusam William Wheeler Rowland Hurdman	1c p f
	Richard Moyses	Richard Hall Robert Sollers Richard Fowler	1m f.
	William Knight	Thomas Hurdman Richard Winslowe Christopher Blande Thomas Thornton	1m. f.
	Daniell Gyles	Townshipps of Stoulton & Norton which **** Nashe	1m f.
	Thomas Hunt	William Smyth William Browne Thomas Whoper Thomas Lock	1m f.
	Henry Cripton	Richard Baker Thomas Andrews Edmund Surman William Chester	1m. f.
Castlemorton	John Band	Mr Bright Paull Smyth Mr Anslowe	1 m f
	? Pack Norne	Gyles Nanfan gent Thomas Nanfan William Hill Hugh Parsons	1c p f
	Thomas Wrenford	Thomas Wrenford gent. Richard Grindle Samuell Millard	1m. f.
	William Lawrans	Thomas Hussard William Shaw	1 m f.
	John Bray	Townshipp	1m. f.
Malverne Magna Madresfield & Newland	Thomas Parr	John Beachamp John Nerd	1c p f
	Philipp Greene	Anthony Barnes William Knight Rowland Jefford Richard Webb	1c p f
	William Holland	Richard Stockall John Neede Nicholas Phelps John Manley	1c p f

	William Stockall	Widdow Hill	
		Marklun Webb	ɪm f
		Nicholas Gogh	
	Richard Baxter	Nicholas Langston	
		Francis Hallard	ɪm. f.
		Elizabeth Neede	
	Robert Brooke	Edmund Snellson	
		Francis Reade	ɪ m f
		Richard Leeth	
	Thomas Dipper	Richard Reade	
		John Warner	ɪ m. f.
	William Bennett	Townshipp	ɪ m f.
Light & Mathen	John Black	Richard Browne	
		John Dunn	
		Henry Clarke	ɪc p f
		Elizabeth Morston, widdow	
	Thomas Chadborne	Henry Mintridge gent	
		Mar (?ten) Hallwide	ɪc p f
		Richard Cooke	
	Richard ?Dovys	George Worvield	
		Francis Browning	ɪc p f
		Richard Collick	
	Henry Nash	John Greene	
		Richard Ovett	
		Sibbell Greene, widow	ɪm. f
		Richard Pitt	
	John Chadborne	Thomas Hollyman	
		Roger Browne	ɪm f.
		Widdow Elvins	
	Sellam Godfrey	Edmund Whittington gent	ɪc p f
	Edward Willman	Widdow Dobe	
		William Hall	ɪm. f.
		Thomas ?Colines	
	Thomas Ostman	Townshipp	ɪm. f.
Spetchley	John James	Townshipp	ɪm. f.
Powick	Thomas Nicholas	John Whitton gent	
		Daniell Tyns	
		Richard Collick	ɪc ɪp f
		Widdow Clent	
	Thomas Holding	John Brooke	
		Widdow Holding	ɪc p f
		Widdow Gallimore	
	William Staunton	John Blueton gent	
		Th Elidys	
		William Gondreton	ɪ c p f
		William Staunton	
	John James	Eliazer Jackson Clarke	
		John Moore	ɪ m. f.
		John Seaverne	
	John Crispe	Widdow Showler	
		Richard Lecy	ɪ m.f.
		George Worvield	

	Richard Beard	Nicholas Blixter	}	1 m. f.
		Richard Pennell		
	Thomas Gates	Townshipp		1 m.f.
Redmarley D'abitot	John Riley	Henry Spiller, gent.	}	1 m. f.
		John Riley		
		William Gunnell		
		Thomas Pirton		
	John George	Charles Harbert	}	1 cp f.
		Thomas Cooke		
	John Baston	Thomas Dabitott, gent.		1 m. f.
	William Woadley	Edmund Bradford	}	1 cp f.
		Widdow Halford		
		John Jakeman		
		William Baldwyn		
		William Hall		
	William Baldwyn	John Cowper, gent.	}	1 m. f.
		Richard Baston		
		William Beale		
		Widdow Goode		
		Elienor Jones, widdow		
		Widdow Wheeler		
	Thomas Pirton	William Pestell	}	1 cp f.
		Thomas Duggmore		
		Thomas Showlton		
		William Hall		
		Feorice Cooper		
	Mark Goode	Townshipp		1 m.f.
Severn Stoke	Richard Pace	Mr Bawton	}	1 c p f
		Richard Sallway		
	John Hunt	Edmund Gyles	}	1 c p f
		William Fowler		
		Mr Wheeler		
		Roger Turlyon		
		Thomas Twinbarrow		
	Ralph Cristian	William Beast		1 m f
	Richard Lygorne	William Mayle	}	1 m f
		RichardHunt		
		Thomas Allyn		
		Robt Buttler		
		Luke Squier		
		John Durston		
	Richard Tufton	Richard Hiccop sen.	}	1 m f
		Widdow Walker		
		John Payne		
		William Riccards		
	Richard Hiccop	The Townshipp		1 m f
St Michael in Bedwardine	John Ellis	Mrs Anne Smyth widdow	}	1 m f
St John in Bedwardine	Richard Frewen	Mr White of Temple, London	}	1 c p
		? *** Gower		
	Edward Staunton	Thomas Taylor		1 c p

Pendock	John Jakeman	Thomas Beale sen. Thomas Beale jun. John Greenway John Barnard	1 c p
	John Mayer	John Jakeman John Tomkins Henry Barnard Thomas Cooke	1 c p
Upton Sup. Sabrin	Allen Grafton	Edmund Lygon gent James Hill	1 c p
	Richard Gwattkins	William Woodward gent Robert Richards John Jefferies Griffith Edwards Ed. Pettford Thomas Dighton	1 m f
	Thomas Jossop	Christopher Winbury Thomas Hancox Richard Dunn John Cotterell Anthony Surman Thom Celley	1 m f
	James Lingham	James Hill Thomas Boend James Lingham	1 m f
	John Best	John Hasell John Best Iddow Chaundler Daniell Rawlinson Michael Hunt	1 c p
	Th Woodward	William Hackett John Vane Th Finch Michaell Dilling	1 m f
Wichenford	John Macam	The Townshipp	1 c p
Tibberton	William Washborne	Richard Bough gent	1 m f
	Th Whooper sen	Roger Hemings Thomas Hooper John Palmer William Horne And the rest of the inhabitants	1 m f
Welland	John Salter	John Archer gent Widdow Pratt Richard Pewtris	1 c p
	William Allen	The township with the Berrow	1 m f

Souldiers 136
Corsletts 54
Musqttes 82

Captain Clent's company

Township	Soldiers	Men charged with armour	Armour
Abberley	Anthony Bettes	Anthony Bettes William Whooper Francis Wall	1 c p
	Thomas Brasier	James Mason Margaret Glassand, widdow John Brasier William Steadman	1 c p
	Humfrey Winwood	John Spilbury John Nott Richard Wood Edmund Nott De Ley ?Hill	1 c p
	John Bynt	Francis Webb Henry James Humfrey Wall	1 c p
	Richard Smthes	Richard Nott Robert Hay sen. Walter James Thomas Burraston	1 c p
	Martyn Hay	Robert Vincent Anne Sowthall Daniell Hay	1 m f
	Richard Inett	Thomas Berry John Fareley	1 m f
	Henry Hay	Thomas Spilbury William Handley William Hill of Lynedon John Gibson	1 m f
	Thomas Sutton	Richard Yarrington William Lewes Walter Comber	1 m f
	Humfrey Bryan	Henry Peniell	
	Richard Burraston	Thomas Powell gent Widdow Burraston Widdow Brasier Anthony Calder John Hill	1 c p
	William Symonds	The Townshipp	1 corslett 1 musq
Battenhall Whittington Sidbury	Richard Winterfield	The township with the rest of the inhabitants	1 c p
Belbroughton	John Taylor	Henry Smyth Thomas Gopp William Wheeler	1 c p
	Thomas Gopp	Jervase Hortle	1 m f
	William Cole	Gilbert Cole Mathew Walford	1 m f
	John Prine	The Townshipp	1 m f

Bewdley	Richard Walker	Thomas Waynwright Peter Branche John Ward	1 c p
	Henry Hubbard	Edmund Bulson William Hopkins gent	1 c p
	Henry Radford	William Clare John Wilkes John Tyler John Ballard	1 c p
	George Barrett	Raphaell Smyth Edward Walker Fen. Gilding	1 c p
	Humfrey Wattmore	William Millton James Nash Thomas Webb	1 c p
	William Cropp	John Burton Widdow ?Skey William Hill William Tyther William Jakeman	1 c p
	Nathaniell Tandy	John Clareson Mrs Bromwich Thomas Clare	1 m f
	John Tiler or John Willys	Walter Hill Robert Viccarede William Spilbury	1 m f
	William Spilbury	Walter Pooler John Soley John Wakerman	1 m f
	Thomas Farley	Silvanus Sares John Suford John Hayles Symon Wood	1 m f
	John Grove	Henry Banks Thomas Corbett John Clarke jun. William Barlow (or Barton) John Given John Millton	1 m f
Churchill and Kingford	Thomas Willets	Thomas Dickens Thomas Willets Thomas Bayliss Roger Bennett	1 m f
Clifton cum membris	John Davies	Roger Rufford Bennett Hill	1 c p
	John Ropier	William Nott John Weston	1 m f
	William Brotherton	Richard Hanley John Aingell	1 m f
	John Hill / Henry Burraston	Phillipp Jones Walter Perkins Richard Davies John Turner	1 m f

	John Mason	William Stallard	} 1 m f
	Walter Hinksman	John Ingram	
	Simon Hanley	} The Townshipp	1 c
	Richard Henley		1 m f
Chadsley	Richard Osborne	John Barber	
Pedmore		Gilbert Penn	
Rushocke		William Scott	} 1 c p
		John Cowper	
	William Bache	Richard Smyth	
		Widdow Smyth	
		Francis Bennett	} 1 c p
		John Butten	
	John Bacon	William Mowle	
		Humfrey Norris	
		Daniell Laight	} 1 c p
		Alice Nash widow	
	Anthony Yates	Edward Male	
		Edward Millard	
		John Patchett sen. and jun.	} 1 c p
		Thomas Tirer	
	Thomas Bache	William Hunt	
		John Scott	
		John Penn of Drayton	} 1 m f
		John Penn of Cackbold	
	John Taylor	Thomas Taylor	} 1 m f
		John Bache	
	William Rayboll	Thomas Dawkes	
		John Cooke	} 1 m f
		John Parker	
	Thomas Paynton	Sylvester Taylor	} 1 m f
		John Newey	
	Thomas Skelding	The townshipp	1 m f
Doverdale	Hugh Hale	Mrs Brace widdow	1 c p f
Elmley Lovett	John Juce	Mr John Tyrer one ha ? ft	
		John Lyndon	
		Francis Webbley	} 1 m f
		John Doolittle	
	Thomas Insole	Thomas Cannell	
		John Best jun	
		Charles Harwood	} 1 c p
		John Griggsonne	
	Charles Bacon	Thomas Mowle	
		Edward Royall	} 1 c p
		Edmund Smyth	
	John Best	The Townshipp	1 m f
Eastham	Edmund Newman	Richard Nichols	} 1 c p
cum membris		William Nichols gent	
	William Wyar	Thomas Hide	
		Elizabeth Downe, widow	
		Richard Walker of Eastham	} 1 c p
		Richard Sheffield of Kyer Wye	

	Edward Soley	Anne Perkes, widdow	
		Edmund Hill	1 m f
		John Fidoe	
	Richard Hunte	John Archer	
		John Wynnall	1 c p
		William Starky	
		Richard Ames	
	William Spilbury	William Nott	
		Robert Fidoe	1 m f
		Rowland Soley	
	Richard Lewes	Anthony Holder	
		Richard Castle	1 m f
		Thomas Freeman	
		Robert Fidoe	
	John Sheffield	The Townshipps	2 m f
Holt and Witley	John Wicken	Thomas Thorley gent	
		Richard Kinnersley Esq.	1 c p f
		Walter Colles	
	Hugh Doolittle	The Townshipp	1 m f
Hartlebury	Symon Uffmore	Urban Eyre	
		Walter Dunn	1 c p f
		John Lircock	
	William Tagg	John Clent of the moore	
		Richard Mowle	1 m f
		William Showler	
		Thomas Michell	
	John Fidkin	John Clomsone	
		Robert Ballard	1 m f
		John Wall	
	John Walker	Elzabeth Manning, widow	
		Thomas Maning of Torton	
		John Tinker	1 m f
		James Packington	
		William Hill	
	Walter Chamb'leyne	The Townshipp	1 m f
Haggley	John Sparrey	William Grove	1 c p
		John Taylor of Sturbridge	
	William Toy	John Dancer	1 c p
		John Fesson	
	Richard White	Thomas Wannerton	1 m f
		William Penn	
	William Penn	The Townshipp	1 m f
Kidderminster Burrough And Forren	Thomas Beste	John Dawkes gent	
		Thomas Colles	1 c p
		Gilbert Lawnder	
		Richard Hunt	
	George Langmore	John Radford	1 c p
		Ellys Arch	
	Fewcris Penn	William Seine	
		John Payton	1 m f
		Thomas Berrye	

	Thomas Lewes	Humfrey Grove	}	ɪ m f
		John Corbin		
	Thomas Hornblower	Humfrey Burlton		ɪ m f
	John Dawkes	Thomas Ballange	}	ɪ m f
		Edward Baynam		
		Abraham Plimley		
	Humfrey Doolittle	Edward Richards	}	ɪ c p
		William Browne		
		Walter Uffmore		
		John Freeston		
	John Walker	Robert Southall	}	ɪ m f
		William Garmson		
		John Longmore		
	John Foxall	John Browne	}	ɪ m f
		Anthony Bowyer		
		Bettridg Dellicoat widow		
	Symon Potter	John Persall	}	ɪ m f
		Nicholas his sonne		
	John Millard	The Townshipp		ɪ m f
Lyndridge cum membris	John Mills	Roger Poston	}	ɪ c p
		William Nashe		
		John Hall		
		Thomas Thyler		
		Gilbert Harper		
	William Walker	John Mann	}	ɪ c p
		Thomas Taylor		
		John Berrye		
	John Walker	Edward Pennell Esq	}	ɪ c p
		Thomas Walker		
	Nicholas Comber	Anne Munn widow	}	ɪ c p
		George Tyler		
		William Greene		
	Richard Aingell	Marie Bromidge widow of Bewdley	}	ɪ m f
		James Richards		
		William Mannox		
		Walter Worrall		
	Edward Millard	Anthony Foster	}	ɪ c p
		John Rock jun		
	George Taylor	John Soley	}	ɪ c p
		Richard Hunte		
		Symon Stockall		
	Thomas Burye	Roger Pennell	}	ɪ m f
		John Myles		
	Thomas Smyth	Mrs Lowe	}	ɪ m f
		Roger Pennell		
	Rowland Fidoe	John Bishop gent	}	ɪ c p
		John Cooke		
		Widdow Mannox		
	Humfrey Grundall	The Townshipp		ɪ m f
Mamble cum membris	William Farley	John Fidoe	}	ɪ c p
		William Smyth		
		Richard Ellys		
		Edmund Mawlten		

	Edward Osland	Edward Hall Elise Sheapheard, widdow Robert Terrie Thomas Bishopp	} 1 c p
	Thomas Hill	Mr Finch as gardian to Robert Acton of ?Steldon	} 1 m f
	William Lirrigoe	Sammuel Richards William Rowley	} 1 m f
	Roger Cowper	John Berrye sen. Henry Pennell John Berrye jun.	} 1 m f
	Mathias Terrye	Thomas Burraston Henry Newman Edward Osland	} 1 m f
	William Robbins	John Lyrrigoe Thomas guett [?Inett] Robert Tolley Richard Hubball	} 1 m f
	John Nott	Richard Wyer Charles Hunte William Mannoxe George Huncksman	} 1 m f
	James Hill John Callow	} The Townshipp	2 m f
Martin Hussingtree	Francis Yarnall	Sir Edward Wheeler Mr Haslecock	} 1 c p
Martley cum memeris	Thomas Nott	Daniel Dobbins gent	1 c p
	William Doughtie	Audrye Jones, widdow John Browning	} 1 c p
	William Lewis	Walter ?Welsh, Widdow ?Arden Widdow ?Horner	} 1 c p
	Richard Marshall alias Myllard	John Alderne Edmund Alderne	} 1 m f
	Thomas Tillam	Thomas Tillam Thomas Cave	} 1 m f
	John Nott	John Buttler John Nott John Fidoe	} 1 m f
	Robert Chappell	Edmund Hinksman James Nash	} 1 m f
	Thomas Wall of Hillanton	Richard Ingram John Arden	} 1 m f
	Humfrey Justice	William Yarrington	1 m f
	John Chamberleyne William Gryg	} The towne of Oyer	2 m f
Ombersley	Richard Portman	Mr Kettlesleye Richard Saunders of Mayhouse James Randle	} 1 c p
	Thomas Baker	John Burton James Younge	} 1 m f

	Thomas Palmer	Thomas Bourne	
		Richard Bourne	} 1 m f
		Henry Jones	
	Thomas Saunders	Thomas Tollye	} 1 m f
		John Wall	
	Roger Walker	John Havord	} 1 m f
		John Insoll	
	John Hayford	Thomas Saunders	
		Richard Winnall	} 1 m f
		Richard Heminge	
	Walter Moyle	Richard Okeley	
		William Saunders	} 1 m f
		William Randle	
	John Gay	Robert Tomes	
		Richard Randle	} 1 m f
		John Portman	
	John Tomes	Thomas Bourlton	} 1 m f
		? Young	
	Richard Mann	} The township with Oldbarow	2 m f
	John Insall		
Oddingley	Richard Yarnoll	The townshipp	1 m f
Old Swinford and Sturbridge	Thomas Rock	John Taylor	
		John Baker	} 1 c p
		Jesper Newbrooke	
	Ambrose Underhill	Nicholas Addenbrooke	
		George Wince	} 1 c p
		Nicholas Sparrey	
	Richard Cox	The Townshipp	1 m f
Suckley cum membris	Robert Merchant	Edward Moore gent	
		The tenant(s) of Mrs Hall and	
		Mr Prettyman or some of them	} 1 c p
		Together with the Widdow	
		Palmer	
	Richard Heminge	Symon Bath	
		William Webley	} 1 c p
		Richard Sandy(s)	
	John Spooner	John Hall	
		Francis Gornay	} 1 c p
		and Insoll's farme	
	William Webley	Lancelott Hall	} 1 m f
		Widdow Smyth	
	Christopher Guillam	Widdow Hall	
		Roger Heming	} 1 m f
		George Palmer	
	Richard Best	Henry Ovett	
		Anthony Dallye	} 1 m f
		Widdow Richard(s)	
	Roger Palmer	Hugh Hide	
		George Hales	} 1 m f
		Raphaell Haywood	
	John Hulland	Paul Rumney gent	1 m f

	William Lynton	Widdow Oliver	
		Symon Bache	1 m f
		William Palmer	
		John Smyth	
	William Johnson	The Townshippe	1 m f
Shrawley cum membris	John Corfield	Thomas Wicken	
		Thomas Hanburye	1 c p
		Walter Portman	
		William Joanes	
	John Streck	Thomas Hill	
		John Hill	1 m f
		Robert Stafford	
	Thomas Seaverne alias Sauken	Brian Seaverne	
		John Marten	1 m f
		Thomas Martyn	
	Robert Seaverne	John Gyles	1 m f
		Anthony Yarrington	
	Robert Chamb'leyne	Robert Brooke gent	1 m f
		Walter Stone	
	John Hill	Lancelott Arden	
		John Yarnton	1 m f
		Edward Cooper	
	Robert Viccaridge	The Townes of Oyer	1 c p
	John Stone		
	Brian Seaverne		2 m f
Stone and Over Mitton	Edward Fillett jun.	Richard Oldnall	
		John Hill	1 c p
		William Clymer	
		William Corfield	
	John Hill	Humfrey Hill	1 m f
		John Oldnall	
	John Thatcher	William Hunte gent	
		Thomas Huck	1 m f
		Edward Prine alias Grove	
	Hugh Prettye	The Townshipp with Pedmore And Kingford	1 m f
Tenbury cum membris	John Holland	Thomas Gittoes	
		Richard Marston	1 c p
		John Cowndley	
		William Millichepp	
	Richard Lane	Edward Barkeronely	
		Richard Lane	1 c p
		John Phillpott	
		James Winton	
	John Ward	Katherine Sheapheard widow	
	Edmund Gittoes	Thomas Ambler	
		James Jones	1 m f
		Thomas Lieth	
	Richard Jones	Nicholas Eaton	
		Thomas Finson	1 m f
		Roger Acton gent	
		Thomas Holt	

	William Holt	John Corbett	}
		Hugh Thomas	
		Thomas Dallahey	1 m f
		Thomas Bray	
	Nicholas Grubb	Richard Porter	
		Thomas Porter	
		Thomas Gittoes	1 m f
		John Amys	
		William Barnaby	
	John Holland of	Richard Downe	1 m f
	Kyer Wood	Roger Aingell	
	Humfrey Lane of	James Tombes	
	Sutton	Francis Lane	1 m f
		Richard Lane of Kyer Wood	
	George Bebb	John Britton	
		John Gumsey	1 m f
		John Britton	
	Richard Marsh	Richard Smyth	
		Widdow Hackett	1 m f
		Roger Gittoes	
	John Ferrington	The towne of Oyre	2 m f
Warndon	Humfrey Solley	John Maries	1 m f
	John Brooke	Widdow Boyce	
		William Staunton	
		Roger Sheriff	1 c p
		Thomas Greene	
Warley	Richard Thorn	William Feldon	
		William Westwood	1 c p
		Thomas Partridg	
Wolverley	John Wood jun.	John Holbarrow	
		John Pitt	1 c p
		John Prettye	
	John Wood sen.	John Baskervield	
		Thomas Hollyman	1 c p
		Edward Thomas	
	William Talbott	Thomas Goodyer	
		John Lyddle	1 c p
		Humfrey Longmore	
	Henry Whitefoot	Symon Juckes	1 m f
		Henry Browne	
	John Raston	William Willetts	
		William Warren	1 m f
		Edward Newnham	
	Anthony Hunt	The Townshipp	1 m f

Souldiers 177
Corsletts 63
Musqtts 114

Appendix 2

Gentry assessed for Horse 1642

■ = Commissioner of Array, 1642
▲ = known Royalist Army officer

	14 August	Revised List, late August
Thomas Coventry ■	10	
Thomas Littleton	6	2
Sir John Packington ■ ▲	6	2
Edward Sebright ■	6	1
Sir Rowland Berkeley ■ ▲	4	1
Samuel Sandys ■ ▲	4	1
John Washbourne	2	1
John Nanfan ■	2	1
Sir William Russell ■ ▲	6	
Thomas Rouse	2	
Mathew Carne	3	
Sir Henry Herbert ■	4	1
Joseph Walsh ■ ▲	2	1
John Keyte, junior	4	
Thomas Savage ■ ▲	4	1
Martin Sandys ▲	2	
Edward Vernon ■	1	1
Henry Townshend ■	1	1
Edward Savage	2	
Edward Broad	1	1
Thomas Child	4	
Robert Steyner	1	
Edward Rouse	1	
William Langston	1	
Henry Norwood ▲	1	
William Mucklow	1	
Richard Foley	1	
Henry Ingram ■ ▲	1	1
William Walsh ▲	1	
George Cole	1	
James Littleton	1	
Thomas Chetle	1	1
John Dickins	1	

	14 August	Revised List, late August
John Atwood	1	
Sir John Rouse ■	1	1
Edward Bushell	1	
Francis Sheldon	1	
Francis Finch ■	1	1
Edmund Fortescue	1	
Roger Cook	1	
Sir Ralph Clare ■		1
Sir Thomas Nott		1
Thomas Lucy		1
Henry Bromley		1
Edward Pitt ■		1
William Curteen		2
Humphrey Salloway		1
William Child ■		1
Sergeant Wyld		1
Sherrington Talbot ■		1
John Savage		1
Mrs Abigail Packington		1
John Winford		1
Walter Blunt		1
Mr Gower, Mr Cook, Dr Longdon		1
Sir Michael Hutchinson		1
Thomas Greaves		1
William Jeffreys		1
Mrs Anne Robins		1
Thomas Hornihold		1
Thomas Good		1
Edward Dingley		1
Thomas Jeffreys		1
I. Dickins, W. Langston		1
William Stephens		1
John Dormer		1
George Wintour		1
Samuel Knightley		1
Robert Gower		1
Mrs Anne Fleet		1
Daniel Dobyns		1
Roger Lowe		1
George and John Lench		1
Thomas Barnsley and Edward East		1
William Brown and M. Parsons		1
Richard Foley		1
Mr [Thomas] Russell of Malvern		1
Francis Haselwood		1
Philip Brace ■		*
Mr Char		*
T. Jolly and Patchet		*
Francis Hannford		
Samuel Atwood and Mrs Lydiat		1
Mrs Cooke of Staunton		1

	14 August	Revised List, late August
J. Freeman of Bushley and		
Thomas Bushell		1
John Bourne		1
Rowland Bartlett		1
Thomas Acton of Bockleton		1
Edmund Turvey		1
Thomas Gower, his son and		
Thomas Chase		1
Robert Gower		1
Edward Barrett of Wick		1
Number of Horse	95	68/71

Appendix 3

Royalist gentry 1646

■ = Commissioner of Array, 1642
▲ = known Royalist Army officer

Gentry captured in 1646 at siege of Worcester

Grafton	Earl of Shrewsbury
Grafton	Lord Talbot (his son)
Shelsey	Sir Edward Lyttleton ■
Droitwich	Sir Edward Barrett ▲
Elmley Lovett	Henry Townshend ■
Woodgreen	Edward Perrott
Sedgeberrow	Anthony Langston ▲
Beoley	Edward Sheldon
Worcester	Sir Martin Sandys ▲
Abberley	Joseph Walsh ■ ▲
Malvern	Thomas Russell
Hindlip	William Habingdon
Pedmore	Colonel Herbert Price ▲
Worcester	Bishop John Prideaux
Earl's Court	Henry Ingram ■ ▲
Strensham	Sir William Russell ■ ▲
Cotheridge	Sir Rowland Berkeley ■ ▲
Astley	Sir John Winford
Holt	Henry Bromley
Burton	Thomas Acton
Blackmore Park	Thomas Hornyold
Worcester	Robert Wylde
Crowle	John Cockes
	Major Thomas Wylde ▲
	Major John Ingram ▲
	George Acton
Abberley	William Walsh ▲
	George Walsh
Spetchley	Thomas Berkeley
Hanley	William Langston
Pershore	French
Worcester	John Lund

At Hartlebury

Hewell Grange	Lord Windsor
Ombersley	Colonel Samuel Sandys ■ ▲
	Captain William Sandys ▲
	Captain Martin Sandys ▲

Compounders in spring 1646

Hampton Lovett	Sir John Packington ■ ▲
Ribbesford	Sir Henry Herbert ■

Prisoners enforced to compound

Salwarp	Sherrington Talbot ■
Hanbury	Edward Vernon ■
Doverdale	Philip Brace ▲
Wichenford	John Washbourne
Rushock	Francis Finch ■
Hagley	Sir Thomas Lyttleton
Beoley	William Sheldon ▲
Harvington	Mrs Packington

Appendix 4

Worcestershire Regiments During the Civil Wars

These lists have been compiled primarily on the basis of Townshend and the List of Indigent Officers as published by Stuart Reid.[1] Not all references based on the Indigent Officers list may be contemporary.

NB. * indicates listed by Townshend in 1643. The home addresses are based on the place of registration at the time of the List of Indigent Officers. Contemporary reference to 'Worcester' may also include more general references to Worcestershire, and shows the considerable degree to which these regiments were locally raised.

1642
1. Worcestershire Trained Bands
As mustered on 22 August 1642.

Worcester
Captain Brace
Captain Richard Pitt
Pershore
Captain Speite
Droitwich
Captain Scudamore Pitt
Bewdley
Captain Clent

2. Samuel Sandys' Regiment of Foot (1000 men)
Raised November 1642. This regiment was part of the core of the Worcester garrison in 1643, which served with the field army during the summer and was transferred to Colonel Knotsford, Governor of Evesham, in April 1644. In July 1644 it was absorbed into Gilbert Gerrard's Regiment of Foot. Major Moore later served in the reconstituted regiment in 1646.

Major	Francis Moore (Severn Stoke)
	Lieutenant Richard Hunt
Captain	Francis Clare (Kidderminster)
	Lieutenant Walter Colles (Worcester)
Captain	— Clarke
Captain	Edward Emms
Captain	Richard Field
Captain	— Heling *
Captain	— Littleton (sic)
	Lieutenant Lewis Butts

Captain — Millington
             Lieutenant Edward Freeman (Worcester)
Captain William Sandys (reported by Symonds to be the uncle of Samuel Sandys)*
             Lieutenant John Salmon (Worcester)
Captain Frederick Windsor *
Captain Frederick Moore *

Captain Lieutenant Charles Gibbons

Other Lieutenants
George Copely
Austin Evans

Ensigns
Thomas Davis

Quartermaster
John Edwards

1643
3. Sir Martin Sandys' Regiment of Foot (Worcester Town Regiment)
The militia regiment of Worcester was largely employed on garrison duties but served in the spring campaign in Gloucestershire.

Colonel Martin Sandys
Lieutenant Colonel Edward Solley
Ensign Francis Hughes

Companies
Captain Thomas Batch
Captain — Knight
             Ensign William Oakly
Captain Richard Mascall (of Rose and Crown Inn, Foregate Street)
             Ensign Humphrey King
Captain Humphrey Tyrer

Lieutenants
Thomas Mascall
Francis Sharman
Nicholas Symonds
— Webb

Sergeants
Thomas Allen
John Baker

Drummer
Edward Addams

also
Christopher Woodward
Thomas Fownes
Thomas Walker (1644)
Thomas Hackett (1644)

4. Samuel Sandys' Regiment of Horse (600 - 700 men)

Raised 1643. Note that this is very different from the regiment combined from other units in 1644.

Lieutenant Colonel Windsor Hickman *

Troops

Major	Thomas Wild
	Cornet Thomas Hunt (Worcester)
	Quartermaster Walter Gunter (Worcester)
	Quartermaster Robert Pine (Worcester)
Captain-	
Lieutenant	John Sandys (uncle of Samuel Sandys) *
Captain	Christopher Fielding
Captain	Thomas Fisher
Captain	John Hanbury
	Quartermaster Francis Hulford (Worcester)
Captain	Anthony Langston (Sedgeberrow) *
	Quartermaster William Mopson (Worcester)
Captain	Robert Manley
	Cornet John Cartwright (Worcester)
Captain	Martin Sandys (Colonel of Worcester Militia)
	Lieutenant Robert Scargill
	Cornet Ralph Thurston
Captain	Thomas Savage * (later major)
	Cornet Edward Barret (Worcester)
	Quartermaster John Durston (Worcester)
	Quartermaster John Martin (Worcester)
Captain	Anthony Stratford (Bushley)

Other Lieutenants
Edward Doughty
Giles Rowles (Worcester)

Other Cornets
Humphrey Burton (Kidderminster)
William Batch (Worcester)

Other Quartermasters
John Canner
John Goffe
John Lunne (Worcester)
Gilbert Trowe
Francis Wainwright

5. Sandys' Regiment of Dragoons

Raised 1643 but recruiting not completed and transferred to Horse.
Captain Thomas Symonds (Claines)

6. Russell's Horse

Raised from December 1642 – April 1643. Comprised *c.*500 men. ?Transferred to Hamilton.

Troops
Sir William Russell
Sir James Hamilton

Sergeant Major Henderson
Captain John Blunt
Captain Joseph Walsh
Captain George Colte
Captain Francis Blunt
Captain Dennis

7. Combined Troops of Horse and Dragoons in the Garrison of Worcester 1642–3
(c. 620 men)
Drawn from a number of regiments, principally those of Sir James Hamilton formerly raised and funded by Russell.

Sir James Hamilton	(70 horse)	(Hamilton's Horse)
Sergeant Major Carr		
Quartermaster Walter Sergeant		
Sir William Russell's Horse	(70 horse)	
Captain John Blunt	(70 horse)	(Hamilton's Horse)
Captain Joseph Walsh	(70 horse)	(probably Hamilton's Horse)
Cornet Watkins		
Captain George Colte	(42 horse)	(probably Hamilton's Horse)
Sir William Russell's Dragoons	(70 dragoons)	
Captain Francis Blount	(100 dragoons)	
Captain Dennis	(60 dragoons)	(Hamilton's Dragoons)
Sergeant Major Henderson	(70 dragoons)	(Hamilton's Dragoons)

8. Sir William Russell's Regiment of Foot
Total c.766 men[2]
* indicates listed by Townshend for June – August 1643. The rest are based on the list of Indigent Officers 1663 and represent service up to 1646. The regiment incorporated the survivors of Hamilton's regiment. Only three of these officers were listed in the garrison regiment of 1646.

Lieutenant Colonel Davies *		
Captain Lieutenant Harris *	(155 men)	
Captain Spencer *	(77 men)	
Captain Robert Middlemore *	(93 men)	(Mosely)
Lieutenant Richard Williams (Worcester)		
Captain Chasnie *	(40 men)	
Captain Robert Hughes*	(58 men)	(serving also in 1646)
Lieutenant Richard Normcroft		
Captain Thomas Sheldon *	(74 men)	(Worcester)
Captain Sparry *	(43 men)	
Captain Rumney *	(82 men)	
(served at siege of Gloucester)		
Captain Richard Moore*	(48 men)	(Powick)
Captain Hanbury *	(76 men)	
Surgeon Richald Addis *		

Other Officers listed in Indigent Officers
Companies

Major	Harvey
	Lieutenant Henry Fitch
Captain	John Ingram (serving in 1646)
	Lieutenant Walter Collins (Worcester)
Captain	Edward Osborne
Captain	Conway Whittorne (serving in 1646)
	Ensign Thomas Mellicheap

Other Lieutenants
John Moses (Worcester)

Other Ensigns
John Moore (Worcester)
John Twittey (Worcester)

Quartermaster
Thomas Blumson

9. Sir John Beaumont's Foot
Raised in Staffordshire in 1642 and became part of the Evesham garrison in 1643. Destroyed at Tewkesbury June 1644.

Lieutenant Colonel John Godfrey (Colonel from September 1643)

Companies
Major   William Courtney
Major   Raphiell Neale (under Godfrey)

Captain   Anthony Dormer
Captain   Robert Fleetwood
Captain   Gilbert Thomas
           Ensign Thomas Ennis
Captain   Francis Tyrringham
Captain–
Lieutenant Thomas Gwatkin

10. Sir James Hamilton's Horse
Raised in Worcestershire in early 1643 with a total strength of 322. This locally-recruited regiment left the county in the Spring and large elements were captured at Devizes. The survivors formed the core of Sir William Russell's regiment.

Lieutenant Colonel Lewis Carre
   Quartermaster John Walter
Lieutenant Colonel Profitt
   Quartermaster John Smith (Worcester)

Troops
Major   John Blunt (Soddington, Worcs)
         Lieutenant John Manly (Worcester)
         Cornet William Taylor [or Peter Blunt's troop]
         Quartermaster Richard Powell (Worcester) [or Peter Blunt's troop]
Captain Peter Blunt (Worcester)
Captain Edward Brent (Worcester)
         Lieutenant George Brent (Worcester)
Captain Henry Colt (PoW Devizes)
         Quartermaster John Bernard (Worcester)
Captain William Walsh (PoW Devizes)
         Lieutenant John Norgrove (Worcester)
         Cornet Watkins
         John Walker (Worcester)
Captain Francis Watkins (Hanbury, Worcs)
         Cornet Francis Ellis

Other Lieutenants
Matthew Hall (Worcester)

Other Cornets
William Bridges

11. Sir James Hamilton's Foot
According to Symonds, this reached a strength of 1,000 men. It left the county with the rest of Hamilton's regiments and was lost at Devizes.

12. Sir James Hamilton's Dragoons
Raised in Worcestershire 1643 with a strength of 370, but never fully mounted. It left the county in Spring 1643 with the rest of Hamilton's regiments.

Companies
Lieutenant Colonel Hamilton
Sergeant Major Henderson
Captain Robert Bullock
Captain — Dennis
          Quartermaster Thomas Ridley
Captain Michael Harland
Captain Richard Moses (Worcester)
Captain David Musset
          Lieutenant John Collyer (Worcester)

1644

13. Sandys' Regiment of Horse
(400 men)
This establishment represents the combination of earlier regiments of Horse in August 1644. Served with the field army in 1645. The Western Royalist army of 1643 regularly attached a troop of dragoons to each of its regiments of Horse.

Troops

Colonel Sandys	(100 men)
Colonel Knotsford	(50 men)
Reformado troop	(50 men)
Sir Rowland Berkeley	(50 men)
Sir Gilbert Gerrard	(50 men)
Captain Brereton	(50 men)
Captain Fitter	(100 dragoons)

14. Sir Gilbert Gerrard's Regiment of Foot *(1,000 men)*
Raised in Lancashire in 1642 and became the garrison regiment of Worcester in 1644, combining units from other local regiments. Command was passed to Gilbert's brother, Ratcliffe Gerrard on his death in 1645. List 14a is as provided by Townshend for August 1644. List 14b is based on the List of Indigent Officers. Whilst all the references in this may not be contemporary it is probable that many of the company commanders were the 'seven captains' as listed at Worcester in 1644.

14a. 1644
Companies

Sir Gilbert Gerrard	(100 men)
Captain William Sandys	(100 men)
(the Hartlebury garrison)	

Sergeant Major Richard Bishop	(80 men)
Captain Gerrard	(80 men)
7 other Captains	(80 men each)

14b. 1645
Probable strength in 1645. Taken from the post-Worcester listing from List of Indigent Officers. The strength of 15 companies equates with the stated strength of the Worcestershire garrison. The regiment was largely destroyed at the battle of Naseby.

Lieutenant Colonel Ratcliffe Gerrard
Major Richard Bishop (PoW Naseby)

Companies
Captain Edward Asheton
Captain William Booth
Captain John Byrom
  Thomas Pilkington (Worcester)
Captain Hugh Floyd
  Lieutenant Rowland Floyd
  Ensign Maurice Floyd
Captain Gilbert Gerrard (son of Ratcliffe)
  Lieutenant Richard Arthur
Captain John Gerrard (son of Ratcliffe)
Captain Patrick Gerrard snr.
Captain Patrick Gerrard jnr.
Captain John Mozey
Captain Edward Paynton
Captain John Potters
  Lieutenant William Waldron
Captain William Stanley
  Ensign Francis Domer
Captain Wlliam Warburton
Captain Gabriel Young
  Ensign Robert Holt
Captain William Young

Other Lieutenants
William Powell
Henry Whittingham

Other Ensigns
— Blayney
— Perrin

15. Sir Gilbert Gerrard's Horse
Originally part of Charles Gerrard's Horse, later part of Worcester garrison.

Captain Henry Cupper (Woodcote, Worcs)
Captain Thomas Walwyn

Lieutenant Nicholas Lency

Quartermaster John Browne
Quartermaster Robert James

16. Sir John Knotsford's Horse

Part of Evesham garrison in 1644. Joined Oxford army in June 1644 and returned to Evesham in July. Then absorbed into Sir Gilbert Gerrard's Horse.

Captain Francis Knotsford
Captain Thomas Westly
  Cornet William Oldham
Captain-Lieutenant John Manly
Cornet Richard Knotsford (Worcester)
Quartermaster John Haynes

The Garrison of Worcester in 1646

The details are provided by Henry Townshend.

Foot

17. ColonelWashington's Regiment of Foot

Formerly Colonel James Usher's Regiment of Dragoons. It then passed to Washington and was converted to a Foot regiment after Marston Moor, due to a lack of suitable mounts.

Governor's Company
  11 officers
  95 men
Lieutenant Colonel. Hurston
  6 officers
  54 men
Major Nathaniel Grey
  6 officers
  44 men
Captain Henry Norwood
  7 officers
  45 men
Captain Bellamy
  5 officers
  38 men
Captain Robinson
  6 officers
  36 men
Captain Armourer
  5 officers
  36 men
Colonel Knotsford (former governor of Evesham in 1644)
  5 officers
  36 men
Captain Dormer
  5 officers
  50 men

Total: 56 officers
          440 men

18. Sir William Russell's Regiment of Foot

Only three of these officers were listed in 1643.

Russell's company
   63 men

Lieutenant Colonel Goffe
   6 officers
   42 men

Major Ingram (also serving in 1643)
   6 officers
   42 men

Captain Hughes (also serving in 1643)
   5 officers
   38 men

Captain Calthrop
   4 officers
   24 men

Captain Poultney
   6 officers
   36 men

Captain Whithorne (also serving in 1643)
   5 officers
   35 men

Total: 39 officers
          280 men

19. Colonel Samuel Sandys' Regiment

Few officers are named but, apart from Moore, there seems to be little correlation to the regiment raised in 1643.

Major Francis Moore (in command as Samuel Sandys was at Hartlebury)
   7 officers
   61 men

Captain Byron
   6 officers
   45 men

Captain William Moore
   11 officers
   76 men

Lieutenant Raynsford
   8 officers
   58 men

Total: 32 officers
          240 men

Reformadoes 120
cannoneers   58
(28 cannon
6 drakes
— 'sling-pieces')
master gunner Nathaniel Nye

20. Horse

Governor's troop	51
Henry Ingram, High Sheriff	71
Sir Joseph Knotsford	32
Captain Armorer	17
Lieutenant Colonel Roberts	19
Total:	224

Staff Officers	18

Second Civil War

21. Worcester Militia 1648 (Parliamentary)
On 4 August 1648 the following were appointed officers of the Worcester militia:
Major Foulke Estopp (commissioned as a Parliamentary captain of Horse in October 1644)
Captain Edward Coxe
Captain Theophilus Alie (d. 1679/80)
Captain William Hughes

Third Civil War 1651

22. Worcestershire Militia 1651 (Parliamentary)
Colonel John James
Major Theophilus Alie
Captain Andrew Yarranton
Captain Foulke Eastop
Captain Boyleston

23. Lord Talbot's Troop of Worcestershire Horse at Battle of Worcester 1651 (Royalist)
(c.60 men)
Colonel Lord Talbot
Lieutenant Colonel Mervin Touchet
Major William Carlis
Captain Lieutenant Richard Kemble
Captain William Penn

Post-War

24. Worcester Militia 1656
(80 men)
Captain Talbot Badger
Lieutenant — Roberts
Cornet John Buck

25. Worcester Militia 1661
Muster Master
Major Thomas Muckley
Provost Marshall
Richard Pitt

Companies
Alderman Vernon (Worcester)

Further Reading

M. Ashley, *The English Civil War* (Stroud, 1990)

R. Ashton, *Counter Revolution: the Second Civil War and its Origins, 1646–8* (London, 1994)

M. Atkin, *The Civil War in Worcestershire* (Stroud, 1995)

M. Atkin, *Cromwell's Crowning Mercy: the Battle of Worcester* (Stroud, 1998)

M. Atkin, *A Storm of Fire and Leaden Hail: the Civil War in Evesham* (Evesham, 2004)

J. Barratt, *Cavaliers: the Royalist Army at War 1642 – 46* (Stroud, 2000)

S. Bond, *The Chamber Order Book of Worcester 1602–1650*, Worcs. Hist. Soc. new series, vol.viii (1974)

L. Boynton, *The Elizabethan Militia 1558 – 1638*, (1967)

C. Carlton, *Going to the Wars*, (London, 1992)

C.G. Cruickshank, *Elizabeth's Army* (Oxford, 1966)

R. Hutton, *The Royalist War Effort 1642–46* (London, 1982)

P. L. Isemonger, *The English Civil War: a Living History* (Stroud, 1994)

J. Kenyon, *The Civil Wars of England* (London, 1996)

J. Morrill *The Impact of the English Civil War* (London, 1991)

S. Reid, *Officers and Regiments of the Royalist Army* (Leigh on Sea, no date)

R.E. Sherwood, *Civil War in the Midlands 1642–1651* (Stroud, 1992)

P. Styles, 'The Royalist Government of Worcestershire during the Civil War, 1642–6', *Trans. Worcestershire Archaeol. Soc.*, 3rd series v (1976), 23–39

P. Tennant, *Edgehill and Beyond: the People's War in the South Midlands 1642–1645* (Stroud, 1992)

J.W. Willis Bund, *The Civil War in Worcestershire 1642–1646 and the Scotch Invasion of 1651*, (Birmingham, 1905)

J.W. Willis Bund, (ed.), *Diaries of Henry Townshend of Elmley Lovett, 1640–1663*, Worcestershire History Society (1915–20)

J. Wroughton, *An Unhappy Civil War: the Experiences of Ordinary People in Gloucestershire, Somerset and Wiltshire 1642–46* (Bath, 1999)

Abbreviations

APC	Acts of the Privy Council
BL	British Library
Bond	S. Bond, *The Chamber Order Book of Worcester 1602–1650*, Worcs. Hist. Soc. new ser., Vol.viii (1974).
CCAM	Calendar of the Committee for the Advancement of Money
CCC	Calendar of the Committee for Compounding
CJ	Commons Journal
CSPD	Calendar of State Papers Domestic
HMC	Historical Manuscripts Commission
Townshend	J.W. Willis-Bund, (ed.), *Diaries of Henry Townshend of Elmley Lovett, 1640–1663*, Worcestershire History Society (1915–20).
WRO	Worcestershire Record Office

Acknowledgements

I have to thank the staff of the Worcestershire Record Office, Worcester City Library, the National Archives, Lord Sandys and Paul Stanley for their help in compiling the sources for this work. I owe a special debt of gratitude to my colleagues in the Worcestershire Historic Environment Service – to David Guyatt for his help in transcribing Appendix 1 and also in helping decipher parts of other scripts, to Neil Lockett for transferring the information to a database on the GIS (as summarised on p. 24) and to Steve Rigby for the other maps. Thanks also to Ms Mary Burkett for permission to reproduce the painting of Sir William Russell on p. 76 and to Dick Hart and Colin Thompson for their information on recent metal detector finds. Mark Goodman provided unfailing help, especially on the development of the Trained Bands. Any errors that remain are, however, entirely mine. Final thanks go to my wife, Susanne, for her patience during the writing of the book and for producing the index.

Notes

Preface

1 For which see M. Atkin, *Worcestershire and the Civil War* (Stroud, 1995); *Cromwell's Crowning Mercy: the Battle of Worcester 1651* (Stroud, 1998).

2 P. Styles, 'The City of Worcester' in *The English Civil War: Local Aspects*, R.C. Richardson (ed.) (Stroud, 1997), p. 210.

3 The National Archives SP28/187 and 188.

4 R. Hutton, *The Royalist War Effort 1642–46* (London, 1982); J. Wroughton, *An Unhappy Civil War: the Experiences of Ordinary People in Gloucestershire, Somerset and Wiltshire 1642–46*, (Bath, 1999).

5 J.W. Willis-Bund, (ed). *Diaries of Henry Townshend of Elmley Lovett, 1640–1663*, Worcestershire. History Society (1915–20).

6 The National Archives SP28/187 and SP28/188.

Chapter One

1 Gervase Markham, 'The Muster Master', *Camden Miscellany* XXVI, 1975, p. 57.

2 J. Barratt, *Cavaliers* (Stroud, 2000), p. 3.

3 C.G. Cruickshank, *Elizabeth's Army* (Oxford, 1966), p. 291.

4 J.W. Willis Bund, Calendar of the Quarter Sessions Papers vol.1 (1900), p. 44.

5 The National Archives SP14/179; Bund *op. cit.* 1900, p. 197.

6 S.Bond, *The Chamber Order Book of Worcester 1602–1650*. Worcester Historical Society. New series, vol. viii (1974) p. 214.

7 APC 8 June 1631, p. 376.

8 Bund *op. cit.* 1900, p. 269.

9 *ibid*, p. 455.

10 *ibid*, p. 105.

11 *ibid*, p. 248.

12 *ibid*, p. 345.

13 *ibid*, p. 309.

14 *ibid*, p. 453.

15 *ibid*, p. 322.

16 CSPD 9 February 1638, p. p. 241.

17 L. Boynton, *The Elizabethan Militia 1558 – 1638*, (1967), p. 261

18 Bund *op. cit.*, 1900, p. 429 and 430; F.S. Pearson, 'The churchwarden's accounts of the parish of Northfield', *Birmingham Archaeol. Soc. Transactions*, 34, 1908, p. 70.

19 CSPD 1628–9, p. 43; Rushworth II, p. 243.

20 Boynton *op. cit.*, pp. 156, 170; Cruickshank *op. cit.*, pp. 91–2.

21 Boynton *op. cit.*, p. 258.

22 WRO 261.4, BA 1006: 625; F.S. Pearson, *op. cit.*, p. 71.

23 Cruickshank *op. cit.*, p. 92

24 Stowe Mss 574, f.26.

25 Bond, p. 50, Worcs. Hist. Soc. new ser. vol. viii, 1974, for 18 December 1621, p. 175

26 W.H. Stephenson, *Records of the Corporation of Gloucester* (Gloucester 1893), p. 45.

27 WRO BA845/5 (Berkeley Papers).

28 Bund *op. cit.,* 1900, pp. 44 and 461.

29 APC 24 May 1626, p. 496.

30 Bond, p. 197.

31 Worcestershire Quarter Sessions, 1628, p. 461

32 APC 10 July 1626, p. 73.

33 Gervase Markham *op. cit.*, p. 61.

34 CSPD 1 February 1639–40, p. 417.

35 Boynton *op. cit.*, p. 247.

36 APC 24 May 1630, p. 395.

37 APC 10 July 1626, p. 73.

38 APC 16 May 1628, p. 427.

39 Bond, *op. cit.*, p. 203.

40 *ibid*, p. 206.

41 *ibid*, p. 204.

42 *ibid*, p. 207.

43 As in 1626, 1628 and 1635: Acts of Privy Council 1626, pp. 71, 79; BM Pamphlet 190g. 13(i); Boynton *op. cit.*, p. 258

44 W. Barriffe, *Military Discipline*, (1661, reprinted Partizan Press, 1998).

45 CSPD 27 January 1638, p. 195

46 *Directions for Musters*, 1638, p. 3.

47 W. Barriffe, *op. cit.*, p. 135

48 Bond, *op. cit*, p. 293.

49 CSPD 1638, p. 277.

50 Boynton *op. cit.*, p. 287.

51 R.H. Silcock, *County Government in Worcestershire 1603–1660*, London PhD Thesis, p. 172.

52 J. Corbet, *An historical relation of the military government of Glouce*ster, 1645 (in J. Washbourn, *Bibliotheca Gloucestrensis* (Gloucester 1825), p. 11

53 Barriffe, *op. cit.*, p. 135.

54 *ibid*, p. 1.

55 John Dryden, *Cymon and Iphigenia* (1700).

56 CSPD 9 February 1638, p. 241.

57 CSPD April 1640, p. 98.

58 WRO A10, Box 2, Vol.2, ff. 208 and 223.

59 The National Archives SP16/462; Bond, p. 337.

60 Townshend, II, p. 19.

61 C. Hopkinson, *op. cit.*, p. 76.

62 Townshend I, p. 5.

63 Townshend I, p. ix.

64 CSPD April 6 1639, p. 20.

65 Townshend I, p. 4.

66 *Warwickshire Antiquarian Magazine* 1859, p. 77, quoted in S. Peachey and A. Turton, *Common Soldier's Clothing of the Civil Wars*, vol.1 Infantry, 1995, p. 8.

67 CSPD 20 July 1640, p. 495.

68 WRO 705:93 BA845/5 (Berkeley Papers).

69 Townshend II, p. 122.

Chapter Two

 1 Birmingham City Archives HCC 564: 398267; HCC 562: 398265.

 2 CSPD 1632, pp. 289, 342 and 424.

 3 S.R. Gardiner, Constitutional Documents of the Puritan Revolution 1628 – 1660 (Oxford 1889), pp. 166–168.

 4 M. Bennett, *The Royalist War Effort in the North Midlands 1642–46* (Loughborough PhD thesis, 1986), p. 216.

 5 As identified by Willis Bund from the initials recorded on the Commission of 5 September 1642

 6 Townshend II, p. xxvi

 7 Chamberlain's Accounts 1640 –1.

 8 Bond 1974, p. 350.

 9 *ibid*, p. 353.

10 Gardiner *op. cit.*, p. 181.

11 HWRO 850 Salwarpe, p. 1054 (A53)

12 Townshend II, p. 66

13 HWRO 899:31, BA669/1.

14 BL E107 (14).

15 HWRO 3669/1 (iv); Townshend II, p. 68.

16 Commons Journal II, p. 710.

17 Quoted in C.D. Gilbert 'Kidderminster at the Outbreak of the English Civil War', *Trans. Worcestershire Archaeol. Soc.* 3rd ser. 11 (1988), p. 37.

18 R. Baxter, *Reliquiae Baxterianae* 1696, part 1, pp. 40–1.

19 *ibid*, p. 43.

20 Townshend II, p. 69

21 Commons Journal, II, p. 720.

22 Townshend II, p. 72.

23 Townshend II, p. 73.

24 HMC 13th Report Portland MSS, App. I, p. 52.

25 Townshend II, p. 72.

26 *ibid*, p. 70.

27 *ibid* II, p. 69.

28 *ibid*, p. 139.

29 *ibid*, p. 139.

30 *ibid*, p. 75.

31 Bond 1974, p. 353.

32 Townshend II. p. 80.

33 *ibid*, pp. 86 – 7.

34 *ibid*, p. 86.

35 T.R. Nash, collections for the history of Worcestershire, vol I (1781), p. 499.

36 Corbet *op. cit.*, p. 16.

37 BL Harleian Mss, 6904, 122 quoted in C. Carlton, *Going to the Wars* (London, 1994), p. 207.

38 Townshend II, p. 79.

39 *ibid*, p. 87.

40 *ibid*, pp. 87– 9.

41 *ibid*, p. 89.

42 *ibid*, pp. 66 – 7, 81.

43 R. Hutton, *The Royalist War Effort 1642–1646* (London 1982), p. 11.

44 WRO City Accounts 1640–9, A10 Box 3; *CJ* II, pp. 761, 763 – 4.

45 *A Perfect and True Relation of the great and bloudy skirmish fought before the City of Worcester upon Friday, September 23 1642* by William Bowen (Worcester City Library W 942.4406).

46 WRO 850 BA6100/2.

47 Heath, Chronicle Part 1, 40.

48 The National Archives SP28/187, f.387.

49 The National Archives SP28/188, f.44–5.

50 The National Archives SP28/188.

51 As identified by Nash *op. cit.*, in vol. II, pedigree of Sandys family opp. p. 220.

52 BL E239 (22) *Special Passages*, 6 – 13 September 1642.

53 W.R. Buchanan-Dunlop, 'Seventeenth Century Puritans in Worcester' *Trans. Worcestershire Archaeol. Soc.*, XXIII (1946), 33–7.

54 HMC 14th report, App. 8, p. 203.

55 VCH II, p. 68.

56 CSPD 1644, p. 355.

57 Townshend II, pp. 94–5.

58 BL Harl. Mss 6851 ff79 – 94.

59 WRO 845/5: Commission of Charles I to Sir William Russell, 25 September 1643.

Chapter Three

1 W.E. English, 'Occupations in Worcestershire wills 1451 – 1660', *Worcestershire Archaeol. and Local History Newsletter*, no.39, 1987, p. 17.

2 P. Edwards, *Dealing in Death* (Stroud, 2000), pp. 107–8.

3 M. Toynbee, 'Royal Ordnance Papers', *Oxford Record Society*, 43, 1956, pp. 68, 73, 77.

4 M. Toynbee, 'Royal Ordnance Papers', *Oxford Record Society*, 49, 1962, p. 427.

5 Birmingham City Archives HCC 574: 398276.

6 With thanks to Birmingham Field Archaeology Unit.

7 M. Atkin, *A Storm of Fire and Leaden Hail: Evesham in the Civil War* (Evesham, 2003), p. 14.

8 M. Atkin, *The Civil War in Worcestershire* (Stroud 1995), p. 54–66.

9 J.B., *Some brief instructions for exercising of the Cavalry or Horse – Troopes*, London 1661, p. 34–5.

10 Birmingham City Archives HCC 577: 398279.

11 BM Harl. Mss 6851, f.129–30.

12 Gilbert *op. cit.*, p. 43.

13 B. Whitelocke, *Memorials of the English Affairs* (Oxford, 1853) I, p. 182.

14 Hutton *op. cit.*, 1982, pp. 92–3.

15 Worcestershire Quarter Sessions WRO BA 110: 85/54.

16 Letter of Poyntz to Ormonde, 1 June 1643 quoted in Carlton, p. 290.

17 SP 28/253 B/13.

18 R. Baxter 1696, *Reliquae Baxterianae*, Part I, p. 53.

19 A.J. Hopper, *The Readiness of the People: the formation and emergence of the Army of the Fairfaxes, 1642–3* (University of York Borthwick Paper 92, 1997), p. 11.

20 S. Peachey and A. Turton, *Common Soldier's Clothing of the Civil Wars*, 1995, p. 10; W.J. Cripps, *The Royal North Gloucesters* (London, 1875), p. 20.

21 S. Pepys, *An Account of His Majesty's Escape from Worcester Dictated to Mr.Pepys by the King Himself*, in C. Thomas (ed.) *Boscobel* (London, 1894), pp. 139–40.

22 BM Harl. Mss 6851 f.139.

23 Bond 1974, p. 364.

24 *ibid*, p. 393.

25 *ibid*, p. 365–6.

26 *ibid*, p. 365.

27 *ibid*, p. 380.

28 *ibid*, p. 404.

29 John and William were both mistakenly described as uncles to Samuel Sandys by Richard Symonds, *Diary of the Marches of the Royal Army*, ed. C.E. Long, (Cambridge, 1997), p. 12.

30 CSPD 1644, pp. 324 and 326.

31 Townshend II, pp. 108–9.

32 Townshend II, pp. 161, 167.

33 Commission of 20 January 1643, private papers of Sandys family.

34 Townshend II, p. 104.

35 BM Harl. Mss 6851, f.129–30.

36 Birmingham City Archives HCC 587: 398331.

37 P. Styles, 'The Royalist Government of Worcestershire during the Civil War 1642–6', *TWAS*, 3rd Ser., V (1976), p. 34.

38 BL Add. Ms 18980, ff 8 – 9, 20.

39 Townshend I, p. xxiv.

40 CSPD 1644, pp. 512 – 3 for reference to Russell's regiment in county.

41 Atkin 2003 *op. cit., passim*.

42 Townshend II, p. 134.

43 P. Styles 1976 *op. cit.*, p. 25.

44 Townshend II, p. 103.

45 *ibid*, p. 127.

46 *ibid*, p. 128.

47 BM Harl. Mss 6851, f.135.

48 Townshend II, p. 136.

49 BM Harl. Mss 6851, f.135.

50 Townshend I, pp. 151–2

51 Bodleian Library MSS Firth C6 – C8, quoted in C.D. Gilbert, 'A Sermon in Civil War Worcester', *TWAS* 16,1998, 177–182 (p. 180).

52 Gilbert 1998 *op. cit.*, p. 178.

53 Bod. Lib. Firth Mss C6 f.52 quoted in Hutton, p. 128.

54 Townshend II, p. 171.

55 R. Symonds, *Diary of the Marches of the Royal Army during the Great Civil War* (ed.) C.E. Long, *Camden Society* 1859, vol. 74, p. 13.

56 Bond 1974, p. 382.

57 J. Dorney, *A Brief and Exact Relation*, 1643, in J. Washbourn *op. cit.*, p. 212.

58 R. Morris, *The Siege of Gloucester 1643*, (Bristol, 1993), p. 23.

59 Townshend II, p. 145.

60 *ibid*, p. 151.

61 M. Atkin and W. Laughlin, *Gloucester and the Civil War: A City Under Siege*, (Stroud, 1992), p. 138.

62 Letter of Charles I to Samuel Sandys 31 March 1644, (Sandys Private Papers).

63 Townshend Vol.3, p. xxix

Chapter Four

1 C.E. Long (ed.), *Richard Symonds's Diary of the march of the Royal Army* (Cambridge, 1997), p. 12.

2 Bond 1974, p. 362.

3 *ibid*, p. 364.

4 Townshend II, p. 125.

5 *ibid*, p. 154

6 *ibid*, p. 150.

7 F. Larkin, *Stuart Royal Proclamations* (Oxford 1983), II, pp. 824 and 1019, referred to in C. Carlton, *Going To The Wars* (London, 1992), p. 197.

8 WRO BA 1006, parcel 627.

9 Townshend II, p. 146.

10 *ibid*, p. 132.

11 WCO, p. 364.

12 Townshend II, pp. 125–6

13 BL Harl. Mss 6851, f.129–30.

14 Townshend II, p. 154.

15 A. Fea, *The Flight of the King* (London, 1897), Tract IV, pp. 227, 200.

16 W.E. English, 'Occupations in Worcestershire wills 1451 – 1660', *Worcestershire Archaeol. and Local History Newsletter*, no.39, 1987, p. 17.

17 Birmingham City Archives 398282.

18 Townshend II, p. 123.

19 *ibid*, p. 107.

20 BL E.266 (24): *Perfect Occurrences*, 21 November 1645.

21 J. Tincey, *Ironsides* (Oxford, 2002), p. 21.

22 Letter of Earl of Essex to the Committee of Both Kingdoms, quoted in J. Adair, *Roundhead General* (London, 1969), p. 155.

23 Edward Earl of Clarendon, *The History of the Rebellion and Civil Wars in England* (ed. W. Dunne Macray, 1888), Book VIII, p. 53.

24 R. Baxter, *Saints Everlasting Rest* (5th ed, 1654), chapter 7, section XV, p. 139.

25 The National Archives SP28/187.

26 The National Archives SP28/187 f.163.

27 The National Archives SP28/187 f.396.

28 General G. Monck, *Observations upon Military and Political Affairs* (London, 1671), p. 26; J. Turner, *Dallas Armata* (London 1683), p. 275.

29 The National Archives SP28/187 ff. 414, 420.

30 Ottley Papers vol.VIII, p. 247.

31 Townshend II, p. 225.

32 The National Archives SP28/187 and 188

33 Townshend II, p. 102–5; Tennant, pp. 106–7; BL Harl. Mss 6804, f.140.

34 BL Harl. Mss 6804, f.139.

35 BL Add. Mss. 18981, f.265.

36 Letter of *c.* 8 September 1644 in J. Lewis, (ed.), *May It Please Your Highness: the correspondence of Prince Rupert* (Newtown 1996), p. 73.

37 WRO 1714/899/192 ff545–7.

38 The National Archives SP 28/187.

39 The National Archives SP 28/187.

40 J.W. Willis Bund, *The Civil War in Worcestershire 1642–6 and the Scotch invasion of 1651* (Birmingham, 1905), p. 56.

41 HMC 10th Report, Appendix 6, p. 175.

42 EBR, n.497, p. 83.

43 C. Carlton, *Going to the Wars* (London, 1992), p. 283.

44 D. Symons and E. Besley, 'Two Seventeenth Century Coin-Hoards from Worcestershire', *Trans. Worcs. Archaeol. Soc.*, 3rd series 10, 1986, pp. 81–3.

45 Quoted in N. Wilkes, *A History of Eckington* (Eckington, 1996), p. 153.

46 J. Thompson, *The Other Army* (Leigh on Sea, no date), p. 6.

47 Townshend I, p. 128.

48 Worcestershire Sites and Monuments Record, WSM 33551 and 28825.

49 Letter of Nehemiah Wharton, 26 September 1642 in H. Ellis (ed.), Letters from a subaltern officer ..., *Archaeologia*, XXV, 1853, p. 326.

50 CJ II, p. 753; *Letter Books of Sir Samuel Luke 1644–5*, H.G. Tibbutt (ed.) (HMSO, 1963), no.163, p. 667.

51 Townshend I. p. 172.

52 A.J. Rowland, *Military Encampments of the English Civil Wars 1639 – 1659* (Bristol, 1997), p. 9.

53 Townshend I, p. 115.

54 *Letter Books of Sir Samuel Luke 1644–5*, H.G. Tibbutt (ed.) (HMSO, 1963), no.223, p. 121.

55 Townshend II, p. 174.

56 *ibid*, p. 175.

57 *ibid*, pp. 174, 201.

58 *ibid*, p. 162.

59 *ibid*, p. 167.

60 CCC May 1651, p. 2789.

61 Townshend II, p. 215.

62 CSPD 1649–50, p. 271.

63 The National Archives SP28/187

64 Townshend II, p. 123.

65 CCAM 23 June 1649, p. 1103.

66 Townshend I, p. 106.

67 Townshend II, p. 253.

68 *Letter Books of Sir Samuel Luke 1644–5*, H.G. Tibbutt (ed.) (HMSO, 1963), no.404, p. 197.

69 C. Firth and G.Davies, *Regimental History of Cromwell's Army* (Oxford, 1940), vol.1, p. 390.

70 Townshend II, p. 141.

71 Bond 1974, p. 394.

72 *ibid*, p. 398.

73 *ibid*, p. 367.

74 Whitelocke, *op. cit.*, p. 96.

75 M. Atkin, *A Storm of Fire and Leaden Hail* (Evesham, 2003), p. 15–16.

Chapter Five

1645–6

1 Commission from Charles I. Private Papers of the Sandys family.

2 Townshend II, p. 215.

3 Bond 1974, p. 393; BL Add. Ms 18980, ff. 8 – 9, 20.

4 CSPD 1644–5, p. 269.

5 M. Atkin, *A Storm of Fire and Leaden Hail: the Civil War in Evesham* (Evesham, 2003).

6 WRO 899:244, BA2101.

7 Townshend II, p. 236.

8 C. Carlton, *Going to the Wars* (London 1992), p. 150.

9 Townshend II, pp. 191–2.

10 *ibid*, p. 175.

11 *ibid*, p. 205.

12 *ibid*, p. 221.

13 Letter to Prince Rupert 3 March 1645, quoted in Gilbert, 'The Worcestershire Clubmen of 1645', *Trans. Worcs. Archaeol. Soc.* 3rd Ser. Vol.15, 1966, p. 212.

14 *The Letter Books of Sir Samuel Luke 1644–5*, H.G. Tibbutt, (ed.) (HMSO, 1963), p. 689.

15 Townshend II, p. 222.

16 *Kingdom's Weekly Intelligencer*, BL E274.2, 274.24.

17 Letter of 22 March 1645 to Sir Samuel Luke, published in J. Webb and T.W. Webb (eds.), 'A Military Memoir of Colonel John Birch', *Camden Soc.* 7 (1873), pp. 216–17.

18 D. Gilbert, 'Two Royalist Garrisons in Worcestershire Parts 1 and 2', *Worcestershire Archaeol. and Local History Newsletter*, nos 39 and 40, 1987 and 1988.

19 *Kingdom's Weekly Intelligencer* for 22–29 April 1645, BL 279 (11).

20 R. Hutton, *The Royalist War Effort 1642 – 6*, (London, 1992), p. 174n; Roy, *The Royalist Army*, p. 218.

21 Townshend II, p. 235.

22 HMC 9th Report Appendix 2, p. 437.

23 Letter of Charles I to Samuel Sandys 30 September 1645 in Sandys Private Papers.

24 CSPD 1645, p. 157.

25 Townshend II, p. 239.

26 *ibid*, p. 237.

27 *ibid*, p. 240.

28 *ibid*, p. 240.

29 *ibid*, p. 241.

30 A.G. Matthews, *Walker Revisited*, 1948, p. 137.

31 R.N. Dore (ed.), *The Letter Books of Sir William Brereton* (Lancs. and Cheshire Record Soc., 1990), 128, no.1003.

32 BL E310.6, 309.23.

33 Townshend II, p. 243.

34 Letter of Charles I to Samuel Sandys 26 February 1645 in Sandys' Private Papers.

35 Townshend I, p. 106.

36 WRO 899:244, BA2101.

37 Atkin 1995 *op.cit.*, pp. 105–16

38 The National Archives SP28/187, ff.161–167; SP28/187, f.387; SP28/188, f.44.

39 The National Archives SP28/187, f.170.

40 Townshend I, pp. 112–113.

41 *ibid*, p. 119.

42 *ibid*, p. 131.

43 Bond 1974, p. 408.

44 *ibid*, p. 413.

45 Townshend I, p. 124.

46 *ibid*, p. 173.

47 *ibid*, p. 133.

48 *ibid*, pp. 128–9.

49 *ibid*, p. 190.

50 *ibid*, p. 156.

51 *ibid*, p. 142.

52 *ibid*, p. 192.

53 C. Carlton *op. cit.*, p. 214.

Chapter Six

1 The National Archives SP28/187, f. 164.

2 Quoted in R. Ashton, *Counter Revolution: the Second Civil War and its Origins, 1646–8* (London, 1994), p. 339.

3 Worcestershire Quarter Sessions 1651, WRO BA 110: 85/54.

4 Ashton, p. 348.

5 Lords Journal X, p. 120–1; Rushworth *Hist. Coll.* VII, p. 1023.

6 For details of the campaign and Battle of Worcester see M. Atkin, *Cromwell's Crowning Mercy: the Battle of Worcester 1651* (Stroud, 1997), *passim*.

7 *Letter of Cromwell to Harrison*, 3 May 1651, in W.C. Abbot, *The Writings and Speeches of Oliver Cromwell*, ii, p. 411.

8 *Letter from Cromwell to Lenthall*, 4 September 1651, in Abbott, ii, 462.

9 CSPD 31 March, 1651, p. 120.

10 HMC 12th Report, Appendix IX, p. 499.

11 HMC 12th Report, Appendix IX, p. 498.

12 CSPD 1649–50, p. 278.

13 Worcestershire Quarter Sessions 1651, WRO BA 110: 85/54.

14 See P.J. Brown, 'The Military Career of Andrew Yarranton', *Trans. Worcs. Archaeol. Soc.* 13 (1992), pp. 193–202.

15 CCC 1643–60, Part IV, p. 2867.

16 CSPD 15 August 1651, p. 332.

17 B. Whitelock, *Memorials of the English Affairs* (1682, repr. Oxford, 1853), p. 503.

18 *ibid*.

19 *ibid*, p. 504.

20 WRO. Letter of Charles I, 24 August 1651.

21 CSPD 27 August 1651, p. 376.

22 Yarranton was subsequently accused of accepting bribes to take the men back into the militia and protect them from prosecution: Brown *op. cit.*, pp. 195–6.

23 CCC 28 October 1656, Part III, p. 1824.

24 Worcester Quarter Sessions 1675, WRO BA 110: 171/5.

25 T. Blount, *Boscobel* (1660), pp. 10–11.

26 Committee for Advancement of Money 27 October 1654, p. 1479.

27 Whitelock, *op.cit*, p. 505.

28 *Letter from Cromwell to Lenthall*, 8 September 1651 in Abbott, p. 467.

29 J. Washbourn, *Bibliotheca Gloucestrensis* (1825), p. cxxiv.

30 HWRO *Audit of the City Accounts 1640–1669.*

31 R. Baxter 1696, *Reliquial Baxterianae*, Part I, p. 69.

32 E. Clarendon, *The History of the Rebellion and Civil Wars in England.* W. D. Macray (ed.) (Oxford, 1888) vol. 5, p. 191.

33 Worcestershire Historic Buildings, Sites and Monuments Record, WSM 12545.

34 VCH Worcs III 1913, 409, quoted in E. Besley, *English Civil War Coin Hoards* (British Museum, 1987), p. 104.

35 Clarendon, *op.cit*, p. 187.

36 C. Durston, *Cromwell's Major Generals* (Manchester, 2001), p. 141.

37 *ibid*, p. 43.

38 CSPD 15 August 1659, p. 111.

39 CSPD 14 September 1659, p. 195.

40 CSPD 4 January 1660, p. 298.

Chapter Seven

1 W.Bray (ed.), *Diary of John Evelyn*, vol.1 (London, 1907), p. 341.

2 Townshend I, p. 37.

3 Worcestershire Quarter Sessions, 1661, WRO BA 110: 185/13.

4 Worcestershire Quarter Sessions, 1677, WRO BA 110: 128/103.

5 Worcestershire Quarter Sessions, 1681, WRO BA 110: 139/32.

6 Worcestershire Quarter Sessions, 1681, WRO BA 110: 139/33.

7 Worcestershire Quarter Sessions, 1681, WRO BA 110: 139/35.

8 Townshend I, p. 38.

9 Townshend I, p. 59.

10 Townshend I, p. 65.

11 Worcester Chamberlain's Accounts 1659–60; Townshend I, p. 66

12 Townshend I, p. 71.

13 Townshend I, p. 56.

14 Townshend I, p. 78.

15 J.R. Tanner, *English Constitutional Conflicts of the Seventeenth Century 1603 – 1689*, (Cambridge University Press, 1928), p. 224.

16 CSPD 17 July 1662, p. 442.

Appendix 1

1 WRO 705:93, BA 845/5. I am grateful to David Guyatt for transcribing this document.

2 R. Huggett, J. Huggett and S. Peachey, *Early 17th Century Prices and Wages* (Stuart Press, 1992), p. 10.

Appendix 4

1 Townshend I and II; S. Reid, *Officers and Regiments of the Royalist Army*, (Leigh on Sea, no date).

2 Townshend II, pp. 152 – 4. Note, however, that these figures were part of a complex dispute and therefore may not be entirely reliable.

3 Bond 1974, p. 443.

Index

Abberley 76, 122
Abbotts Morton 100
Abrell, James, pewterer 149
Acton, Thomas 141
Acts of Parliament
  (1659) 149
  (1662) 152
Addams, Edward, drummer 73
Alie, Capt. Theophilus 139
Allen, Sgt Thomas 89
altar rails *33*
Alvechurch 100
ammunition, inventory of 40, 42
ammunition casting 108
Amscote (Warks) 100
archers and archery 16
artillery 76, 83
Assessment(s) 75, 76, 79, 80, 81,
  82, 83, 87, 88–9, 92, 94–100,
  106, 108–9, 116, 121
Association (regional) 113, 115–17
Astley, Lord Jacob 27, 122–3, 124
Astley, Joseph 154
Aston, Sir Thomas 80, 100, 122,
  127
atlases *80*
Aynsworth, Thomas 98

Baber, William and Jane, powder
  makers 76–7, 108
Badger, Capt. Talbot 148
Bagshawe, Arthur 153
Baker, Sgt John 89
Baker, John, tax collector 88
Baldwin, Henry, carpenter 108
Bard, Sir Henry 85–6, 94
Barnes, Thomas 127
Barriffe, William 22, 23, 25
Bartlett, Rowland 100
Basing House (Hampshire) 48
Baxter, Richard, preacher
  29–30, 40, 41, *43*, 54, 57, 68,
  69, 96, 110, 131, 132, 147, 148
Beaumont, Sir John
  (1607–1643) 56, 65, 77, 79,
  84, 183
Benbow, Capt. 141
Berkeley, Sir Rowland 33, 44,
  74, 101, 141
Berry, Major General James 148
Betsworth, Col. 127
Bewdley 30, *60*, 83, 139
  bridge demolished 96, 138
  burials of soldiers *131*
  cap industry *71*, 108
  'capmen' 135

clergy 57
corpses 105
defences 68
garrison *60*, 61, 75
inventory of ammunition 42
magazine 40
soldiers billeted 26
Trained Bands 46
billeting 13, 49, 50, 75, 83, 92,
  96, 102, 103, 104, 106, 107,
  134, 135, 140
billmen 15
bills (weapon) 13, 15, 18, 27
Blackwell (Warks) 100
Blakenhurst Hundred 19
Blockley parish 15
Blount, Edward 141
Blount, Francis 55
Blount, Peter 141
Blount, Robert 141
Blount, Sir Walter 141, 142
Blunt, Capt. Francis 86, 132
Blunt family 44
Booth's Rising (1659) 150, 153
Boscobel Woods 135
Boyleston, Capt. 139, 149
Boys, Capt. 26, 157
Brace, Capt. Philip 46, 49
Bradley, Simon 54
Brancill, John, joiner 61, 135
Bransford Bridge 145
Bredon Hill *60*, 122
Bricklehampton 54
Bridgnorth (Shropshire) 86, 99,
  132
Bristol
  battle of 132
  military yard 19
  siege of 84
Broade, Edward 48, 68, 135
Broadwas 22
Broadway, St Eadburga's
  Church *33*
Broadwindsor (Sussex), George
  Inn 92
Bromsgrove *60*, 96, 100
  clergy 57
  inventory of ammunition 42
  magazine 40, 155
Brooke, Lord 42, 57
Brooke, Thomas 106
Brown, Col. John 52
Browne, James, linen weaver 15
Browne, Thomas *123*
Buck, Gervase, JP 138–9
Bundy, Roger 153

burials, of soldiers 53, 85, *85*,
  105, *131*, 132
  skeleton at Huddington 147
Burn, John 55
Burroughs, Mr, rector 57
Bushell, Thomas 61
Byron, Sir John 32, 50, 51, 52

calivers 13, *14*, 15, 16, 18, 19,
  42, *45*
camp followers 92, 104
camps, temporary 68, 102
cannon 47, 64, 109
Cannon, Capt. 105
cannon balls (cannon shot) *55*,
  61, 64
Capel, Lord 84, 89
cap industry, at Bewdley 108
capmen 135
Carlis, Col. William 143–4
Catholicism 30, 49, 81–2, 118
Chaddesley Corbett 99, 147
Chamberlain, Henry 15
Charles I *29*, 31, 46, 47, 49, 59,
  74, 81, 134, 135, 151, 152, 153
  Irish rebellion quelled 30
  loans and taxes 29–30
  maps left at Inkberrow
    Church by *80*
  medal given by *128*
  Trained Bands 13, 16, 19, 20,
    21, 25, 27, 32, 47
Charles II 28, 32, 135–6, 150,
  151
  battle of Worcester (1651) 44,
    47, 101, *131*, 140, 144, 147
  Coronation 154
  disguise 70–1
  Restoration 151, 152, 154–5
Charlton 122
Cheshire 149
Child, William 33
Claines 105
Clare, Sir Francis 81
Clare, Sir Ralph 33, *41*, 74, 76,
  79, 100, 121, 141, 142, 149
Clark, Samuel 150, 153
Clarke, William, clothier 141
Clarson, Thomas 19
clay tobacco pipe *114*
Clent, Capt. John 24, 25, 46,
  157, *157*
clergy 57
clergy company 155
clothing 17, 26, 27, 61; *see also*
  uniforms

Clubmen Movement 117–18,
  118, 119–20, *121*, 122
clubs, wooden 16, 27, 42
'Coat and Conduct' tax 13, 17,
  29, 39
coin hoards 101, *101*
coins, in purse 147
Coitte, Richard 15
Colchester (Essex) 19
Coldstream Guards 153
Collins, William 139, 150
colours 17, *17*
Commission of Array 31, 32,
  33, 34–5, 36, 37–8, 39, 42,
  43–4, 47, 49–50
Commission of Safety 91–2, 129
'Committee of Both Kingdoms'
  59
Committee for Compounding 149
Committee for Maimed
  Soldiers, seal of *152*
Committee of Safety 73, 74, *75*,
  82, 94, 142
Commonwealth Exchequer
  Papers *55*, *93*, 98, *98*, 100, *123*
companies 11
conscription 68–9, 72, 83
Cooke, James 105
Cookesley 13
Corbet, John, chaplain 25, 48, 118
Cotheridge, butts 16
Council of War 74, 83
Coventry 27, 41
Coventry, Thomas, 2nd Lord (d.
  1661) 32, 33, *34*, 44, 147, 154
Cradley 118
  coin hoard 101
Crispe, Col. Richard 81
Cromwell, Oliver (1599–1658)
  102, 136, *137*, 138, 139, 140,
  144, 145, 147, *149*
Cromwell, Richard 150
Croome Church, tomb of
  Thomas, 2nd Lord Coventry
  34
Cropredy, battle of (1644) 73
Cropredy Bridge 96
Crow, Richard, mason 26

Dansey, William 142
Daye, Mary 98–9
death toll 131–2
'decimation tax' 147
De Gheyn, Jacob *14*
Denbigh, Wales 85, 100, 121, 132
Denbigh, Earl of 109
Dennis, Capt 105
desertion 13, 27, 68, 72, 73, 79,
  82, 88–9, 94, 100, 128, 129
Devereux, Capt. 98
Devereux, Robert *see* Essex, Earl
  of

Devereux, Sir Walter 41, 42, 59,
  117
Digby, Lord 121
Dingley, Edward 121, 122, 152
Directions for Musters 17, 21, *21*,
  25, 48
Dobbyns, Daniel 44, 59
Dodderhill 13
Doddingtree Hundred 19, 25,
  30, 64, 94
Dormer, Capt. 65, 112
Dormston 100
Dorset Trained Bands 27
Dragoons 48, 55, 71, 127, 135
  Boyleston's 149
  Hamilton's 75–6, 89, 182, 184
  Sandys' 75, 181
  Washington's 89
  Worcester garrison 136, 182
drill 19–20, 21–3
drill books 21, *21*
Droitwich
  'broad ribbon' for colours 17,
    17
  conscription 69
  garrison *60*, 75
  hides provided by 89
  inventory of ammunition 42
  magazine 40
  Parliamentary forces
    occupation 65
  plundering 100
  St Mary Witton 57
  soldiers billeted (in salt
    cellars) 26, 61, 96, 103
  supplies for Parliamentary
    army 112, 127
  Trained Bands 46
drummers 73
Dryden, John 25–6
Dudley, Edward, Lord 32, 33
Dudley, Col. William 'Dud' 61,
  135
Dunbar, battle of (1650) 136
Dyson, Henry 153, *153*

Eckington 100
Edgehill, battle of (1642) 32, 44,
  51, 54, *55*, 73, 77, *132*
Edinburgh 103
Edwards, Rowland, tailor 26
Elmbridge 13
Elmley Castle 101
Elmley Lovett 26, 94, 95
Elvins, Edward, clothier 138,
  139
Enyon, James 81
Essex 73, 102
Essex, Robert Devereux, Earl of
  (1591–1646) 32, 36, 51–2, 53,
  53, 54, 55–6, 69, 96, 102
Essex, Sir Thomas 54

Estopp, Major Foulke (Fowlke)
  134, 139
Evesham
  Abbey belltower *115*
  apprenticeship 101
  battle of (1645) 73, 113, *114*,
    120
  billeting of soldiers in 26, 134
  Bridge 65, 77, 97, *97*, 109
  defences 105, 113, *114*
  defences levelled by Waller 96
  Fair 106
  field army in 106
  garrison 56, *60*, 61, 64, 65,
    75, 77, 79, *82*, 83, 95, 99,
    100, 104, 112, 120, 122,
    128, 183
  inventory of ammunition 42
  Langstone House *108*
  magazine 40, 46, 155
  musket and pistol balls found
    at Greenhill *90*
  prison 149
  rebellion in 97
  seizure of *111*
  Swan Lane, defences *114*
  Washington's Dragoons 89
Exchequer *see* Commonwealth
  Exchequer Papers
Excise Committee 95
Eyre, Col. Anthony 155

Fairfax, Sir Thomas 69, 110,
  127, 134, 136, 151
'Faithful City' 50, *130*, 131
families of soldiers 92, 104, 129
Faringdon (Berks) 27
Feckenham Forest 30
Field, Stephen 147
field signs 17, 70
Fielding, Capt. 13
Fifth Monarchists 149, 154
Finch, Francis 33, 74
Fisher, Major 121
Fladbury *60*, 98, *98*, 99, 127, 134
flags 17, 70
flintlocks 69–70
Flyford Flavell 53–4, *55*, 127
Foley, Richard, ironmaster 61,
  64, 100
Folliott, Sir Henry 15
food prices, for Worcester
  garrison 129
Foot
  new regiments 47
  pre-war Trained Bands 11,
    15, 18, 26
Forest of Dean 60, 84, 85, 91
Fowler, Sergeant Major 13
Fox, Col. 'Tinker' 48, 64, 83
Frankley 48
Freeman, Capt. John 85, *85*

free-quarter 83, 89, 91, 96, 98, 102, 104, 116, 121

Gardiner, Samuel, mayor 46, 55, 57
Gardner, Christopher 109
garrisons 60, 65, 68, 74, 75, 76–9, 82, 100, 104, 120, 123–4
  arms 61, 64
  Association demands 116–17
  camp followers and families 92, 104, 129
  supplies 94
  supported by parishes 94–5
  unpaid taxes collected by 94
  see also Evesham; Hartlebury; Madresfield; Worcester
Genifer, John 19
gentry
  assessed for Horse 174–6
  Royalist 177–8
George, John and Anne 101–2
Gerrard, Sir Gilbert, governor of Worcester 68, 82, 83, 84, 100, 105, 106, 111, 112, 120, 184–5
Giffard, Charles 144
Giffard family 147
Gloucester (Glos.) 73, 138
  battle 132
  'blue' regiment 70
  Kingsholm 84
  military yard 19
  money raised for Worcester 145
  siege of 73, 84–5, 91, 106
  Town Regiment 73
  Trained Bands 18
  troops from 136
Gloucestershire 48, 84, 109, 112, 148
Godfrey, Lt Col. 77, 79
Goffe, Thomas, bailiff 25
Goring, Lord 46, 155
Gough, William 15
Goughe, Roger 20
Grand Jury 36, 38, 40, 83, 116
gunpowder 40, 42, 61, 89, 127
Guyatt, James, sergeant 20

Hackett, Henry, parson 57
Halater, John, parson 57
Halfshire Hundred 19, 25
Hall, John, vicar 57
Hall, Richard 152
Hall, William 100
Hamilton, Sir James 35, 84, 105
  regiments raised by 72, 74, 75–6, 89, 91, 132, 182, 183–4
Hamilton, John 46
Hamilton, Lord 13
Hanbury, Capt. 84

hand grenades 64
Harcot, Major 135
Hardwicke, Humphrey 57
Harrison, General 136, 138, 139
Hartford Green 149
Hartlebury 75, 128
  garrison 60, 61, 65–6, 73, 75, 82, 95, 106, 107, 124, 127, 135
  Royalist mint 88
  Scottish army 112
  sheep plundered by Scots 100
hedgebills 25, 42
Heming, George 108–9
Heming, Walter, clothier 141
Hempsted church (Glos.), tomb of John Freeman 85, 85
Henderson, Sgt Major 89
Herbert, Sir Henry 33
Herefordshire 16, 27
Hertfordshire, Trained Bands 73
Hide, Lt Col. David 105
Hide, John, miller 19
Higgins, Richard 13
Hill, James 75
Holland, William 15
Hollar, Wenceslas, maps by 80
Holt, butts 16
Hooper, Thomas 23
Hornblower, Thomas 100
Hornyold, Thomas 141, 143
Horse (cavalry) 25, 26, 116
  gentry assessed for 174–6
  new regiments 48
  pre-war Trained Bands 11, 16–17, 18, 19
  supplied by parishes 95
horses, for cavalry and draught 76, 94, 99, 102, 136
  costs 89
  fodder for 95
  losses of 53–4, 55
  shoeing 61
Howard, Lord Edward 32
Howard's brigade 85
Huddington, skeleton 147
Hughes, Ensign 72
Hughes, Francis 151
Hungerford, Fitzwalter, sergeant 20
Huntingdon 85

impressment 13, 15, 19, 26, 56, 65, 69, 116, 117
Inett, Richard 139
Ingram, Henry 33, 44, 74
Inkberrow Church 60, 80
inspections, of arms and armour 23
Irans, Augustine 105
Ireland 132
  casualties 15
  service in 13, 134, 135

Irish rebellion 30
Irish troops 84, 125, 128, 130
iron-working industry 61, 64
Ives, Emanuel 100

James, Col. John 136, 138, 139
James I 18
Jewkes, William 127

Kaye, William 54, 55
Kemble, Capt. Lt Richard 144
Kempe, George, mayor of Evesham 97
Kempsey 94, 102, 127
Kempson, Lt Col. 134
Kendrick, Col. 145
Kentish Horse 99
Kidderminster 60, 68, 80, 131, 138, 139
  apprenticeship 101
  byelaws 39–40
  camp follower buried in 92
  casualties 132
  clothiers 57
  fighting around 122
  inventory of ammunition 42
  magazine 40
  rioting 35
  Royalist tendencies 135
  Waller's Horse 96, 99
King, William 42
King's Norton 100
King's Regiment 153
Kingsholm, Gloucester 84
Kingston, Capt. John 141
Knotsford, Francis 142
Knotsford, John 79, 83, 97, 129, 186

Lambert, General 149
Lancers 16, 18
Lane, Richard 144
Langston, Anthony 121
Laudian reforms 30
Lechmere, Nicholas 59, 101, 152
Lechmere family 59
Legge, Lt Col. Robert 112, 113
Leicester, siege of (1645) 85
Leigh Court 61, 117, 120
Leigh Sinton 118
Lenches 134
Levellers 126, 134
Liggen, Col. 122
Light Horse 16–17, 18
Lilburne, Col. 134
Lincolnshire Trained Bands 27
Littleton, Sir Edward 33
Littleton, John 33
Liversay 99
London, Artillery Gardens 21; *see also* Tower of London

London Trained Bands 19, 98
longbows 16
Lords Lieutenant 11, 12, 13, 20, 21, 32, 36, 156
Ludeley, skirmish *55*
Luke, Sir Samuel 107, 117
Lygon, William 59, 109, 127, 152
Lygon family 59
Lyttleton, Charles 134, 149–50, 153
Lyttleton, John 13
Lyttleton, Sir Thomas (1593–1650) 13, 31, 35, 48, 49, 76, 83, 134, 152
Lyttleton family, of Frankley 30, 149

Madresfield, moated site and garrison 60, 61, 68, 75, 120, 124
siege of 105, 122, 127
magazines 12, 19, 20, 40, 42, 47, 50, 61, 68, 76, 116, 139, 155
maimed soldiers 15, 55, 152, *152*
Malvern 118
Malvern Chase 30
Mamble, Constable of 30
Mansfeldt, Count 13
Markham, Gervase 20
marriages 108
'Mars: his triumph' 21
Marston Moor, battle of 83, 89, 112, 132, 155
Massey, Capt. 82
Massey, John, drummer 26–7
Massie, Col. Edward (1620–1674) 73, 78, 95, 112, *112*, 113, 118, 152
match 40, 42, 64
Mathon 100, 118
Maurice, Prince 78, 84, 86, 105, 111, 113, 116, 119, 120, 121, 122
Maystaffe, Thomas 54
medal, reward for good service *128*
Merrick's regiment 54
metal-working 61, 94
military yards 19
militia, pre-war 11; *see also* Trained Bands
Militia Act (1662) 155
Militia Ordinance 32, 36, 40
Millward, Capt. 127
Milward, George, clothier 138
mints, Royalist 64, *88*, 106
Monck, General 150, 151, 153
Monmouth caps *71*, 108, 135
Moore, Major 128
Moore, Simon, vicar 138
Morice, Walter, clothier 141
Morris, Thomas 53, *93*, 98
Muckley (Muclow), Major Thomas 155

musket balls 20, 22, 40, *55*, 64, *90*, 102, 155
costs of 89, 155
musketeers 13, *14*, 15, 21–3, 69, *71*
muskets *14*, 15–16, 19, 23
'bastard' 13, 16
cost of 89
matchlock 61, 69
stocks for 61, 135
muster masters 12, 20, 35–6, 116
Muster Roll
(1621) 18, *18*, 19
(1640) 23
(1641) 11–12, 21, *22*, 23, 24, 27, 157–73
muster rolls 12
musters 12, 13, 15, 18, 19–20, 21, 22, 44, 46
Mynne, Colonel 84

Nanfan, John 33
Naseby, battle of 79, 85, 110, 120, 132
New Model Army 69, 84, 92, 110, 112, 133, 135, 147
local men in 120
red coats 70
Restoration 153
siege of Worcester 125
tents for 103
Worcester, battle of (1651) 136, 141, 153
Newbury, battle of (1643) 85
Newport Pagnall, garrison 104, 107
Northampton, William, Earl of 18
Northern Horse 100
Northfield 16
Norwich (Norfolk) 19
Nott, Sir Thomas 134

officers 20, 48, 49, 76, 116, 128, 135
behaviour of 105
pay 73, 92
pre-war Trained Bands 11
Okey's regiment 135
Ombersley 60, 127, 139, *140*
Ordinance (1644) *109*
Oswaldstow Hundred 18, 19, 25
Oxford army 61
Oxford (Oxon.) 60, 61, 64, 85, 94, 95, 96, 97, 113

Packington, Sir John 33, 44, 55, 59, 74, 79, 136, 141, 142
parishes
garrisons supported by 94–5
pikes and armour 42–3
soldiers supplied by 11–12, *24*, 25

Parliamentary Committee for Worcestershire 59, 68, 109, 113
Passey, Lt Col. 84
Patman, Capt. 122
pay 20–1, 81, 88–9, 91, 92, 111, 125, 128–9, 135, 148
Pearse, T. 98
Pembroke, Earl of 12
Penn, William 144
Pennel the Elder, Edward 141
pensions 15, 152–3, *153*
Pershore *60*
Bridge *95*
Clubmen meeting 117
garrison 79
goods requisitioned 53, *93*, 98, 99
Horse stationed at 79, 109
house burnt down 112
Royalist army camped around 81
soldiers billeted 26, 61
Trained Bands *18*, 46
Pershore Hundred *18*, 19, *24*, 25
Petty Constables 12, 13, 28, 39
pikeheads 64
pikemen 13, *14*, 16, 70, *70*, 157
pikes 13, 15–16, 18, 25, 157
Pinvin, skirmish 109
Pirton 102
pistol balls *90*
Pitchcroft, Worcester 19, 25, 31, 38, 39, 42, 46, *47*, 125, 138, 140
Pitt, Capt. Richard 46, 155
Pitt, Capt. Scudamore 46
Pitt(s), Edward 33, 74
Plimley, Abraham 57
plundering *87*, 91, 93, 98–9, 100–1, 102, 104, 116, 122, 145
poor relief 101
Posse Comitatus 11, 27–8, 72, 111, 115, 116
powder flask tops *71*, 102
powder mills and powder making 61, 76–7
Powell, Henry 26
Powell, James 77, 108
Powell, Richard 152
Powick 118, *123*
Bridge *51*, *90*
cavalry sword *90*
Church *143*
garrison 140
skirmish 32, 50, 51, *51*, 52, *58*
Powys, Edward, bookbinder 136
Poyntz, General 69
priming bottle top *71*
Privy Council 12, 13
propaganda 57, *58*, 59, 120

Purefoy, Col. 57
Pye, Sir Walter 79
Pym, John 27

Quakers 149
Quarter Sessions 15, 23, 31, 36, 39, 91, 116, 136, 152
Queenhill parish 79

Rainsborough, Col. Thomas 105, 126, 130
Rea, Capt. Thomas 50, 51, 57
Redmarley 84
reformadoes 128
Restoration 150, 151–6
Richardson, William 77, 108
Rich's Horse 145
Ripple, battle of (1643) 60, 78, 79, 105
Rock parish 122
Romney, John 141
Rous, Col. Edward 44, 59, 109, 113, 152
Rous, Thomas 59
Rous family 59
Rous(e), Sir John 33, 42, 74
Royalist Association 118, 120
Rumney, Capt. 85
Rupert, Prince 48, 50, 52, 61, 74, 75, 82, 83, 104, 108, 120, 122
Russell family 30, 49, 81
Russell, Sir Thomas 42
Russell, Sir William (1602–1669) 16, 31, 33, 35, 40, 42, 50, 59, 64, 76, 152
at battle of Ripple 78
conscription by 69
Foot regiment 69, 76, 84, 85, 88, 94, 128, 182–3, 187
governor of Worcester 55
home at Strensham 67
Horse regiment 44, 68, 76, 84, 88–9, 181–2
mis-appropriation of funds 92
payment of troops 92
Powick skirmish 52, 53
regiments raised by 68, 72, 76, 81, 82, 87, 125
rivalry with Sandys 81–2
spending by 80

St John, Lord 54
saltpetre 40, 61, 77, 108, 127
Salway, Humphrey 36, 39, 44
Sampson, John 15
Sandys, John 73
Sandys, Martin 59, 72, 73, 74, 89, 105, 125, 128, 136, 180
Sandys, Richard 55, 73
Sandys, Samuel (1615–1685) of Ombersley 32, 33, 35, 36, 54, 73, 136, 152

at Hartlebury 84
deserted Worcester 128
Dragoons regiment 75, 181
Foot regiment 56, 74, 82, 83, 84, 85, 128, 179–80, 187
governor of Evesham 74, 77, 82
governor of Worcester 28, 111, 124
Horse regiment 44, 72, 75, 77, 83, 84, 85, 112, 120, 121, 181, 184
quarrel with Prince Maurice 121
regiments raised by 68, 72, 76, 79, 81, 82, 87, 125
rift with Sandys 75
rivalry with Russell 81–2
Sandys, Thomas 86
Sandys, Capt. William 73, 106, 124
Sandys family 73
Sannes, Capt. Richard 55
Saunders, Capt. 135
Saunders, Thomas 98
Savage, Giles 42
Savage, Major 84
Savage, Thomas 33, 44, 74, 101, 149
Savage family 44
Saye, William 98, 98, 127
Scarlett, Edward, cannoneer 76
Scotland 132
marriages regulated 108
service in 17, 23, 26, 92
Scots, Scottish army 100, 101, 108, 112–13, 135, 136, 138, 139–41, 144, 145–7, 155
Scudamore, Col. Barnabas 117
Sebright, Sir Edward 33
Second Civil War 134, 188
Sedgeberrow family 121
Selby 27
'select militia' 147, 149
Sequestration Committee 73
sergeants 20
Severn Stoke, medal 128
Sharman, Lt 72
sheep pikes 25, 42
Sheldon, John 86
Sheldon, Ralph 141, 142
Sheldon, William 86, 141, 149
Sheldon family, of Beoley 30
Sheriffs Lench 81
Sherrard, Henry 27
Ship Money tax 29
shoes 71
Shrawley Wood 82, 89
Shrewsbury 84, 89
Shrewsbury, Earl of 118
Shropshire 60
garrisons 61, 152

Simonds, Capt. Thomas 75
Smith, Emanuel 100
snapsacks 17, 28
Snow, John, tentmaker 103
Soley, Thomas 138
Solley, Lt Col. Edward 49, 50, 72, 131, 151
Speed, J[ohn] 12
Speite, Capt. John 46
Spetchley Park 102
Spiller, Sir Henry 33, 74
Stamford's regiment 85
Stapleton, Col. 145
Starr, Col. 127
Stayner, Capt. Robert 105
Stephens, William 50
Stokesay (Shropshire) 85
Stourbridge, ironworks 61, 64
Stourton Castle 68
Stow on the Wold 65, 123, 124
Stratford 75
Strensham
defences at moated manor house 65, 67, 79
garrison 60, 61, 65, 75, 100, 112
Russell's house (Manor) pillaged 53, 55
taxes 95
Stutty, Christopher 26
substitutes, for service in Trained Bands 13, 25, 27
Suckley 118
swords 16
cavalry 90
Symonds, Richard 72, 74, 75, 87, 106

Talbot, Lord Francis (Earl of Shrewsbury) 136, 141, 142, 143, 144, 147, 188
Talbot, Sherrington 33, 36, 38, 74
Talbott, Capt. 13
taxes 20, 29–30, 55–6, 72, 88–9, 94, 95, 101, 109, 112, 113, 117, 120, 127, 128–9, 147–8, 152
Taylor from Bransford 128
Tenbury, coin hoard 101
tents 102–3, 103
Tewkesbury 68, 73, 78, 79
Third Civil War 155, 188
Thornhagh's Horse 135
Throckmorton 127
Tibberton 23
Tillam, John 20
tobacco-growing, Vale of Evesham 30
'tonnage and poundage' 29
Touchet, Mervin 141, 143
Tower of London
magazine 61
mint 88

Townshend, Henry 33, 36, 44, 74, 82, 102, 104, 106, 108, 116, 124, 125, 127, 128, 129–30, 149

Trained Bands 30–59, 75, 83, 179
  archers in, and bows used by 16
  clergy company 155
  colours for 17, *17*
  drill 19
  equipment 15–16
  foreign service 11, 13, 19, 25, 26
  Horse (cavalry) 16–17, 25, 26
  organisation 18
  Parliamentary 134–50
  pre-war 11–28, 46
  Restoration 151, 153
  service in 18–19
  soldier with caliver *45*
  substitutes 13, 25, 27
  support services 17
  training 20, 25
  uniforms (clothing) 17–18, 26, 27, 70
  widows to fund arms 102
  Worcester (Militia) 35–6, 46, 68, 71–2, 135, 150, 155, 188 (*see also* Worcester Town Regiment)

Trimpley
  fort 68
  skirmish 122
Turton, Col. Richard 57, 135
Twistleton, Col. 145
Twyning, John 105

Underhill, Capt. 152
uniforms 17–18, 61, 108, 138
Upton on Severn 65, 78
  garrison *60*, 61, 140
Upton Warren 13

Vale of Evesham
  soldiers billeted in 81, 106
  tobacco-growing industry 30
Waller's occupation of 96, 98, 99
Vaughan's brigade of Horse 85, 100, 121, 122
Vavasour's Brigade 85
Vere, Sir John 13
Vernon, Alderman 153, 154
Vernon, Edward 33
volunteer regiment 47, 72, 75, 76

Walker, Richard, 'scout-master' 144
Waller, Sir William (1597–1668) 28, 65, 73, 78, 93, 96, *96*, 97, 98, 99, 103, 106, 152

propaganda leaflets 57, 59
regiments raised by 109
Walsh, Joseph 33, 44
Walsh, Walter 142
Walsh, Capt. William 92
Ward, Robert, *Animadversions of Warre* (1639) 23
Waring, Edward 20
Warmington (Warks) 55
Warwick (Warks) 41, 42, 68, 73, 75
Warwickshire 46, 75, 96, 109, 112, 120
  Trained Bands 12, 27, 44
Warwickshire Commission of Array 31, 42
Wash, Charles 142
Washburn, John 141, 143
Washington, Sir Henry (1615–1664) 79, 81–2, 89, 125, 126, 127, 128, 186
Watson, John, commissary 106
Webb, Lt 89
Welsh Horse 139
Wem (Shropshire) 57
Western Association 109
Westminster Trained Bands 48
Wetherall, Peter, sergeant 20
Whalley, Col. 105, 125, 127, 134
Wharton, Nehemiah 52, 53, 54, 102
Wheeler, John, bailiff 113
wheellock pistols 16
Whitby, Oliver, chaplain 82
White Ladies Aston *22*
Wichbold 13
Wickhamford 127
Wigmore, Robert 141
Williams, Sir Thomas 15
Windsor, Lord Thomas 32, 36, 153, 155
Winford, Sir John 141
Wintour, Sir John 85
Wogan, Capt. Edward 135
women 102
Woodbury Hill *60*, 117, *118*
Woodward, Edmond 20
Worcester
  accommodation in 106
  ammunition stocks 40–1
  battle of (1651) 101, 131, 136–47, *142*, *148*, 188
  Bridge *130*, 154
  The Butts *66*, 126, *126*, 129
  Cardinal's Hat Inn, Friar Street 73, *75*
  Cathedral 48, 50, 53, *54*, *133*, 154
  charges for billeting in 107
  Charles II's lodgings *146*
  city walls 20, *64*, 65, *66*, 138

clergy 57
College Green 99
The Commandery *35*
Committee of Safety 73, 74, 82, 94
Cross Inn 99
Deanery 147
defences *12*, *62–3*, 72, 105, 108, 113, *124*, *126*, 130, 138, 140
expenses paid by 105
field army quartered on 81
Foregate 130, 139
Fort Royal *66*, 140, 144
garrison 61, 64, 65, 68, 76–7, 83, 84, 91, 94, 95, 104, 129, 182, 186–8
garrisoned by Clark's regiment 150
Guildhall 23, 53, 105
magazine 20, 47, 50, 68, 76, 116, 139, 155
Newlands 105
part-time soldiers 111–12
pay of the garrison 91
powder mills and powder making 76–7
Rainbow Hill 125, 126, 131
Red Hill 126, 145
Restoration of Charles II 151, 154
St Johns 16, 125
St Peter's, Sidbury 130
Salwarpe parish 140
siege (1646) 44, 73, 76, 81, 102, 103, 105, 106, 122, 124, *124*, 125–6, *126*, 127–31, 143, 177–8
soldiers billeted in 26
suburbs cleared *12*, 65, 81, 104, 106
Talbot Inn, Sidbury 50, 64
Tolsey 20, 46
Town Hall 36, 68, 73, 82
Wheeler's Hill 103
see also Pitchcroft; Trained Bands; Worcester Town Regiment
Worcester Town Regiment 17, 70, 72–3, 76, 82, 89, 92, 94, 112, 128, 131, 151
Wright, Henry, draper 140
Wylde family *35*, 59
Wylde, John, Sergeant-at-Law 36, 39, 40–1, 44

Yarranton, Capt. Andrew 138, 139, 145
Yates, Francis 144